CW01464636

A History of the Scottish Liberals
and Liberal Democrats

A History of the Scottish Liberals and Liberal Democrats

David Torrance

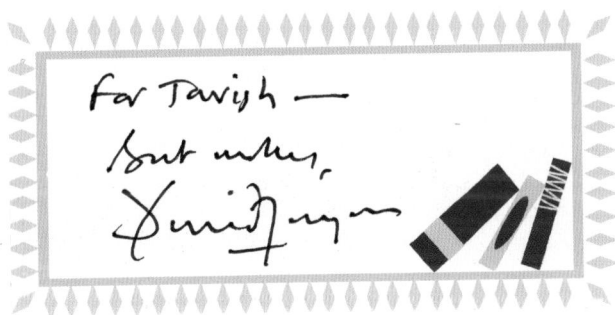

EDINBURGH
University Press

Edinburgh University Press is one of the leading university presses in the UK. We publish academic books and journals in our selected subject areas across the humanities and social sciences, combining cutting-edge scholarship with high editorial and production values to produce academic works of lasting importance. For more information visit our website: edinburghuniversitypress.com

Edinburgh University Press Ltd
The Tun – Holyrood Road
12 (2f) Jackson's Entry
Edinburgh EH8 8PJ

Typeset in 10.5/13pt Sabon by
Cheshire Typesetting Ltd, Cuddington, Cheshire, and
printed and bound in Great Britain

A CIP record for this book is available from the British Library

ISBN 978 1 3995 0638 0 (hardback)
ISBN 978 1 3995 0639 7 (paperback)
ISBN 978 1 3995 0640 3 (webready PDF)
ISBN 978 1 3995 0641 0 (epub)

Published with the support of the University of Edinburgh Scholarly Publishing Initiatives Fund.

Contents

Introduction:
Scottish Liberalism and Scottish Society

For almost a century, Scotland and the Liberal Party (and its Whig[1] antecedents) were as one. Between the Great Reform Act of 1832 and the general election of 1922, only once did Scottish Liberals fail to emerge as Scotland's single largest party. More often than not it had both a majority of seats and votes. Party and nation became synonymous, with Scottish Liberal policy and thought influencing national identity and permeating public discourse.

The same would also become true of, successively, the Scottish Conservative and Unionist Party, the Labour Party and the Scottish National Party over the century that followed the strange death of Liberal Scotland. But none of those parties came close to matching either the extent or consistency of the Liberals' electoral hegemony. And even after the Scottish Liberal Democrats – as the party became following a merger with the Social Democratic Party (SDP) – had been reduced to Scotland's third (or even fourth) party, between 1989 and 2015 it continued to exert a disproportionate influence over the politics of Scotland, particularly in the constitutional sphere.

All of this might come as a surprise to those familiar with a sizeable literature on Scottish politics and history. Library bookshelves bulge with tomes on the Scottish National Party (SNP) and Labour, but not the Liberals or Unionists despite their shared dominance of Scottish politics until the mid-20th century.[2] Writing in 1998, the political scientist Peter Lynch (an exception to this rule) noted that the Scottish Liberals had 'seldom come to the attention of academic observers', with the 'notoriously thin' literature on political parties in Scotland 'thinnest in relation to the Liberals and Liberal Democrats'.[3] The historian I. G. C. Hutchison also noted a similar 'deficiency' in the literature, which tended to overemphasise the Home Rule question and 'Red' Clydeside.[4] Hutchison, however, has chronicled the Scottish Liberals of 1832–1924 in judicious detail. More recently, Ewan Cameron has picked up that baton, while in the field of political science the late James Kellas paid more attention to the party than most. Even dedicated histories of the Liberals neglect the Scottish party. Chris Cook mentions Scotland only in the context of the Scottish Parliament, while David Dutton merely in general geographical and electoral terms.[5] Reading both, you could be forgiven for assuming that no separate organisation even existed north of the border.

Viewing the Liberals as an English party with (Scottish and Welsh) bits added misses the important point that for long periods it was often the other way around. Scotland was not merely part of the 'Celtic fringe' but the Celtic core of Liberal strength and dominance in Great Britain. Between 1880 and 2019, nine of the UK party's leaders sat for Scottish constituencies without necessarily being Scottish (Gladstone had some Scottish ancestry, Asquith none), while Lord Rosebery, another Liberal premier, was thoroughly Scottish. As a result, Scottish policy concerns –religious, social or constitutional – impinged upon UK as well as Scottish party considerations.

It seems important to begin by asking 'what is liberalism?' Its British or UK tenets are well known – individualism, free trade, constitutional reform and social progressivism – and Scottish Liberalism does not differ markedly in any respect. Writing in 2016, Craig Smith characterised the 'Scottish Liberal tradition' as having emerged from the Reformation, Scottish Enlightenment and 19th-century reform movement. Its 'great theme', he added, was 'individualism':

> Scotland's experience of Calvinism imbued its culture with a strong respect for the individual. In the Scottish Enlightenment this moved from the sphere of religion into that of social life as [David] Hume, [Adam] Smith and others argued that their developing commercial society offered far greater opportunities for individual self-expression than previous times. In the nineteenth century in the hands of John Stuart Mill, it became the core of the most celebrated moral case for a free society.

A free society could only be achieved via 'moral egalitarianism' (the belief that all people were of equal moral status) and individual self-respect, the idea – best articulated in Samuel Smiles' Victorian best seller *Self-Help* – that hard work and thrift could set an individual (and their family) free.

To this tradition Adam Smith had added the free exchange of goods between responsible individuals, better known as free trade, from which the poor would benefit most. Key in this respect was limited but stable government and the rule of law. Despite Scottish Liberalism's focus on rugged individualism, it also valued a sense of community or, in 21st-century terminology, 'localism'. This championed communal organisation and strong, independent local government, together with philanthropic attention to the less advantaged. Mutual co-operation between management and workers was another consistent theme.[6]

Some of the classical Scottish political issues which are examined in the pages that follow are not exclusive to the Liberals. Some belong firmly in the late 19th century (disestablishment of the Church of Scotland and land reform), some in the late 20th century (civil liberties and human rights). On the other hand, constitutional reform of some sort has been a constant thread linking the 19th, 20th and early 21st centuries (Home Rule or devolution within a federal framework).

All these aspects of the Scottish Liberal tradition have been under-examined. This volume, therefore, aims to plug a long-standing gap in the Scottish literature by examining the rise, dominance and fall of Liberalism in Scotland, from the Whigs of the mid-19th century through to the Liberal Democrats of the late 20th and early 21st centuries. It is envisaged as the first of four books looking at Scotland's main political parties, all of which lack up-to-date single-volume histories.

Having not yet discovered a way to make a living from researching and writing political history, I appealed for financial support, which was generously forthcoming from the Scottish Liberal Club, Scottish Trust for Liberal Democracy, Lord Steel of Aikwood, Lord Stephen, Sir Danny Alexander, Craig Harrow, Jim Fiddes and the late Lord Maclennan. Being good Liberals, none attempted to interfere with my judgements or assessments, responsibility for which is mine alone.

In an earlier form, Chapter 9 appeared in *The Story of the Scottish Parliament: The First Two Decades Explained*, edited by Gerry Hassan (EUP, 2019), while material throughout this volume concerning the 'nationalist-unionism' of the Scottish Liberals formed part of my PhD thesis, subsequently published as *Standing up for Scotland: Nationalist Unionism and Scottish Party Politics, 1884–2014* (also EUP, 2020). More modest portions of the present text are derived from this author's earlier publications, *The Scottish Secretaries* (Birlinn, 2006) and *David Steel: Rising Hope to Elder Statesman* (Biteback, 2012).

When it comes to the present volume, I have several debts to mention if not repay. My colleague Dr Edward Hicks kindly sourced academic journal articles while my friend James Douse brought other secondary sources to my attention. Stephen Daisley also provided access to some useful archival material. Several friends and interviewees commented on draft chapters and provided useful comments and corrections: Frances and Grace Bennie, Cllr Robert Brown, Lord Campbell of Pittenweem, Matthew Clark, Sandra Grieve, Dr Peter Lynch, Bernard Ponsonby, Lord Purvis of Tweed, Lord Rennard, Euan Roddin, Lord Steel of Aikwood, Lord Wallace of Tankerness and Sir Graham Watson. Last but not least, thanks to Floradh Laura NicLachlainn Chamshron-Leòdhais and Andrew Eaton-Lewis for hosting me during a windswept week at Àras nam Fir Chlis on the Isle of Lewis, where much of this book was first written.

Dr David Torrance
Peckham, South London
November 2021

NOTES

1. The Whigs were aristocrats opposed to the excesses of either monarchical or parliamentary government.
2. The present author has attempted to address this deficiency as regards the Scottish Conservative and Unionist Party, as indeed have James Mitchell, David Seawright and Alan Convery.
3. P. Lynch (1998), 'Third Party Politics in a Four Party System: The Liberal Democrats in Scotland', *Scottish Affairs* 22, 16.
4. I. G. C. Hutchison (2001), *Scottish Politics in the Twentieth Century*, Basingstoke: Palgrave, xi.
5. See C. Cook (2010), *A Short History of the Liberal Party: The Road back to Power*, Basingstoke: Palgrave Macmillan and D. Dutton

(2004), *A History of the Liberal Party*, Basingstoke: Palgrave Macmillan.
6. Craig Smith, 'The Scottish Liberal Tradition', Reform Scotland website, 13 January 2016.

1

'The Party of National Patriotism': 1832–1880

The Scotland of the early 1830s was a Tory nation, although that was about to change, and change dramatically. Before the *Reform Act (Scotland) 1832*, its parliamentary electorate comprised a few thousand adult males. Following its passage, the number of Scottish MPs increased from 45 to 53 and the franchise grew seventeen-fold to around 64,500 voters out of a population of around 2,300,000.

The historian H. J. Hanham viewed these reforms as the democratic transition from 'a string of pocket or rotten boroughs and counties' to restoration of 'representation to the nation at large'.[1] Scottish voters responded by supporting Whigs or Radicals 'who had come to be regarded as the champions of the national interest'. D. W. Urwin also saw the 1832 Act as the legal basis of what he called the 'somewhat unwieldy political alliance known as Scottish Liberalism'.[2] Drawing on a deep anti-Toryism resulting from that party's resistance to reform, Whigs won all but 10 of Scotland's 53 seats at that year's election.

As I. G. C. Hutchison, another historian, has argued, the 'very comprehensiveness' of that victory meant only Whigs could subsequently be blamed for any failure to deliver on promised reforms.[3] Indeed, the Whigs subsequently lost ground through poor organisation, something at which the mid-19th century Scottish Conservatives then excelled. There was an attempt to form a Scottish Liberal Association in the mid 1830s but it came to nothing. Scottish Liberals complained that money flowed north from the Carlton Club (to the Scottish Conservatives) but nothing was forthcoming from the Reform Club. The lack of a Scottish Liberal organiser was particularly felt at the 1841 general election.

Nevertheless, the Liberals controlled between 21 and 23 of the 23 Scottish burgh seats between 1832 and the Second Reform Act of 1868, the year a 'Liberal Party' was created formally under Gladstone's leadership. Later, they came to dominate county seats too. Between the two Reform Acts, the Liberals never controlled fewer than 31 of Scotland's 53 constituencies.

Party labels were not yet fixed and there existed degrees of Liberalism in Scotland. One historian of the party identified three main types:

Whig-Liberal: Those who supported the 1832 settlement and continued to do so; viewed as too conservative by more radical colleagues.

Moderate-Liberal: Often synonymous with Whigs but not as pejorative; sometimes used to describe Free Church Liberals.

Advanced or Radical-Liberal: These Liberals were usually voluntaries or secularists who supported disestablishment and triennial parliaments; usually opposed to what they perceived to be the Liberal establishment.[4]

To T. C. Smout, Victorian Liberals were a 'consortium' of three different social and political groupings: Whigs, radical middle-class Liberals and working-class 'Lib-labs'.[5] The label 'Liberal' was, therefore, best seen as an umbrella term covering a variety of interests which were, on occasion, prepared to stand against one another. Five out of the 20 constituency fights at the 1852 general election, for example, were exclusively between Liberals.

As the above descriptions also suggest, religious matters dominated. Broadly speaking, Tories wanted to preserve the status of the Church of Scotland (or 'the Kirk') while some (but not all) Liberals supported reform or outright disestablishment. If there were differences over policy matters, for example education, they tended to flow from these broader religious debates.

The 1843 'Disruption' of the Kirk, the central event in 19th-century Scottish affairs, concerned the interplay between church and state, and thus played a part in shaping both the Liberal and Conservative parties in Scotland. One interpretation sees the Liberal Party as a proxy for a unified Church in the years after

1843 in its ability to allow an expression of 'national' values. But with the emergence of the Free Church, Whig hegemony in Scotland was challenged for the first time. As Gordon F. Millar observes:

> Liberals were conscious of the fact that they belonged to the same body, whatever their differences on which direction it should go in might be. At various times a certain issue provided a rallying point. In the 1840s this had been Corn Law repeal. Twenty years later it was parliamentary Reform. Where an individual Liberal placed himself in relation to such an issue expressed what kind of Liberal he was. All Liberals believed in 'Reform'', however that might be defined.[6]

So between the Disruption and the *Representation of the People Act 1868* (known as the Second Reform Act), the Liberals were 'at the very core of Scottish life, involved in everything from debating the country's educational provision to discussing whether a tenant farmer should, or should not, be allowed to shoot the hares and rabbits that ran over the land he rented'.[7] T. C. Smout, however, believed the party's moralising generalities 'shrouded a vacuum at its centre, where other countries had practical politicians and constructive politics'.[8] To Lindsay Paterson, 'Liberalism became the Scottish national ideology, firmly grounded in a cautious evangelical radicalism'. And such was its electoral strength, even bitter internal disputes 'over the true allegiance of Liberal politics' could not dent the party's Tory-beating prowess.[9]

Scottish Liberal MPs of whatever hue were usually Episcopalians or members of the Kirk. In 1847, the 11 elected to represent Scottish counties were lawyers, military men, merchants or manufacturers. In the burghs, there was more religious variety. Of the 22 elected in 1852, there were six members of the Free Church and three 'Voluntaries' in addition to the 11 mainstream Presbyterians or Anglicans.[10]

At that latter election (1852), a combination of Free Church, Voluntary and Radical votes kept the Whigs at bay in Scotland's larger towns. Liberals were also aided by a split in the Conservative Party in 1846 over the repeal of the Corn Laws, as well as a growing middle-class urban population. The Scottish Liberal Party thus provided a political home for this expanding professional vote. The demon drink was also a factor. The Forbes MacKenzie Act of 1853 restricted hours of public drinking in Scotland, reflecting a tilt towards temperance also seen in major English cities such as the Liberal stronghold of Birmingham.

Millar identified three 'salient' factors which influenced the development of Scottish and Liberal politics in the mid-1850s: education, Scottish nationalist sentiment and the Crimean War. The first of those was particularly bitter. The Conservatives wanted to defend the existing Church of Scotland-based parochial system of education; the Free Church wanted that system opened to its adherents; while the Voluntary church movement wanted a national system free of religious influence. All attempts at legislative reform in the 1850s were based on a belief that the status quo was not an option.

Importantly, votes on Bills in 1850 and 1851 exposed differences of opinion between the Free Church supporters and Voluntary doubters. On another legislative attempt in 1855, the doubters ended up voting with Conservative opponents. As Scotland became a more secular country, there was less tolerance among Radical or Advanced Liberals for the sectarianism of certain colleagues. This tension was to persist until the general election of 1857.

There was also a national dimension to these education debates, not least because English Members could wield such influence over the outcome of a purely Scottish issue (a familiar dynamic in the territorial politics of the UK). That said, those behind the National Association for the Vindication of Scottish Rights (NAVSR, founded in 1853) or the movement to erect a monument to William Wallace (begun in 1856) were more likely to be Tories than Liberals.

Indeed, prominent Liberals like Sir Henry W. Moncreiff declined to join the NAVSR. The Liberal-supporting *Scotsman* newspaper was also dismissive. For Liberals such as the former Edinburgh MP Duncan McLaren who did take part, it was an opportunity to attack the Anglicising and politically dominant Whigs.[11] Other 'national' claims found broader agreement among Liberals, chiefly Scotland's right to increased representation at Westminster given its growing population and contribution to Treasury coffers.

To Ian McLeod, Liberalism was no less than Scotland's 'national declaration of reborn nationhood', intrinsically linked to the 'holy trinity' of institutional autonomy preserved in 1707: Kirk, law and education:

> Scottish institutions directed the course of Scottish Liberalism in the 19th Century so long as Liberalism stayed true to its fundamental Mid-Victorian commitment to institutional reform. So long as that remained so, the politics of Scotland would remain distinctly Scottish. Disestablishment was a Scottish issue in the way that 'the 8-hour day' could never be.[12]

Or, as one adherent later put it: 'I am a Liberal because I am a Scotchman.'[13]

The third and final salient factor was the Crimean War. Wartime jingoism jarred with the 'peace movement' agitation of the voluntary wing of the party represented by figures like McLaren, while the conflict also produced calls for more efficient leadership in government. By the time Lord Derby took office in 1858, Whigs and religiously moderate Radicals were in the ascendency in Scottish burghs, while in the counties Liberals had picked up support from Conservatives due to the patriotic appeal and domestic conservatism of Lord Palmerston. By the 1859 general election, the Liberal Party had reunified at Westminster (indeed historians consider Palmerston to be the first 'Liberal' Prime Minister) and in Scotland only 8 out of 53 constituencies were contested.

Given the turbulence of the 1840s and '50s in Scottish politics, Millar detected a 'rest and be thankful' attitude in the Scottish Liberalism of the 1860s, particularly the 'self-congratulatory tone' of some 1865 election addresses. John Vincent spoke of a 'federal alliance' between Liberals in England and the party in Scotland and Ireland. But although the 'whole structure of the permanent Liberal majority' depended on the party's 'standing start' in Scotland and 'opportunities' in Ireland, Scotland and Ireland received scant attention from Palmerston et al. at Westminster. And while constituencies might be 'radical enough in doctrine', in Scotland 'they liked a laird as much as they disliked landlordism'. Before 1868, therefore, Scottish Liberal MPs were mainly derived from the 'upper crust', while Scottish legislation was neglected at Westminster, something which later generated demands for reform.[14]

Hutchison, meanwhile, viewed pre-1868 Scottish Liberalism as standing for:

... ethics and morality in government, both at home and abroad, and put personal freedom and individual civil liberties before aristocratic and feudalistic privilege. Retrenchment in state expenditure was essential to promote these goals, as it would eliminate corruption and patronage, instead encouraging governmental efficiency.[15]

To this, usefully, all sections of Scottish Liberalism could subscribe. The 1868 general election – which followed the Second Reform Act – saw more Tory-held seats in Scotland fall to Liberals. The enlarged burgh electorates in places like Glasgow and Dundee led to greater political organisation, while a new working-class electorate began to make itself known and therefore exert influence over reform-minded Liberals, much like supporters of the Free Church a quarter century before.

By then, H. J. Hanham viewed the Liberals in Scotland as the 'party of national patriotism'. 'Such political issues as arose were usually thrashed out, not between the two parties but within the Liberal party,' he added, 'with the result that Scottish politics had a unique air of permanence.'[16] At the same time, the issues upon which electoral contests turned were pan-UK, international or local rather than 'Scottish'. That said, in 1869 Scottish Liberal MPs addressed a letter to Gladstone protesting the management of Scottish affairs. He appointed a commission under Lord Camperdown, which recommended the appointment of an under-secretary for Scotland at the Home Office.

Filling it, however, proved difficult, with Hanham identifying the 'deplorably low' quality of Scottish MPs. Not a single Member from Scotland (as opposed to Englishmen sitting for Scottish constituencies) was a member of the Cabinet between 1835 and 1885, so leadership roles instead rested upon unelected peers like the Earl of Aberdeen and Duke of Argyll.[17] Hanham admired some features of Scottish Liberalism such as the 'independence and sense of public duty' of local provosts (the Scottish equivalent of mayor) and bailies (local government officials), but not the caution that 'bred apathy' and a 'reluctance to change'. Scottish Liberal associations tended to choose retired soldiers, sailors, Indian civil servants, merchants and manufacturers as candidates, rather than men of 'dash and ability'.

By the 1870s, most Scottish Liberal MPs in burgh constituencies were aged over 50 and it was looked upon as 'something of a revolution' when in 1874 Charles Cameron of the *North British Daily Mail* was returned for Glasgow aged only 33. Hanham also observed the 'oligarchic' nature of Scottish associations, with a few families monopolising seats for decades. In Caithness, for example, the two Liberal families of Sinclair of Ulbster and Traill of Rattar shared representation between 1832 and 1885.

If such families were unsuccessful in one seat, they would simply move to another in which they had some familial or landed connection. 'Scotland is a small country closely knit by kinship, the universities, the bar, the churches and the press,' concluded Hanham, writing in 1959, 'and it is scarcely surprising that the family atmosphere of individual Liberal associations also characterised Scottish Liberalism in general'.[18]

And such was the stability and success of the Liberals in Scotland that it came to be regarded as a 'refuge' for prominent party figures who found it difficult to retain a seat in England: not only the towering figure of W. E. Gladstone, but also George Goschen, Erskine Childers, H. H. Asquith, Winston Churchill, Augustine Birrell and John Morley.

In the later 1860s, Gladstonian leadership 'integrated the regional sections of the party' on the same principles of 'solidarity, concord, and co-operation, as it did the various classes within the party'.[19] During the 1870s, party organisation in Scotland was also formalised, the impetus being an unexpected Tory landslide in 1874. The Liberals lost 12 seats to the Conservatives amid weakening internal unity due to the rise of the Radicals. Furthermore, most constituencies had no local association or agent with which to mobilise supporters.

In 1876 William P. Adam,[20] a Liberal whip, created the West and South-West of Scotland Liberal Association (WSWSLA) with offices in Glasgow, and the following year the East and North of Scotland Liberal Association (ENSLA) based in Edinburgh, with a secretary (John James Reid) who acted as agent for the whole of Scotland. The ENSLA tended to be more Whiggish in character and the WSWSLA more Radical. When the Radicals later tried to raise matters such as land reform and disestablishment at meetings of the two new associations, they were accused of trying to divide the party. Though some constituencies resisted Adam's external interference, they were gradually induced to set up formal associations.

Intimately involved in these organisational developments was Lord Rosebery.[21] He had joined the House of Lords in 1868, the same year Gladstone became Prime Minister for the first time. As R. J. Akroyd has written, until 1880 Rosebery 'skillfully manipulated people and exploited the new machinery of politics to carve out a position of preeminence in Scotland which he used as a springboard into British and Imperial politics'.[22] Not since Henry Dundas had a major Scottish politician possessed an identifiable interest in Scotland and its affairs.

In February 1877, shortly after a tour of the United States, Rosebery helped William Adam inaugurate the ENSLA, of which he became president by popular acclamation. At its first general public meeting at the Edinburgh Music Hall in November 1877, UK Liberal leader the Marquis of Hartington spoke and inaugurated the new association (as he had its west-coast equivalent). When the Perth delegation raised concerns about the 'scant' attention paid to Scottish affairs at Westminster; Hartington could only reply that the previous Conservative government had been worse.

In his own remarks, Rosebery said it was 'not an association for producing manifestos and political cries' like the Conservatives, nor was it 'a sickly and despotic society to exact a catechism and demand an exact profession of faith from every member that enters it'. Rather the ENSLA would be a means of communication, information and organisation. He also cautioned against complacency:

> I once fancied that Scotland was so Liberal that no exertions were needed – that we had no need of proselytising – that all we had to do was to keep the faithful within the fold. But surely the last election undeceived us as to that.[23]

Lord Hartington – who also pledged to deal with the disestablishment question 'on its merits alone and without reference to any other considerations'[24] – was in Edinburgh to contest the Rectorship of Edinburgh University. Such contests were in the late 19th century useful barometers of political opinion. Candidates were usually prominent British politicians, and Rosebery was keen that Hartington should defeat his Conservative opponent (Richard Cross, the Home Secretary), which he did by a large margin.

Everything then came together. Accepting the freedom of Glasgow in November that year, Hartington witnessed Rosebery's popular appeal; the following year Rosebery was invited to contest the Aberdeen University Rectorship; and, at the same time, William Adam and Rosebery urged Gladstone to contest Midlothian at the next general election. Rosebery's victory in Aberdeen (beating, again, Richard Cross) 'solidified his position in Scotland and in the Liberal Party',[25] while the Midlothian campaigns established Rosebery as a power-broker in UK politics.

Gladstone officially accepted the Midlothian Liberal Association's invitation to contest the constituency in January 1879 and subsequently conducted two memorable campaigns (November–December 1879 and March–April 1880) in which Rosebery was intimately involved.[26] When the Grand Old Man's train arrived at Waverley Station, Rosebery 'helped Mr Gladstone alight and took Mrs Gladstone on his arm to the carriage'. And when the Gladstones arrived at Dalmeny, they were met and escorted by a torchlit procession of some 200 estate retainers.

Influenced by his experience of electioneering in the United States, Rosebery planned Gladstone's schedule and the content of his speeches. He also ensured his guest networked with the convenors and committee of the Midlothian Liberal Association as well as local nobility.[27] Rosebery wrote to the ENSLA's John James Reid:

> I believe if [Gladstone] accepts, our best plan would be to organise a great Liberal Banquet to him in the Corn Exchange on the model of that given to Lord Beaconsfield in 1868. That would be a recognition by Scotland of his efforts for Liberalism in the past & of his fresh anxiety to serve Scottish Liberalism in this matter. But it must be done so as not to interfere with the Liberal leaders – Granville and Hartington, & therefore I underline the second point.[28]

When Gladstone duly spoke at Edinburgh's Corn Exchange on 29 November 1879, Rosebery was in the chair. He also funded the campaigns out of his own pocket, which led to accusations that he was violating restrictions which barred peers from active involvement in elections to the House of Commons. One (Scottish Liberal) pamphleteer suggested that Rosebery would be rewarded with a promotion in the peerage.

The charge was difficult to refute given Rosebery's speech-making, funding, organisation and hospitality on Gladstone's behalf, but he got away with it, most likely on account of his and the Liberal leader's huge popularity. Chairing the ENLA AGM in January 1880, Lord Elgin wryly observed that the previous complaint (from political opponents) that the Liberals 'represented a mere rabble, a disorganised mob' had given way to a new charge that 'they were inclined to sink all their differences and enter into a sort of conspiracy to dismiss from the place they occupied honourable and patriotic men in whom the country had complete and entire confidence'.[29]

The campaign had worked wonders for party unity. Organisational changes instigated by Adam and Reid, meanwhile, began to yield results. Prior to the 1880 election, Reid toured constituencies 'interfering with local committees to an extent which would hardly have been tolerated in England',[30] assisted by a private political fund from which to distribute largesse. As Michael Dyer put it: 'Popular trust in the politically ambiguous Gladstone and candidates pledged to him provided a simple reference point for the emerging mass electorate, transcending the complexities of local Liberal factionalism.'[31] The disestablishment issue barely registered. A survey found that 'the almost universal desire of Liberal candidates was to express no definite opinion on the subject'. Only eight out of 60 candidates unequivocally supported disestablishment.[32] Gladstone endorsed Hartington's 1877 pledge (though he took care to attend Presbyterian churches), after which it slipped down the campaign agenda. On Scottish questions, he was brief and deliberately vague.

Adam's main challenge had been the cities of Glasgow, Edinburgh and Dundee, where multi-member constituencies encouraged disputatious Liberal factions 'to compete rather than co-operate'. Adam promoted unity by persuading different factions to back incumbents and encouraging the creation of over-arching electoral organisations. In Edinburgh, a United Liberal Committee was established while, by 1879, Glasgow's Whig and Radical factions were reconciled through the appointment of Charles Tennant as president of the Glasgow Liberal Association, 'which had been stripped of its ideological bias'.[33]

All of this aided the Grand Old Man's nationally significant campaign in Midlothian. 'The progress began, continued and ended in triumph,' wrote Michael Fry. 'Every meeting was attended with almost mindless adulation, every telling point cheered to the echo, every restated moral principle given jubilant affirmation.'[34] Hutchison reckoned voters in as many as 20 Scottish constituencies could have heard Gladstone speak during late 1879.[35]

When the Midlothian result was announced on 5 April 1880, more than 15,000 people gathered in central Edinburgh to see and hear their new MP (he had beaten Lord Dalkeith by 1,579 votes to 1,368). Gladstone later gushed that Rosebery was:

> ... very decidedly a remarkable man, not a mere clever man: and is to be evidently the leader of the Liberal party in Scotland, & that in a sense beyond any, I should think, in which they have heretofore had a leader. From the first time I ever saw him I liked him & thought highly of him: but he has opened out upon me marvellously.

But given his prominent role in Midlothian – the first modern British election campaign – Rosebery had pledged to refuse any position in a Gladstone administration. Instead, Rosebery set his sights on the rectorship of Edinburgh University. During the campaign he was introduced to Charles Cooper, the editor of the *Scotsman*, who would become another key figure in Rosebery's political machine. When he won the rectorial contest on 8 November 1880, the *Scotsman*'s leader column was devoted to his victory speech. It even took precedence over the results of the US presidential election.

NOTES

1. H. J. Hanham (1959), *Elections and Party Management: Politics in the time of Disraeli and Gladstone*, London: Longmans, 158.
2. D. W. Urwin (1965), 'The Development of the Conservative Party Organisation in Scotland until 1912', *Scottish Historical Review*, 44; 90.
3. I. G. C. Hutchison (1986), *A Political History of Scotland 1832–1924: Parties, Elections and Issues*, Edinburgh: John Donald, 33.
4. G. F. Millar (1994), *The Liberal party in Scotland, 1843–1868: electoral politics and party development*, PhD thesis: University of Glasgow.
5. T. C. Smout (1986), *A Century of the Scottish People 1830–1950*, London: Collins, 240.

6. G. F. Millar.
7. G. F. Millar.
8. T. C. Smout, 75.
9. L. Paterson (1994), *The Autonomy of Modern Scotland*, Edinburgh: Edinburgh University Press, 48.
10. Voluntarists were opponents of both the established and Free Church of Scotland. Prominent Liberal Duncan McLaren, for example, was a member of the United Presbyterian Church, the leading Voluntary denomination in Scotland after 1847.
11. See W. Pickard (2011), *The Member for Scotland: A Life of Duncan McLaren*, Edinburgh: John Donald. Duncan McLaren was a wealthy Edinburgh draper, Lord Provost of the city and one of its MPs from 1865 to 1881. Three of his sons also became Liberal MPs. His brother-in-law was John Bright, with whom he formed a close association.
12. I. McLeod (1978), 'Scotland and the Liberal Party, 1880–1900: Church, Ireland and Empire – A Family Affair', M. Litt. thesis: University of Glasgow, 8 & 18.
13. A. Reid (ed) (1885), *Why I Am a Liberal: Being Definitions and Personal Confessions of Faith by the Best Minds of the Liberal Party*, London: Cassell, 64.
14. J. Vincent (1972), *The Formation of the British Liberal Party 1857–68*, Harmondsworth: Pelican, 84–7.
15. I. G. C. Hutchison (2020), *Industry, Reform and Empire: Scotland, 1790–1880*, Edinburgh: Edinburgh University Press, 271.
16. H. J. Hanham, 155–6.
17. Argyll would resign as a minister over the Irish Land Bill in 1881, after which the Earl of Aberdeen soon followed.
18. H. J. Hanham, 165.
19. J. Vincent, 88.
20. Adam was a Scottish MP of long standing. In late 1880 he became Governor of Madras, though was in office for less than a year before passing away.
21. See biographies of Rosebery by Lord Crewe, Robert Rhodes James, E. T. Raymond and, more recently, by Leo McKinstry.
22. R. J. Akroyd (1996), *Lord Rosebery and Scottish Nationalism 1868–1896*, PhD thesis: University of Edinburgh.
23. Meeting on 6 November 1877, Scottish Liberal Party Papers Acc 11765/1.
24. In 1875, Scottish nonconformists had organised themselves under Principal Rainy of the Free Church and Dr Cairns of the United Presbyterian Church to secure disestablishment of the 'national' Church of Scotland via the Liberal Party.
25. R. J. Akroyd.

26. Gladstone had turned down an offer to contest the St Andrews Burghs, a small seat which lacked the prestige of Midlothian.
27. See D. Brooks (1985), 'Gladstone and Midlothian: The Background to the First Campaign', *Scottish Historical Review* lxiv, 56.
28. Lord Rosebery to J. J. Reid, 27 December 1878, Reid MSS, MS 19623 f52.
29. ENLA AGM, 28 January 1880, Scottish Liberal Party Papers Acc 11765/1.
30. H. J. Hanham, 159.
31. M. Dyer (1996), *Men of Property and Intelligence: The Scottish Electoral System prior to 1884*, Aberdeen: Scottish Cultural Press, 123.
32. Unknown (1882), *The Scottish Liberal Members and their Pledges on the Church Question in 1880*, Edinburgh.
33. M. Dyer, 133–4.
34. M. Fry (1987), *Patronage and Principle: A Political History of Modern Scotland*, Aberdeen: Aberdeen University Press, 92.
35. I. G. C. Hutchison (2020), 286.

2

'The Only Relevant Feature of Scottish Political Life': 1880–1906

At the 1880 general election, Liberals had secured their greatest victory, with Scottish voters responding warmly to Gladstone's emphasis on 'individual autonomy and self-help, to Liberal doctrines of free trade and limited government, to attacks on aristocratic and clerical privilege, and to the elevation of free speech and human rationality'.[1] Following a turbulent couple of decades, the Scottish electorate had unified behind the dominant personality of William Ewart Gladstone. Over the next two decades, however, 'what had originally been viewed as hairline fissures in Scottish Liberalism became gaping crevasses, so that the party's triumph became less of a climax and more of a climacteric, ushering in its long-term decline'.[2]

The historian I. G. C. Hutchison identified these 'crevasses' as Home Rule and the neglect of progressive social reform, both of which are analysed later in this chapter. Until 1881, judged Michael Dyer, Scottish Liberalism 'survived as an amorphous agglomeration of local elites with differing interests and values, which coexisted largely because there was no need for them to co-operate on a national or even regional basis'.[3] Gladstone's personality also helped, with the premier achieving the status of a 'household God' through plates, prints and busts, especially on Scotland's eastern coast. Frustrated Unionists talked of 'Gladstonolatry' and the associated practice of 'Gladstonian glamour', whereby the Grand Old Man apparently deployed his charisma to manipulate Liberal fortunes in Scotland.[4]

Significantly, the two Scottish Liberal associations formed in 1876–7 had played very little part in the 1880 election, with William Adam and Lord Rosebery handling any organisational matters between them. After the election, however, negotiations soon began to merge the two associations, something finally achieved on 25 July 1881. The first president of the Scottish Liberal Association (SLA) was, of course, Rosebery, although he resigned soon after on finally joining the government as under-secretary for Scottish affairs.

Hopes of organisational harmony also proved short lived. As James Kellas observed in his account of the party during this period, the subsequent history of the SLA was to show 'a considerable conflict between the Council and Executive', with Radical Liberals soon campaigning for more influence.[5] At its first AGM in October 1881, the SLA's stated aims were 'first, to unite the Liberal party; second, to promote the return of Liberal members to Parliament; and third, to afford steady and unflinching support to a Liberal Government.'[6] It also supplied legal information, settled quarrels, provided literature and arranged for speakers. Formulation of policy was left to associations by virtue of the fact that they were free to choose their own candidates.

Annual general meetings of the SLA were held alternately in Glasgow and Edinburgh at the beginning of each year, while autumn meetings took place in other towns around Scotland. At these, Radicals were able to free themselves from executive control and pass policy resolutions which proved embarrassing to the party leadership. Much of this was hidden from view, at least initially. As G. F. Millar has written, 'the Liberal party had become so dominant as to be the only relevant feature of Scottish political life'.[7] One comment attributed to Rosebery also held true a century later: 'How is it, then, that, as we have seen, the Scottish Conservative candidates adopted by the constituencies can go together to St Stephen's [at Westminster] in a single first-class railway carriage?'[8]

The 1880s saw many fierce debates over policy issues, even before that over Irish Home Rule in 1886. In 1882, land reform became an issue in the Highlands and Islands while disestablishment of the Church of Scotland was again raised in Parliament. Disestablishment's diminished status as a political priority had however been confirmed in 1881. Alluding to the candidature of R. B. Finlay, a tenacious defender of the Church of Scotland, in that year's East Lothian by-election, the chairman of the SLA said that:

On one particular point, the relations between Church and State, that gentleman held opinions different from many other Liberals – indeed very different from his own, but, as they knew, it was not a burning or pressing issue in the country at this time. What they were really looking forward to were questions of the tenure of land, the relations between landlord and tenant and so on, and questions of the procedure of the House of Commons to enable the representatives of the country to do their duty more effectively. These were the real pressing questions of the day.[9]

Another pressing issue in 1884 was renewed pressure for better management of Scottish affairs. Rosebery's appointment as, in his own terminology, 'a back-stairs minister for Scotland', had failed to appease what some have termed the first 'nationalist' phase of modern Scottish politics.

While Gladstone enthused Scottish Liberals, Rosebery was one of their own, and thus inspired a more patriotic rather than moral form of public devotion. J. M. Barrie recalled Rosebery 'firing an Edinburgh audience to the delirious point' when an old man in the hall shouted out: 'I dinna hear a word he says but it's grand, it's grand!'[10] Speaking in the House of Lords in June 1881, he warned that the words 'Home Rule' had 'begun to be distinctly and loudly mentioned in Scotland'. Rosebery quoted Disraeli imploring the people of Scotland to give up 'mumbling the dry bones of political economy and munching the remainder biscuit of an effete Liberalism'. He believed the people of Scotland were, in 1881, 'mumbling the dry bones of political neglect, and munching the remainder biscuit of Irish legislation'.[11]

As a Home Office minister, Rosebery attempted to 'disentangle' Scottish and English business but quickly became frustrated. This put a strain on his relations with Gladstone, to whom he wrote indignantly:

> The Prime Minister was returned by a Scottish constituency, backed by an overwhelming majority of Scottish members. From the day of the first meeting of the new Parliament until the present day of its third session, if I am correctly informed, not one minute of Government time has been allotted to Scotland or Scottish affairs. Can you be surprised that the people of Scotland complain? ...
>
> Unfortunately the view is taken in Scotland that I have a considerable share in the responsibility; and certainly wherever the Scottish halfpence may go, I shall get the Scottish kicks. That is an

eventuality which I am not prepared to face, when I am of opinion that the aggressive boot contains a toe of justice.[12]

By the end of 1882, the two were estranged and Rosebery was prepared to resign. But by the time Gladstone was embarking on his Third Midlothian Campaign they appear to have been reconciled.[13] The Prime Minister paid tribute to Rosebery as 'a man whose patriotism, whose Scottish patriotism, is equal . . . to his ability and to his eloquence'.[14] The disestablishment question also resurfaced, particularly at the beginning of 1885,[15] by which point 'the very success of the party, which eliminated the fear of opposition, caused a great deal of internal trouble'. Some internal groups were even 'prepared to split the party for their sectional interests'.

Scottish Liberal grandees were keen to keep a lid on all of this. Pre-eminent at this time was the SLA's 'dominating personality',[16] the 9th Earl of Elgin who, like Gladstone, was 'an opponent of extravagance and an enemy of display', also sharing the Grand Old Man's abhorrence of foreign or imperial adventures.[17] At the SLA AGM on 23 January 1884, Elgin said it was 'necessary to confine themselves strictly to those subjects which did not permit . . . differences of opinion in the party'.

This and the fact Whigs now dominated the Association prompted the Radicals to take more drastic action, not least because many desired to make disestablishment a 'test' issue at the next general election. The plan was to elect so many committed Scottish Liberal MPs that Gladstone could not ignore it. Nonconformism had grown in support since 1880, and while the Liberal leader tried to settle the issue via a public letter, it simply would not go away. They wanted nothing less than disestablishment and disendowment, with funds 'released' from the latter to finance free education, something enthusiastically supported by the Free Church of Scotland and United Presbyterian Church.

Matters came to a head when, on 15 September 1885, 'Radical Joe' Chamberlain launched his election campaign in Glasgow. Although he (an English nonconformist) too did not want disestablishment to become a 'test' question at the election, the Chamberlainite National Liberal Federation of Scotland (NLFS), established at a separate gathering the same day, had already resolved to make it so. If anything, Chamberlain's intervention in Scottish politics made matters worse, while it also allowed the Conservatives to make 'saving' England and Scotland's established churches a major election issue.

Resolutions were passed, Liberal candidates were bombarded with letters, and a front-page advert in the *Scotsman* on 7 November 1885 carried the signatures of some 1,475 ministers advocating disestablishment, about a third of Scotland's clergy. Those opposed to disestablishment and disendowment used the Church of Scotland's Committee on Church Interests, dominated by Lord Balfour of Burleigh, to issue nearly half a million copies of an *Address to the People of Scotland*, in which Balfour 'declared that the opponents of the establishment were trying to use unrepresentative Liberal associations and packed conferences to trump up a claim of majority support within the Liberal Party'.[18]

To James Kellas, the establishment of the NLFS (which flowed from the Radicals' failure to federate the SLA) represented 'a turning-point in the history of the Liberal Party in Scotland', because for the first time the party's Radical wing had taken control of a major political demonstration while establishing an independent organisation without the blessing of either Gladstone or Rosebery. The *Scotsman* and *Glasgow Herald* were both anti-disestablishment and therefore hostile to the Glasgow-based NLFS, of which Gilbert Beith, president of the Glasgow Central Liberal Association, became president. Beith ridiculed the SLA and promoted resolutions on reforming parliamentary procedure, land law, the House of Lords, local government, local option (local referendums on whether or not an area should sell alcohol) and religious equality. Dr Cameron, who owned the *North British Daily Mail* and the *Oban Times*, was another acknowledged leader of the Radicals.

Although each denied the existence of rival programmes, Chamberlain's speeches directly addressed such matters while Gladstone was often non-committal. The Earl of Fife, a leading Whig landowner, poured scorn on the 'miserable rubbish with which Birmingham [Chamberlain's fiefdom] has deluged the whole of the country during the autumn', going on to speculate as to the best way of eradicating 'these new Socialistic doctrines from the Liberal creed'.[19] Meetings of the Scottish Liberal Association 'became tests of strength between the two parties'.[20] At an SLA gathering in Perth on 16 October, Radical

nonconformists were strong enough to overturn an official resolution calling for a few years' delay. Instead a motion unequivocally calling for the disestablishment of the Church of Scotland
was passed by the overwhelming majority of 415 votes to 7.
Lord Fife resigned as a vice-president of the SLA and party unity
began to disintegrate, with 'double' Liberal candidates emerging
in several Scottish constituencies.

With Gladstone about to head north from his Hawarden home
in nonconformist Wales to open his campaign in Midlothian,
Rosebery urged a clarifying statement. The Grand Old Man had
already informed Principal Rainy (the recognised leader of nonconformism beyond the Liberal Party) that he could not endorse
disestablishment given the effect it would have in England, and
in a long speech at the Free Church Assembly Hall in Edinburgh
on 11 November, he not only ruled it out as a 'test' question
but made clear he would not interpret a majority of Scottish
MPs as an indication of Scottish feeling.[21] Instead, Gladstone
placed Scottish disestablishment 'at the end of a long vista'
arguing, not unreasonably, that something so divisive could
hardly be described as a truly 'national' demand. 'All pleased
and sanguine,' reported Gladstone privately. 'Disestablishment
scare nearly over.'[22] Although the NLFS went on to reaffirm
disestablishment as a test question and many Liberal churchmen had already defected to the Tories, that particular boil had
been lanced.

Gladstone's position had been influenced by his Scottish con-
fidantes: Rosebery, Charles Tennant (a strong Church Liberal)
and Edward Marjoribanks, later chief whip. The SLA's chairman for most of the 1880s, Lord Elgin, was also a friend of
the 'national' church. Lord Aberdeen, who had converted to
Liberalism during the Midlothian campaign of 1879, served as
Lord High Commissioner to the Kirk's General Assembly in
1885 and was very close to Gladstone.

Indeed, Hutchison reckoned this 'extraordinary nexus of
blood and marriage ties' did much to prevent radicalism from
fully capturing the Scottish Liberal Party during the 1880s and
1890s. Lady Aberdeen (a long-time president of the Scottish
Women's Liberal Federation) was Marjoribanks' sister and the
Aberdeens' daughter married John Sinclair, later Secretary for
Scotland and a confidante of Sir Henry Campbell-Bannerman.
'The Aberdeen group provided a solid centre weight in Scottish

Liberalism, balancing not just the radicals but also the Liberal Imperialist section of the 1890s.'[23]

At the general election of November–December 1885, there were 27 double Liberal candidatures in the newly-created single-member constituencies. Rosebery, who 'as an aristocrat with radical sympathies ... neatly bestrode Liberalism's two wings',[24] tried to arbitrate, with some candidates receiving a letter of recommendation from Gladstone, although most went to the polls backed by rival associations. The government's failure to legislate for land reform also caused ructions, with the Duke of Argyll writing to Gladstone regarding fears of a 'Scotch Parnellite Party embracing some 5 county members' becoming 'a formidable addition to the Party of Disorder'.[25] Argyll was spot on, and five crofting candidates were returned in the Highlands and Islands. The Liberals took the hint and subsequently passed the first of several Crofters' Acts, and by the next election all but one of the five had transitioned into orthodox Liberals.

This failure of organisation produced renewed calls for reform, and on 18 December 1885 Rosebery wrote to Lord Elgin saying the time had come for a new Association, most likely along the lines of the NLFS. With the Liberals back in office after a brief Tory hiatus, Rosebery also refused to fill the new office of Scottish Secretary despite having agitated for its creation prior to the election. Sir Reginald Coupland compared Rosebery's 'position as a Scottish nationalist' with that of David Lloyd George in Wales: 'He could and did support the cause on occasion, but he could no longer be its leader.'[26]

At a lavish banquet held in his honour in November 1885, Rosebery said he believed there was:

> one principle with which the future of the Liberal party will have much to do, the principle that where there is a vigorous and a real and a loyal nationality it is not wise to suppress or to ignore that nationality – (cheers) – and that the better policy is to satisfy its just aspirations, for by so doing you will be promoting in the highest and the best sense the efficiency of the unity of the Empire at large. (Cheers.)[27]

These were prophetic words, both in terms of Liberal policy and Rosebery's own career. Instead he took charge of foreign affairs in a Gladstone ministry notable for 'the large proportion of Scotchmen and of Scottish members which it contained', not only the Grand Old Man himself but Erskine Childers (Home Secretary), Henry Campbell-Bannerman (War Office), Lord Aberdeen (Viceroy of Ireland), Sir George Otto Trevelyan (Scottish Office) and Sir Lyon Playfair (Vice-president of the Council). Junior members also included Professor Bryce, Edward Marjoribanks, Lord John Hay and the Scottish law officers.

The cross-party Tory-Liberal campaign for a Scottish Office had seen key tenets of Scottish nationalism take root in Liberal discourse and ideology. The belief that Scotland was a naturally radical country, its egalitarianism derived from the Highland clan system, the General Assembly of the Church of Scotland and a distinctive (and of course superior) Scottish education system. Furthermore, this radicalism was believed to be stifled by Westminster, particularly the House of Lords' inbuilt Conservative majority.

Nationalism in another part of the Union, however, was about to dominate political events in Scotland and the rest of the UK. During his campaign in Midlothian, Gladstone 'uttered the first distinct note of his Irish policy', which was to be 'subject in all respects to the law of Imperial unity'.[28] The *Scotsman* newspaper caused a sensation by revealing more details which, if true, Holmes Ivory (the principal Scottish Liberal election agent) warned Lord Rosebery meant Gladstone would not have 'an earthly chance of carrying Scotland with him'.[29] On 8 April 1886, Gladstone unveiled his Government of Ireland Bill, which proposed a 'Home Rule' (or devolved) parliament in Dublin with responsibility over certain domestic affairs. What was from the vantage point of the 21st century a moderate reform was viewed in the late 19th century as a radical constitutional experiment, and to some Liberals a very dangerous one. The mighty Liberal Party split. Twenty-two Scottish Liberal MPs voted against the Bill, mainly but not exclusively Whig landowners. And of the 12 Liberal Churchmen, 7 voted against.

The Whig-dominated Scottish Liberal Association (whose president, the Earl of Stair, and chairman, the Earl of Fife, both quit over Home Rule) did not support Gladstone in the general election that followed, during which Edinburgh and Midlothian became the setting for speeches both defending and attacking the government's Irish policy. 'Scotland has been the battlefield of the Empire', observed *The Times*, 'in much the same sense as Belgium has been called the battlefield of Europe.'[30]

With many in the SLA taking positions behind enemy lines, the NLFS emerged as an uncritical supporter of the Prime Minister's Irish Bill. In one communication to the Liberal associations of Scotland, the NLFS earnestly called:

> upon the Liberals of Scotland to stand by their great and venerable Leader. And now that an appeal to their suffrage is made, **let them refuse to elect any candidate who declines to support this new departure in Irish politics.** And let them be assured that this crisis involves a new departure also in the direction of great social reforms and the moral and material advancement of the people.[31]

And in another communication issued later that year, the NLFS urged equal treatment for Scotland *and* Ireland:

> We further counsel the Liberal Electors of Scotland to direct attention to the question of Home Rule for their own country. Scotch business gets scant justice at Westminster; Scotch private Bills put large fees in the pockets of English lawyers; and social reforms, demanded for more than a generation, now ripe for legislation, cannot be approached so long as the mind and purpose of the Nation are smothered by the overpowering Conservatism of England. The leading Metropolitan Press does not scruple to exult over this fact; but Scotland cannot quietly submit to be so treated. The true remedy lies in Home Rule – allowing the Scottish people to manage their own affairs.[32]

The NLFS remained, however, too much a West of Scotland organisation, which undermined hopes of it displacing the SLA as the main organ of Gladstonian politics in Scotland.

Scottish Liberal leaders did not trust the NLFS (or Liberal-aligned crofting MPs) to organise the July 1886 general election, so formed a new body called the Scottish Association to Promote Self-Government for Ireland at a meeting of Scottish peers and MPs at the Scottish Whip's town house on 8 June with Rosebery as president. Although it claimed to exist for the distribution of information, the historian Donald Savage viewed it as 'another attempt by the parliamentary Liberals to ensure their hold on the party machinery'.[33]

Nevertheless, poor organisation contributed to the large number of Gladstonian defeats in Scotland at that election, most of which were due to Liberal Unionist defections rather than Conservative victories. Having held 62/70 seats in 1885, the Scottish Liberals were reduced to just 43, still a majority (as in Wales) but, given the hitherto 'national' nature of Liberal support in Scotland, a traumatic reduction. Only England returned a Unionist majority. 'England overrides Wales & Scotland,' mused Gladstone. 'This will bring forward Scotch & Welsh questions on national grounds.'[34] This electoral churn, however, provided an opening for the future Liberal leader and premier, H. H. Asquith, who contested East Fife after Boyd Kinnear, the incumbent, set himself against Home Rule. Asquith stood as an 'advanced Liberal' committed to Irish Home Rule.[35]

Following the election, Scotland effectively possessed two Liberal parties which differed only on the Irish Question. At the SLA's AGM on 29 October 1886, Lord Elgin announced that no one would be excluded from the Association who professed to be a Liberal. But he also attempted to exclude any policy discussions, essentially arguing that the SLA remain neutral on the greatest issue of the day. This made it impossible for Liberal Unionists – those who had voted against the Bill – to take any further part in the Association.[36] Instead, they began to align themselves with the Scottish Conservatives (soon to be, simply, 'Unionists'), who also opposed constitutional reform in Ireland. *The Times* later observed that the SLA had 'practically expelled the Unionists from its ranks, and converted itself into a Home Rule Association'.[37]

Despite support from Radicals in the NLFS (who hoped Gladstone would back disestablishment as a *quid pro quo*), opposition to Home Rule was particularly marked in Scotland, which had religious, industrial and familial links to Ulster's Protestants. This presented a problem for its dominant political party. 'The consequent electoral co-operation between the Liberal Unionists and the Conservatives re-cast the political landscape,' observed Hutchison, 'for it simultaneously reinforced the Unionist support in counties and prised open urban constituencies hitherto deaf to the blandishments of Toryism.'[38]

Michael Dyer has described how in rural constituencies 'the character of Liberalism changed', most of all in the Highlands where the desertion of Whig landowners to the Unionists left 'the development of Liberal interests and organisation to the Crofters'. In other agricultural counties, 'the Liberal coalition passed from landed proprietors into the hands of tenant farmers, burgh tradesmen, newspapermen, United Presbyterian ministers and lawyers, who were active in the village and small-town associations'.[39] Liberal activists now looked to the UK leadership rather than local landowners.

M. K. Thompson has argued that the Scottish Liberal split was more nuanced than simply Whig versus Radical, with both camps framing their positions around differing interpretations of liberalism.[40] Indeed, Duncan McLaren, a nationalistic Edinburgh MP and veteran of both the National Association for the Vindication of Scottish Rights in the 1850s and the campaign for a Scottish Secretary in 1884, accepted the validity of Irish grievances but believed the 'three kingdoms' – Scotland, England and Ireland – should be treated equally, but without grants of legislative autonomy. When the Edinburgh South Liberal Association, of which he was honorary president, declared for Home Rule, McLaren resigned, even pledging to vote locally for whomever (and of whichever party) pledged their opposition to an Irish parliament.[41] Despite this, he gained the soubriquet of 'Member for Scotland', his Liberalism being the 'kind that gave the party its Scottish backbone until 1918'.[42]

Many Scottish Liberals also disliked the protectionism supported by many Irish nationalists, while Gladstone's plan for a government buyout of Irish landowners offended both defenders of property rights and those who felt this a bit much given that Scottish crofters were not to receive similar treatment.[43] Home Rule also eroded Liberal support from the Scottish media, which had been an important factor in sustaining the party's domination of 19th-century Scotland. The break with Gladstone greatly pained *Scotsman* editor Charles Cooper (an ally of Rosebery) professionally and personally. Cooper later welcomed Joseph Chamberlain's alternative plan for several local assemblies subject to the Imperial Parliament.

Home Rule led many Liberals in Scotland to 'consider the Liberal Unionists and Conservatives better defenders of property, patriotism and Protestantism' than their Gladstonian colleagues.[44] Sydney and Olive Checkland characterised Liberal Unionism as 'a bridge over which middle-class man could pass from Liberalism to Toryism without suffering any sense of betrayal'.[45] Indeed, over time, these Scottish Liberals would help form a new centre-right party called the Scottish Unionists after merging with the largely moribund Scottish Conservatives in 1912.[46] Most Scottish Whig peers defected to the Liberal

SCOTTISH LIBERALS AND LIBERAL DEMOCRATS

Unionists, Rosebery and Elgin being notable exceptions. When
it came to the future of Scottish Liberalism, Elgin wrote to
Rosebery arguing that:

> everything should be done to avoid an open split. I think if we come
> to a rupture now, we shall lose a great many men all through the
> country who are valuable especially in organisation work – and it
> will amount to something very like a dissolution of the Scottish
> Liberal Association. It seems to me to be just possible to tide over
> the difficulty for the present if we could find a president whom both
> sides would accept. I think they might accept you if you would
> consent to be nominated. Will you think it over? The association
> in its present form was your work & I think you only left it when
> you took office.

Rosebery (who began to shed his earlier Scottish nationalism)
took up the challenge and revived attempts to form a new
National Federation. Meanwhile the Scottish Liberal Club,
established in 1879 by Rosebery, William Adam et al., managed
to remain united while its London counterparts came out for or
against Home Rule. It even purchased premises on Edinburgh's
Princes Street adjoining the Scottish Conservative Club erected
some years previously.[47]

Negotiations concluded on 22 December 1886, and the
National Liberal Federation of Scotland was formally merged
in the Scottish Liberal Association, coming to be known as the
'Scottish Liberal Association, being a Federation of the Liberal
Associations in Scotland'. Although defections over Home Rule
had made the Scottish party more homogenous, still tensions
between Whigs and Radicals persisted, the former unhappy at
policy now being included in the Association's objectives,[48] and
the latter displeased by the composition of the provisional executive. In the view of Michael Dyer, 'the organisational values
of the Glasgow Radicals informed the revamped SLA, and
the ending of individual membership marked the transition of
Scottish Liberalism from a confederacy of notables to a modern
political party'.[49]

The *Scotsman* was clear that the Federation had 'swallowed
the Scottish Liberal Association' by French Revolutionary tactics.
Lord Rosebery was again president of the SLA, and attempted –
in vain – to hold back the advancing tide of Radical Liberalism
in Scotland. In 1887, Rosebery's candidacy for the rectorship

of Glasgow University was contrived to re-unite Liberal Home
Rulers and Unionists but broke down when he made partisan
speeches in favour of devolution for Ireland. Former UK Liberal
leader Lord Hartington urged Liberal Unionists to back the
Conservative candidate, who duly won. The Liberal Club at
Glasgow University was ransacked and Rosebery considered his
association with Hartington to be at an end.[50]

That autumn, the executive of the SLA dispatched a delegation of Scottish Liberal 'Deputies' to Ireland, where they were
'met at the chief [railway] stations by eager crowds of people
... thanking them for the sympathy of Scotland, and for the
practical interest taken by her in their struggle for constitutional
rights'. In Dublin they met Nationalist leaders and addressed
thousands from the window of the Imperial Hotel. The Deputies
also experienced 'manifest hostility' from Dublin Castle (the
seat of British rule), 'whose spies and detectives were in constant
attendance upon them'. Returning to Scotland, the Deputies
expressed confidence that Ireland could govern itself while
the Union and Empire would 'rest on the sure basis of mutual
interest and goodwill'.[51] A copy of their report was sent to
Gladstone, who naturally approved. The SLA later gave Charles
Stewart Parnell a rather gushing reception at Edinburgh's Corn
Exchange in July 1889.

Sympathy with Irish Home Rule did not, of course, mean the
Scottish Liberals were formally committed to legislative devolution for Scotland, whatever the views of certain MPs and activists. There is a sense the party approached this question with
caution, generating apparently positive mood music in an effort
to make Irish Home Rule more palatable in Scotland, where the
Liberal Unionists had quickly established themselves as a major
force. As Jim Bulpitt observed, this ambiguity formed part of
the Liberals' 'territorial code', allowing the party 'to assume
the leadership of Scottish and Welsh nationalism for over thirty
years without committing itself irrevocably to that cause in
either section'.[52] Some doubted whether, not entirely seriously,
the Liberal Party could cope with the likely consequences of
Home Rule. Speaking in 1886, John Morley said:

> I only ask myself, supposing the Scottish Liberals were to be by any
> calamity withdrawn from the legislative body that deals with the
> affairs of England – poor England! – how we should fare without

you, and I, for one, am not at all willing readily, and without very strong cause, to lose the advantage of the noble Liberalism of Scotland.[53]

While a resolution in favour of 'the application of the principle of Home Rule to Scotland' was adopted at the SLA's annual meeting in February 1888, Lord Elgin made clear the executive's reluctance to commit itself to any 'specific form' of devolution.[54] Further resolutions were passed and Gladstone, during a tour of his Midlothian constituency in 1890, was left in little doubt as to party feeling. In 1889, he had spoken of Scottish Home Rule as 'a sentiment as yet vague and unformed, in embryo'.[55]

Rosebery floated a 'local-national' body of 144 members with certain powers delegated from the Imperial Parliament to Edinburgh,[56] while Gladstone fudged the issue, making Delphic remarks which satisfied no one. On 21 October 1890, the SLA executive told Gladstone it anxiously awaited 'the moment when our leader shall give us the word that shall rally us in the fight', the goal of self-government having 'long been dear to the Scottish people'.[57] It was certainly very popular with grassroots Liberals and, for different reasons, with temperance campaigners, who believed a Scottish rather than Imperial Parliament would more readily make its goals a legislative reality.

By 1890, Lord Hartington had aligned himself with the Unionists and on visits to Scotland claimed 'Scotch Home Rule was cared for by nobody outside the Scottish Home Rule Association'. This, retorted the future Liberal premier Henry Campbell-Bannerman, 'only showed that when [Hartington] came to Scotland, as when in England, he lived in a balloon'. By the 1892 general election, meanwhile, the SLA had assembled a more radical agenda than that adopted by the English National Liberal Federation (NLF) in its Newcastle Programme of 1891. At its Glasgow conference on 7 October 1891, resolutions were passed in favour of an eight-hour day for miners, home-rule-all-round, disestablishment as a test question, abolition of the House of Lords, amendment of the Crofters Act, one-man-one-vote and women's suffrage. As David McLardy said at the SLA Council meeting on 17 February 1892: 'The programme passed at Newcastle might be good enough for Englishmen, but it was not good enough for Scotsmen – it wanted the democratic ring.'[58]

Gladstone, however, was guided more by the NLF than the SLA, no matter how supportive the latter was over Home Rule. Here the SLA's formal separation from English party organisation weakened its influence on UK Liberal policy. As James Kellas has observed, the fact that Welsh disestablishment was incorporated into UK Liberal policy while Scottish disestablishment was not, most likely spoke to the pressure Welsh Radical Liberals were able to exert within the National Liberal Federation: 'The Scots, by remaining aloof,' observed Kellas, 'preserved their political nationality in name but rendered it ineffective in practice.' He continued:

> All the debating and sermonising north of the border could not force the Westminster politicians to accept that Scottish Liberalism really mattered. Had the arguing taken place in the National Liberal Federation instead of in the Scottish Liberal Association, the ordinary Scottish Liberal would have had a voice in the policy of the party as a whole. As it was, Scottish Liberal policy could only have been implemented by a Scottish Liberal Parliament.[59]

The resulting frustration had a broader impact. A Scottish Labour Party had been formed in 1888, unequivocally committed to working-class representation as well as Home Rule for Scotland. The 1892 election also convinced the Scottish Home Rule Association (SHRA) formed in 1886 to break with the Scottish Liberals, 'as much an expression of dissatisfaction with the place of the Scottish Liberal Party in the Liberal Party as a whole, as with the place of Scotland in the United Kingdom'.[60] As the historian H. J. Hanham put it, the leaders of the SHRA had come to recognise that they 'were stronger nationalists than they were Liberals'.[61] They also cried betrayal at 'the reward which Liberal Scotland gets for sixty years of unwavering support to the Liberal Party!'[62] The final straw had been Gladstone's failure to mention Home Rule while campaigning for re-election in Midlothian.

In an 1890 speech to the Scottish Liberal Club, Lord Rosebery had observed that

> Scottish Liberalism is, and always has been, of a somewhat different character from the Liberalism in the rest of the United Kingdom, more matured, more deep, more founded on reflection, more animated perhaps by a conscientious and far-seeing enthusiasm than the Liberalism of any other part of the United Kingdom. And being so based and so animated, I believe it is independent of any one

political question that may momentarily divide the Liberal party, and that it is impossible for any one issue, however grave and important it may seem to us for the moment, permanently to divide the Scottish Liberal party.[63]

This Scottish exceptionalism was met with cheers but the results of the general election two years later were mixed. Although Ireland did not dominate in 1892 as it had in 1886, Conservatives filled Scottish election platforms with Ulster Unionists, whom many Scottish Liberals found distasteful. Rosebery sneered at Ulster Scots 'carrying the Shorter Catechism in one hand and a revolver in the other'.[64]

Despite these tactics, Liberals were able to form another government – Gladstone's final ministry – although the House of Lords remained a barrier to any meaningful reform. In Scotland, Liberals secured 50 seats (winning back 11 but losing 4), prompting one MP, Herbert Paul, to argue that 'dissatisfaction' at the failure of certain measures should be deferred in favour of following 'the old Scottish custom', namely standing 'shoulder to shoulder' with the Grand Old Man.[65]

Moving the second reading of his 1893 Government of Ireland Bill (unfinished business from 1886), Gladstone asserted that it was 'quite right that England and Scotland should have an administrative system with which they can sympathise', to which he wished to add Ireland. This time, however, the Irish were to retain representation at Westminster, something Gladstone told the chairman of the Midlothian Liberal Association was a 'consequence flowing' from the demands made 'by the country – & especially by Scotland and Scottish Liberals'. If this were true, observed Naomi Lloyd-Jones, then Gladstone's strategy backfired. The Second Home Rule Bill 'incensed a number of Scottish Liberals and Home Rulers who saw in it an even more disturbing prospect. For them, Irish inclusion at Westminster would result in Scottish opinion being overridden not only by the English, but by the Irish also.'[66]

In 1894, Rosebery inherited Gladstone's Cabinet and campaign manifesto, including Scottish disestablishment, although that commitment had come to feel like a millstone around his neck. As Lloyd-Jones has also written: 'Scottish Home Rule – like Scottish Disestablishment – imperilled Liberal unity within Britain, yet failed to secure any tangible benefits for the party in Scotland.'[67] Five disestablishment motions were moved in the Commons between 1886 and 1895, all of which attracted strong support from Scottish Liberal MPs. Rosebery also introduced a Bill in 1894, but it fell with his government in 1895. Besides, the issue lacked the salience it once had, especially as the Free and United Presbyterian Churches amalgamated, and the resulting United Free Church moved towards a merger with the Church of Scotland.

A Scottish Liberal Prime Minister at Downing Street did little to settle various party splits north of the border. Rosebery had promised much but delivered little, although he and his Scottish Secretary Sir George Otto Trevelyan did manage to establish a Scottish Grand Committee (SGC) to better manage Scottish legislation at Westminster, while combatting a long-standing grievance that English votes could over-rule a clear Scottish consensus.[68] A Scottish Local Government Bill – which was considered by the SGC – also extended a new system of local councils to Scotland (Rosebery had acted as chairman of the first London County Council in 1889[69]). In 1894 and after two circuits of Edinburgh's Arthur's Seat, meanwhile, Rosebery persuaded the Earl of Elgin to give up his desire to serve at the Scottish Office and become Viceroy of India instead.

By the election of 1895, Scottish Liberalism was bereft of new ideas and expected to lose ground to the Conservatives and Liberal Unionists. This it did, emerging with 39 seats, still a majority but four fewer than in 1886 and therefore viewed as a disaster. Out of government, Scottish party personnel became a confusing nexus of 'ins' and 'outs', those who remained close to Rosebery and others who gravitated towards fresher, younger leadership figures.

James Kellas deemed the experiment of ten years of 'democracy' within the Scottish Liberal Party and its associated attempt to formulate a distinctive Scottish Liberal agenda to have failed. Rosebery resigned in 1896, doubting in a letter to Gladstone whether he had ever actually been in control. On 9 October he addressed a large and enthusiastic audience at Edinburgh's Empire Theatre to make his resignation public. The following year, the Scottish Liberal Association invited Sir William Harcourt, his successor, to address a meeting in Scotland, but when this stimulated opposition among Roseberyites, Harcourt ended up not coming at all.[70]

In 1898 William Ewart Gladstone passed away (the Scottish Liberal Club established a library in his honour),[71] and by February 1899 another new leader with a Scottish power base had emerged, the Stirling-based Sir Henry Campbell-Bannerman. 'CB', as he was generally known, was from a middle-class Glaswegian background, and distinctive in that he was a home-grown Scottish Liberal in an era dominated by 'so many carpet-baggers grateful for the safety of Scottish Liberal seats'.[72] Like many Scottish Gladstonians, Sir Henry favoured Scottish as well as Irish Home Rule, although, practically, he believed the former could only transpire as part of an holistic scheme which prioritised Ireland. 'Scotch home rule must wait', he said, 'until the sluggish mind of John Bull is educated up to that point.'[73]

Home Rule for Scotland – intended to rectify Scotland's sub-ordinate position in British politics – was an integral part of the Radical Liberal creed, of which CB was now head. Deeply 'opposed to privilege, whether of birth or wealth, and proud of Scotland's "democratic" traditions in education and reli-gion' (they favoured disestablishment too), the Radicals had been strengthened by an expanded franchise, the departure of the Liberal Unionists and the reforms initiated by the 'crofter's war' in the Highlands. Led by the Gladstonians A. L. Brown of Galashiels and David McLardy of Glasgow, Rosebery was considered to be a fellow Radical, largely on account of being able to 'speak as a Scotsman to Scotsmen'.

The former premier, however, had other ideas. Roseberyites gathered at Dalmeny to lament the party's radical turn, urging Rosebery to come out of retirement and lead a reformed Liberal party committed to Empire and more efficient government. They believed dropping (Irish) Home Rule would lure back Liberal Unionists, while a focus on social reform could win over increas-ingly politicised working-class voters. This new creed – which viewed social progress as irredeemably bundled up with the British Empire – was to become known as 'Liberal Imperialism' and its adherents 'Limps'.

In 1898 Rosebery had intimated his resignation as presi-dent of the Scottish Liberal Association in protest at the sort of 'faddist' (or Radical) resolutions being adopted by its general council. He changed his mind when the SLA executive agreed to curb policy discussion (thus returning the SLA to its original model) and limit resolutions from constituency associations.

Initially, the Liberal Imperialists believed Sir Henry Campbell-Bannerman to be 'sound' on matters colonial, though they were less enamoured by his uninspiring leadership in the Commons and leaden oratorical style.

When news of war between the UK and the Boer republics of the Transvaal and the Orange Free State reached Scotland in mid-October 1899, however, hairline fissures in Scottish Liberalism once again became gaping crevasses. There were three camps. Liberal Imperialists were almost uncritical supporters of British action in southern Africa, while a number of Gladstonians regarded it as aggressive imperialism. These 'pro-Boers' (a pejorative terms used by Limps) challenged the war on moral and financial grounds, with John Morley arguing that the Exchequer could not afford both expansion abroad and social reform at home. Other, more extreme, Radicals such as the former crofter MP Dr G. B. Clark, lambasted a war brought on 'by fraud, force and folly', not to mention millionaires 'in the fond hope that they would be able to get cheaper labour and bigger profits'.

CB, meanwhile, attempted to chart a middle way, criticising Unionist policy but accepting that the war had to be seen through to a successful conclusion. The divided Liberal Party was compared to 'a dog with the head of Lord Rosebery, an inside of Sir Henry Campbell Bannerman, and a tail of . . . Dr Clark. The whole body would be wagged by the tail, and they would have a mongrel of the very vilest description.'[74] Campbell-Bannerman spoke at Aberdeen in December 1899, supporting two pro-Boer MPs but accepting no Liberal responsibility for the war.

At an SLA gathering the following day, its executive appeared to slight CB, which angered the Radicals. The general council then broke with the executive by expressing confidence in their leader. Upset at the implication he had been behind the slight, Rosebery wrote to Sir Henry, although CB rejected the peace offering. Rosebery finally resigned as SLA president in January 1900, explaining that it was the 'natural corollary' of his resignation as premier in October 1896. 'Since then I have only been a sleeping partner in the association with political liabilities beyond my control,' he wrote to the SLA secretary. 'A relation which is purely formal, but which involves apparent responsibility, is a false position and should not continue.'[75]

Campbell-Bannerman became the new president of the Scottish Liberal Association but took care to retain Roseberyites on its executive so as to avoid a more damaging split. Following the relief of Mafeking in 1900, Rosebery declared that 'we are all Imperialists now' while CB called for magnanimity. The former proved the better judge of the national mood as the Scottish Liberals fought a 'khaki' election 'divided, defensive and largely leaderless'.[76] Having executed a nakedly jingoistic campaign, Unionists deprived Liberals of a Scottish majority for the first time since 1832, with Liberal representation falling from 39 seats to 34. 'The wretched result in Scotland is partly due to bread and butter influences,' was CB's diagnosis, 'especially in the Clyde district, where warlike expenditure is popular, partly to the turnover of the Catholic vote, which was the main cause in my diminished majority, partly to Khaki, and partly to our own factions which have taken some of the heart out of us.'[77] Radicalism, crowed the *Scotsman*, 'has to take a back seat in that part of the realm which hitherto had been its most stubborn stronghold'.[78]

In the words of Michael Fry, 'the Scots Liberals' great century ended on a baffled and disappointed note'.[79] For Ian McLeod, between 1880 and 1900 the Liberal Party 'ceased to be the national party of Scotland' just as Liberals lost their status as the natural party of UK government although, paradoxically, Scottish party figures were more influential in the national party than ever before.[80] Emboldened by the results, the Liberal Imperialists spoke of a second Midlothian campaign with which to re-establish 'sane' Liberalism in Scotland and beyond. Ronald Munro-Ferguson, a leading Limp, resigned as Scottish whip, and the following day Rosebery delivered a rectorial address at the University of Glasgow. His depiction of imperialism as a divine mission enthused Liberals in the second city of the empire but won condemnation further afield, including clerics who denounced the former premier's 'gospel of imperialism'.

A certain hubris had entered the Liberal Imperialist ranks. In his memoirs, H. H. Asquith recounted an occasion in 1900 when he, Augustus Birrell and R. B. Haldane had climbed to the top of a hill near the Firth of Forth to take in views across Fife and East Lothian. Birrell declared: 'What a grateful thought that there is not an acre in this vast and varied landscape which is not represented at Westminster by a London barrister!'[81] The historian C. W. Hill reckoned the hill formed part of the Raith estate owned by MP Ronald Munro-Ferguson (later Viscount Novar), who was also present on the climb, though not a London barrister.

Events in southern Africa, meanwhile, had not quite played out. When reports emerged in June 1901 that the British command had burned Boer farms and placed women and children in squalid camps, Campbell-Bannerman used a speech to denounce what he called 'methods of barbarism', a phrase he repeated in the House of Commons. When David Lloyd George moved a motion to adjourn business and consider conditions in the camps, only 17 of the 34 Scottish Liberal MPs supported CB. Rosebery criticised his unpatriotic remarks, but the mood in Scotland seemed to lean more towards CB's moral outrage at deeply illiberal acts. A by-election in North-East Lanark also appeared to vindicate the Radicals. At an October 1901 gathering of the SLA, Sir Henry said he would neither resign nor retract his remarks.

Undeterred, the Liberal Imperialists launched an autumn campaign which called for the abandonment of Irish Home Rule alongside support for the Empire and greater 'efficiency' in government, but as the war dragged on, the Limps lost their earlier lustre. Rosebery's Chesterfield speech in December 1901 heralded a 'frontal challenge to official Liberalism',[82] after which he and CB met privately in London. It did not go well, with Sir Henry speaking with 'bitterness' (according to Rosebery) at the 'rebellion' which had been 'attempted in Scotland' and 'put down and squashed out by our fellows'. These comments were leaked to the Liberal-supporting *Dundee Advertiser*, for which Rosebery believed CB was responsible.[83]

Rosebery then authorised the creation of a 'Liberal League', inaugurated in London in February 1902 and which 'mounted a full-scale attack on the established party in Scotland'. The Limps focused on organisation, policy and candidates, challenging the Scottish Liberal Association by holding separate meetings. Finance, however, proved problematic, with Rosebery – who called his policy 'sane Imperialism'[84] – complaining that 'Scotland does not give us a shilling – indeed it extracts what it can from our meagre funds'.[85] The war ended in May 1902, and it proved impossible for the League to enthuse Scots concerned at the huge costs already incurred. 'The Liberal party in Scotland was rallying under the leadership of Campbell-Bannerman,' observed S. J. Brown in his authoritative account of the Boer split, 'but it was rallying to the old orthodoxy of peace, retrenchment and democratic reform, and not to efficiency and imperialism.'[86]

A melancholy Lord Rosebery addressed an SLA gathering in Edinburgh in November 1902, at which he still appeared defensive over his earlier resignation as president:

> I am ... told confidentially that I am supposed to have slighted the Scottish Liberal Association by the course which I then took. Well, if I slighted the Scottish Liberal Association, it was a very unnatural act on my part; I have nothing but good wishes, nothing but good feeling, for the Scottish Liberal Association. Who should have more? I founded it; I was its president for some 20 years, its only president, and when I renounced the presidentship, it was not from any feeling of distaste for the Scottish Liberal Association, but because I wanted to carry out to the very end the process of separation from party politics which I had begun in 1896.[87]

For Rosebery 'there had been no second Midlothian – no clear call from the Scottish people, no triumphant return as leader' to refashion the party',[88] rather it had been CB who had successfully invoked Gladstone's rage against the arrogance of imperial power.

S. J. Brown also argued that Scots had prioritised their Scottish rather than British (or imperial) identity, and indeed the early-20th-century Liberals retained something of the 'nationalist' ethos bequeathed by Rosebery. A 'handbook' for Scottish Liberals published in 1900 complained that Scottish affairs suffered from lack of parliamentary time and being 'overruled by the votes of the English members' (it even claimed the 1843 Disruption would have been 'averted' but for English votes). Rather weakly, the handbook also quoted Gladstone's 1889 acknowledgement that were Scotland 'to make a demand on the United Parliament to be treated not only on the same principle but in the same manner as Ireland, I cannot deny the title of Scotland to make such a claim'.[89] The fact that nothing had come of this under two Liberal premiers passed without comment.

At a series of by-elections between November 1902 and 1904 the Liberals regained their Scottish majority. Lord Tweedmouth, chairman of the SLA, overhauled party organisation while the Association promoted younger candidates and trained agents. It also helped that it was the Unionists' turn to be divided, albeit over tariff reform rather than South African wars. Joseph Chamberlain's 1903 call (in Greenock) for preferential taxes to draw the Empire closer together finished off the Liberal League. Popular sentiment rallied in defence of free trade, and the League joined the Scottish Liberal Association and Young Scots Society (see Chapter 3) to form the Scottish Free Trade Union. Even Rosebery spoke at a large Free Trade demonstration in Edinburgh in December 1903. The SLA, therefore, entered the 1906 general election 'with unity in its three main Liberal organisations – the Scottish Liberal Association in the centre, the Liberal League on the right and the Young Scots Society on the left'.[90] Past divisions over Kirk, Ireland and Empire all appeared to have been resolved.

Another handbook issued prior to that historic election expressed the Scottish Liberal Association's confidence that 'the country is on the eve of a great political change, which will bring with it completer freedom, a new economy, coupled with increased efficiency of administration, and a close and sustained attention to the moral and social welfare of our people'. It also made reference to:

> a general scheme of Devolution by the creation for local purposes of Subsidiary Local Legislative Bodies entrusted with certain powers and duties, and subject to the control of the Imperial Parliament, is one which must come sooner or later, and can and will come without causing separation or disintegration of the Empire.[91]

If the electoral consequences of the 1886 Home Rule split had amounted to a realignment on the right, also causing problems for the Scottish Liberals was a realignment on the left. A party increasingly dependent upon working-class support in the west continued to be led by relatively conservative Liberals in the east. By the late 1880s, meanwhile, trade unions and trades councils in Scotland were increasingly turned off by Liberal preoccupations like disestablishment and temperance. According to W. H. Fraser, 1885 was key date for Scottish trades' councils' break with Liberalism, although the Aberdeen Trades Council supported a Radical Liberal in Aberdeen North until as late as 1896.

The *Representation of the People Act 1884* (known as the Third Reform Act) had prompted 'Lib-labs' on the Glasgow Trades Council to field working-class candidates in local and parliamentary elections, thus infuriating the middle-class Liberals who controlled local selection committees. Keir Hardie offered himself as a Liberal in 1888 but had been rebuffed. He nevertheless stood on a largely Liberal platform and made clear that a vote for him would be a vote for Gladstone. To I. G. C. Hutchison, it was apparent that the 'traditional values of the Liberal party in Scotland, such as laissez-faire, constitutional reform, fiscal austerity and moral improvement, were losing their appeal as politics moved to a more class-based foundation'.[92] As R. B. Haldane had remarked in 1894, he had 'not a high opinion of my fellow Scot as a social reformer'.[93]

The Boer War had also brought Radical Liberals closer to Labour politicians through shared platforms at 'stop the war' meetings. In 1904, the Scottish Liberal Association set up a conciliation committee to 'direct its attention, not merely to obviating electoral disputes between Liberal and Labour candidates, but . . . also . . . to unite all the progressive forces' in Scotland. It never operated and, besides, Labour leaders were not interested, a failure W. H. Fraser attributed to the growing class hostility also identified by Hutchison.

Candidate selection did not help. Unlike in England, there was no (Herbert) Gladstone-(Ramsay) MacDonald Lib–Lab electoral pact in Scotland. In Lanarkshire, Liberals refused miners' candidates even in predominantly mining constituencies, and when Labour interventions lost Liberal seats to Unionists, Liberal hostility hardened. By the end of 1906, Alexander Murray, the Master of Elibank and the Scottish Liberal whip, was warning that 'unless the Liberal party stood upon its own legs its very vitals would be consumed and it would fall between two stools, and disappear as an active force in British politics'.[94]

NOTES

1. S. J. Brown (1992), '"Echoes of Midlothian": Scottish Liberalism and the South African War, 1899–1902', *Scottish Historical Review* 71:191/92, 157.
2. I. G. C. Hutchison (2020), *Industry, Reform and Empire: Scotland, 1790–1880*, Edinburgh: Edinburgh University Press, 297.

3. M. Dyer (1996), *Men of Property and Intelligence: The Scottish Electoral System prior to 1884*, Aberdeen: Scottish Cultural Press, 34.
4. See N. Lloyd-Jones (2014), 'Liberalism, Scottish Nationalism and the Home Rule Crisis, c.1886–93', *English Historical Review* 129:539, 862–87.
5. See J. G. Kellas (1965), 'The Liberal Party in Scotland 1876–1895', *Scottish Historical Review* 44:137, 1–16.
6. SLA executive report for 1881, Scottish Liberal Association Papers Acc 11765/2.
7. G. F. Millar (1994), *The Liberal party in Scotland, 1843–1868: electoral politics and party development*, PhD thesis: University of Glasgow, 14.
8. W. Earl Hodgson (1884), 'Why Conservatism fails in Scotland', *National Review* ii 1883–84, 236.
9. I. G. C. Hutchison (1986), *A Political History of Scotland 1832–1924: Parties, Elections and Issues*, Edinburgh: John Donald, 148–9.
10. I. McLeod, 59.
11. HL Deb 13 Jun 1881 vol 262 cc320–21.
12. Lord Rosebery to W. E. Gladstone, 27 June 1882, Gladstone Papers Add MS, 44288 f100.
13. The Third Reform Act created 12 additional Scottish MPs.
14. SLA (1884), *Third Midlothian Campaign: Political Speeches Delivered in August and September 1884 by the Right Hon. W. E. Gladstone, M.P.*, Edinburgh: Scottish Liberal Association, 5.
15. See J. G. Kellas (1964), 'The Liberal Party and the Scottish Church Disestablishment Crisis', *English Historical Review* lxxix, 31–46.
16. D. C. Savage (1961), 'Scottish Politics, 1885–6', *Scottish Historical Review* 40:130, 118.
17. S. Checkland (1988), *The Elgins 1766–1917: A tale of aristocrats, proconsuls and their wives*, Aberdeen: Aberdeen University Press, 206.
18. D. C. Savage, 121–22.
19. See E. A. Cameron (2006), '"A far cry to London": Joseph Chamberlain in Inverness, September 1885', *The Innes Review* 57, 36–53.
20. D. C. Savage, 123.
21. See A. Simon (1975), 'Church Disestablishment as a Factor in the General Election of 1885', *The Historical Journal* 18:4, 791–820.
22. I. G. C. Hutchison (1986), 160.
23. I. G. C. Hutchison (1986), 160–61.
24. M. Fry (1987), *Patronage and Principle: A Political History of Modern Scotland*, Aberdeen: Aberdeen University Press, 91.

25. D. C. Savage, 126.
26. Sir R. Coupland (1954), *Scottish & Welsh Nationalism: A Study*, Glasgow: Collins, 296.
27. Scottish Liberal Club (1885), *The Rosebery Banquet: Edinburgh, 13th November 1885*, Edinburgh: Edinburgh University Press, 17. Following the banquet (attended by Gladstone), the West End of Princes Street was 'brilliantly illuminated' with rows of candles.
28. *The Times*, 3 January 1887.
29. N. Lloyd-Jones.
30. *The Times*, 3 January 1887.
31. NLFS address to members of the Liberal Associations of Scotland, 11 June 1886, Scottish Liberal Party Papers Acc 11765/35.
32. NLFS address to members of the Liberal Associations of Scotland, 1 October 1886, Scottish Liberal Party Papers Acc 11765/35.
33. D. C. Savage, 134. Liberal Unionists created two branches of Hartington's National Liberal Union in Scotland.
34. N. Lloyd-Jones.
35. Asquith later made his legal reputation defending two Scottish radicals, John Burns and R. B. Cunninghame Graham, who had been arrested at a demonstration following the imprisonment of an Irish Nationalist MP.
36. See C. Burness (2003), *'Strange Associations': The Irish Question and the Making of Scottish Unionism, 1886–1918*, East Linton: Tuckwell Press, and I. Cawood (2012), *The Liberal Unionist Party: A History*, London: I. B. Tauris.
37. *The Times*, 31 December 1887.
38. I. G. C. Hutchison (2020), 298.
39. M. Dyer (1996), *Capable Citizens and Improvident Democrats: The Scottish Electoral System 1884–1929*, Aberdeen: Scottish Cultural Press, 51.
40. See M. K. Thompson (2016), 'Defining Liberalism', *The Innes Review* 67:1, 6–30.
41. See W. Pickard (2011), *The Member for Scotland: A Life of Duncan McLaren*, Edinburgh: John Donald, 264–5.
42. W. Pickard, *Journal of Liberal History 50*, Spring 2006.
43. The Northumbrian landowner Sir George Otto Trevelyan, for example, emerged as a Liberal Unionist because of his opposition to the accompanying land bill, but soon returned to the Liberal fold.
44. D. C. Savage, 135.
45. S. & O. Checkland (1989), *Industry and Ethos: Scotland 1832–1914*, Edinburgh: Edinburgh University Press, 85.
46. See C. Burness (2003), *Strange Associations: The Irish Question*

and the Making of Scottish Unionism, 1886–1918, East Linton: Tuckwell Press.

47. N. Torn (2012), *From the birth of 'The Gladstone' to the death of W. E. Gladstone: The Scottish Liberal Club, 1879–1898,* Dissertation: University of Edinburgh.

48. The SLA's fourth official objective became 'to encourage the discussion of political questions in Liberal Associations'.

49. M. Dyer (1996), *Capable Citizens and Improvident Democrats,* 35.

50. R. J. Akroyd (1996), *Lord Rosebery and Scottish Nationalism 1868–1896,* PhD thesis: University of Edinburgh.

51. Report dated 16 November 1887, Scottish Liberal Association Papers Acc 11765/35.

52. J. Bulpitt (1983), *Territory and Power in the United Kingdom: An Interpretation,* Manchester: Manchester University Press, 126.

53. HC Debs 30 May 1913 Vol 53 c495.

54. N. Lloyd-Jones.

55. HC Debs 9 April 1889 Vol 335 c103.

56. *Scottish Review,* April 1890.

57. SLA executive to W. E. Gladstone, 21 October 1890, Scottish Liberal Association Papers Acc 11765/3.

58. J. G. Kellas (1965), 14.

59. J. G. Kellas (1965), 15. The SLA merely sent observers to gatherings of the NLF.

60. J. G. Kellas (1965), 15.

61. H. J. Hanham (1969), *Scottish Nationalism,* Cambridge, MA: Harvard University Press, 119.

62. N. Lloyd-Jones.

63. *Aberdeen Weekly Journal,* 3 April 1890.

64. I. McLeod, 161–2.

65. J. G. Kellas (1965), 14.

66. N. Lloyd-Jones.

67. N. Lloyd-Jones.

68. This parliamentary device was apparently Rosebery's idea, although I. G. C. Hutchison attributes it to Marjoribanks.

69. Responding to criticism of that appointment on account of his nationality, Rosebery remarked 'that if a Scotchman is forbidden to take office anywhere outside his own country we shall introduce a principle so novel, not merely to our nation but to our history, that I do not know in what direction it may turn the current of our affairs' (*The Times,* 20 February 1889).

70. I. McLeod, 209.

71. This still exists, having formed part of Debenhams on Edinburgh's Princes Street until its sale in 2020.

72. The most comprehensive and recent biography is A. S. Waugh (2019). *Sir Henry Campbell-Bannerman: A Scottish Life and UK Politics 1836–1908*, London: Austin Macauley.
73. *Journal of Liberal History* 63, Summer 2009.
74. E. A. Cameron (2010), *Impaled Upon a Thistle: Scotland Since 1880*, Edinburgh: Edinburgh University Press, 81.
75. *The Times*, 5 March 1900.
76. S. J. Brown, 169–70.
77. I. G. C. Hutchison (1986), 177.
78. *Scotsman*, 17 October 1900.
79. M. Fry, 118.
80. I. McLeod, 263.
81. Earl of Oxford and Asquith (1920), *Memories and Reflections I*, London: Cassell, 105.
82. I. G. C. Hutchison (1986), 227.
83. S. J. Brown, 179.
84. *The Times*, 24 February 1902.
85. I. G. C. Hutchison (1986), 227–8. The Liberal League in Scotland was wound up shortly after the 1906 election.
86. S. J. Brown, 181.
87. *The Times*, 3 November 1902.
88. S. J. Brown, 181.
89. SLA (1900), *Current Politics From a Liberal Standpoint: A Handbook for the Use of Liberals*, Edinburgh & Glasgow: Scottish Liberal Association, 120–21.
90. S. J. Brown, 181.
91. SLA (1905), *Current Politics From a Liberal Standpoint: A Handbook for the General Election*, Edinburgh & Glasgow: Scottish Liberal Association, iv–v; 405.
92. I. G. C. Hutchison (2020), 299.
93. I. McLeod, 24.
94. W. H. Fraser (2000), *Scottish Popular Politics: From Radicalism to Labour*, Edinburgh: Polygon, 148.

3

Liberal Scotland:
1906–1922

Sir Henry Campbell-Bannerman had become Prime Minister
in December 1905, after which he brought several Scottish
Liberals, including his protégé John Sinclair, R. T. Reid and
the 9th Earl of Elgin, into his government, the last of that trio
becoming Secretary of State for the Colonies. Not everyone in
the party, however, had been thrilled at the prospect of a 'CB'
ministry. In September 1905, H. H. Asquith, R. B. Haldane and
Lord Grey conferred (while in Scotland) as to the composition
of the first Liberal administration in more than a decade.

The trio were concerned that Sir Henry was already too old
to shoulder the burden of office, thus their 'Relugas Compact'
stipulated that they would not join his government unless CB
moved to the House of Lords, allowing Asquith to become de
facto Prime Minister in the Commons, with Haldane as Lord
Chancellor and Grey as Foreign Secretary. King Edward VII,
who shared their fears, was sympathetic. Although Asquith et
al. were correct as to CB's health, he still called their bluff.
Only Grey received the stipulated seals of office; Asquith instead
became Chancellor and Haldane went to the War Office.[1]

Sir Henry – president of the Scottish Liberal Association since
1900 – also proved himself shrewd enough to capitalise on
Conservative unpopularity by calling an immediate election.
The Liberals won 397 seats to the Tories' 156. In Scotland, the
Liberals won 58 seats to the Unionists' 10, an increase of 24
on 1900. The 1886 split and Rosebery's unhappy premiership
seemed distant memories.

At a meeting of the SLA on 7 February 1906, activists con-
gratulated themselves for having arranged 564 meetings in

57 constituencies during the campaign, something they believed
to have 'contributed materially to produce the excellent results
for Liberalism which were obtained at the polls' (there had
been only 218 meetings in 1900). A general election committee comprising the SLA, East of Scotland Liberal League, the
Scottish Reform Club and the Young Scots Society (of which
more below), had also minimised overlapping activity and competing demands for speakers. For the first time, 'conveyances
and motor cars' had been used to transfer likely Liberal voters
to polling stations. It was, added one of those present, 'a matter
for extreme gratification that the voice of Scotland has been
expressed with such unmistakable emphasis'.[2]

The Young Scots Society (YSS), born out of electoral defeat
in 1900, was widely acknowledged as having contributed to the
1906 landslide in Scotland. An early YSS motto had been 'For
Gladstone and Scotland' which, as James Kennedy observed in
his seminal study of the group, 'encapsulated the Society's dual
aim: to promote both liberalism through support for radical
reform and nationalism through support for Scottish Home
Rule'.[3]

But now Liberals were back in government, the Young Scots
were to be less than helpful, not least in their criticism of the
Scottish Office. This was headed by John Sinclair, who was
considered by some to be politically incompetent but was nevertheless close to the Prime Minister.[4] One Young Scot deemed
the Scottish Office 'too much of an alien organisation', with
legislation 'imposed on [Scotland] against her wishes and desires
. . . framed by an English minister with the assistance of English
lawyers'.[5]

Given the government's massive majority, the YSS could not
understand why Home Rule for Scotland did not appear to be a
priority. Instead, the government pressed ahead with 'unfinished
business' from the previous century: land reform and temperance. Even an education measure harked back to the religious
debates of the 1850s. And only Home Rule failed to reach the
statute book in some form.

LAND REFORM

Land reform had become an article of faith for Scottish Liberals
during the 1890s. Anti-landlordism ran deep in the party, with

landowners being held responsible for having restricted the franchise during the 19th century. The 1843 Disruption had sharpened this feeling – many landowners had refused the Free Church land on which to build its churches – and the Highland crofting revolt had revived it in the 1880s. I. G. C. Hutchison, therefore, viewed the Small Landholders (Scotland) Bill as forming 'a bridge between old and new liberalism which was particularly effective in Scotland'.[6]

But when Lord Pentland (as John Sinclair had become on moving to the Lords) introduced this Bill for a second time in 1907, it not only revived tensions between Liberals and Unionists but also within Scottish Liberalism, not least because it was more radical than parallel English legislation.[7] A clause providing for the enlargement of existing land holdings, whether by agreement or via compulsory powers, enraged gentleman landowners, which included many Liberal grandees in the Commons and Lords. Although Sinclair had Sir Henry's backing (he had alluded to land reform in his first speech as Prime Minister), Lord Rosebery – with his extensive land holdings in the Lothians – fumed that the principle of the Bill was 'essentially a vicious one'. Looking around the Upper House he declared: 'If nobody else goes into the lobby [to vote against it] . . . I will go alone.'

The Scottish Liberal ministers Lord Elgin and Lord Tweedmouth also opposed the Bill in Cabinet. Writing to a colleague, Sir Henry almost seemed to relish that the Bill was not only a 'rock of offence to the Tories' but 'even more to the Lib[eral] Imp[erialist]s, who still rear their head now and then!'[8] But opposition proved too strong and Sinclair withdrew the Bill, its chances of success having declined along with the Prime Minister's health.

Sir Henry Campbell-Bannerman died at Downing Street in April 1908, a few days after resigning as Prime Minister.[9] Although his successor H. H. Asquith (the MP for East Fife since 1886) thought Sinclair had 'the brain of a rabbit, and the temper of a pig', he kept him at the Scottish Office where he met with growing criticism, including from Scottish Liberals. At a particularly rowdy meeting of the Scottish Liberal Association in late 1909, Allan McLardy of Glasgow moved a resolution claiming the Scottish Office was more autocratic than the House of Lords, and branding the Scottish Secretary a 'mere tool in the hands of the permanent officials'.[10]

In November 1909 the House of Lords rejected the Liberal government's Budget in defiance of a convention which prevented the Upper House blocking a financial measure. Sinclair's repeated defeats at the hands of hereditary peers also highlighted that reform was necessary.[11] In January 1910, therefore, Asquith went to the country on the basis of reforming the House of Lords. In Scotland, the result was mildly encouraging, with the Liberals gaining a seat from the Unionists. In England, however, the outcome meant increasing reliance on Irish Nationalist MPs. Asquith then introduced the Parliament Bill and, when an all-party constitutional conference stalled, another election was held in December, at which the Liberals consolidated their position in Scotland.[12]

The Parliament Act became law in 1911 and at the end of that year Lord Pentland moved his Smallholders Bill for the last time. Rosebery again roared in protest, but some minor concessions ensured it finally received Royal Assent – together with the National Insurance Act – on 16 December 1911. A month later Pentland was sacked by Asquith and dispatched to Madras as governor. His wife and *The Times* agreed that Pentland's legislation had bolstered Scottish Liberal support at the two elections of 1910, although it proved a damp squib in practice.[13] By 1914, the new Board of Agriculture for Scotland had created just 500 new small holdings and enlarged fewer than 300 of those already in existence.

Land reform was at least a measure on which the Liberals were willing to take a stand. Ian Packer has argued that the Scottish party's more broadly-based coalition of support – especially after the 1910 elections – meant it was less willing to pursue widespread social reform lest it disrupt support from working and middle-class voters. The party's success relative to England in 1910 also made it less willing to reach any accommodation with the emerging Labour movement. In 1906 a few Scottish Liberals had lost due to 'triangular' contests involving Labour candidates, and in 1910 they had only agreed not to oppose two incumbent Labour MPs.

To the historian Michael Fry, therefore, the Scottish Liberal Party continued to present itself as an 'old fashioned fundamentalist sect' obsessed with 'the unfinished business of the previous century'. Hutchison, on the other hand, acknowledged this rather dated agenda but also detected a growing interest in social reform among the 1906 MP intake, the Women's Liberal Movement and, of course, the Young Scots.

Hutchison also viewed the 1909 'People's Budget' as a key moment in altering Scottish Liberal preoccupations, the resulting controversy allowing them to embrace a social agenda without necessarily alienating more traditional Radicals.[14] The Chancellor, David Lloyd George, was certainly in no doubt that Scottish Liberalism ought to be both 'Radical and National'. Opening the Young Scots Club on Edinburgh's West Richmond Street in 1911, he said:

> The whole tone of Scottish Liberalism has changed enormously for the better since the [Young Scots] Society was founded in 1900, and with the change of tone Liberalism has greatly strengthened its hold on the country.[15]

Lloyd George launched his (English) Land Enquiry in 1912 to develop proposals for new legislation, and this did not preclude 'policies specifically relevant to Scottish conditions'. A separate Scottish Land Report was published on 12 July 1914, with an eye on an election expected the following year.[16] It focused, unlike its English counterpart, on improving the 1911 Act, the ineffectiveness of which was already causing some dissatisfaction among Scottish Liberal MPs.

A policy of taxing land values was strongly supported by many Scottish Liberals. Others were virulently opposed, the most prominent of which was A. C. Murray, brother of the Master of Elibank and the MP for Kincardineshire.[17] He spent 1912 lobbying Asquith and Lord Grey against what he called a 'band of robbers'. Doubtless conscious of this, the land taxers who dominated the SLA were keen to see an unequivocal endorsement in Lloyd George's (Scottish) Land Campaign, which was launched in October 1913.

This split was only resolved when the Chancellor spoke in Glasgow on 4 February 1914. After denouncing various Scottish landowners and promising 'chariots of retribution', he stated that 'the Government have already, through their chief [Asquith], accepted the principle of the rating of site values and they intend to give effect to it by legislation'. In other words, a limited form of land taxation was to be introduced. This was included in the Scottish Report, but in such a minor way that even A. C. Murray raised no objections.[18]

TEMPERANCE

Temperance reform was another legacy issue which remained immensely popular among Scottish Liberals, drawing much of its strength from the support of Presbyterian dissenters. It just so happened that the Secretary for Scotland after 1912, Thomas McKinnon Wood, was a committed Congregationalist (if not a Teetotaller). The idea of 'local option' – granting communities rights of veto over liquor licences via the ballot box – was not new. The Peel Commission on Licensing Laws had recommended it in 1899, and a private members' bill advocating local option and general licensing reform had passed through the Scottish Grand Committee in 1909–10 (this Rosebery creation had been revived in 1907).

The temperance lobby was noisy and chaotic, but the Scottish Secretary was convinced public opinion was on his side. At the Temperance (Scotland) Bill's (third) second reading on 1 April 1912, McKinnon Wood told the House of Commons that just days before a petition signed by 2,000 ministers 'of all denominations' had been delivered to the Prime Minister. The Bill, however, was savaged in the House of Lords and critics accused the Scottish Secretary of steamrollering his opponents. 'Mr. McKinnon Wood has turned the thumbscrew on all members of his own party,' judged the *Scotsman*, 'who have had the audacity to express the heretical view that all wisdom does not reside either in him, or in his Bill.' The Secretary for Scotland came under attack in the Commons in February 1913, and for a while it looked as though the government would ditch the Bill on account of hostility from its own supporters.

McKinnon Wood refused conciliatory moves from both Lloyd George and Winston Churchill, and was heard to threaten resignation if the Bill was dropped. In the end, Lloyd George 'faced the music and got a large majority'. The Scottish Secretary concluded proceedings with a familiar refrain: 'It is perfectly well known that the majority of Scottish representatives are in favour of this Bill, and have been for a great many years, and in that they are supported by their constituents.'[19] This time the Lords reserved its sting for other battles and allowed the measure to go through rather than see the *Parliament Act 1911* invoked.

No 'local option' ballots were held until 1920. 'The rules', judged T. C. Smout, 'were a political curiosity and a testimony to Liberalism's faith in local democracy.' A poll could only be held if 10 per cent of electors requested one and for any change to occur, at least 35 per cent of those on a local roll had to vote, with local prohibition only taking effect if 55 per cent backed a no-licence resolution. Almost 600 polls took place in 1920, with 41 areas voting for prohibition or limitation. Although it proved popular in Liberal-voting, middle-class residential areas, it held little appeal beyond that, particularly in larger urban settlements. Some Liberals also received little credit for having introduced the measure in the first place. Famously, in Dundee, Edwin Scrymgeour defeated Winston Churchill, becoming the first and last Prohibitionist Party MP. Churchill vowed never to return to the city.[20]

HOME RULE

Above all these issues sat Home Rule for Scotland, the dream of many Scottish Liberals for the past three decades. The arguments – as they did over the century to follow – tended to wax and wane, often moving in concert with Ireland, and sure enough between 1912 and 1914 – when Irish Home Rule at last looked close to realisation – Scottish Home Rule sentiment was again a live issue.[21] Not only did it make the Irish Question more answerable, but it could be linked to social reform and allow Liberals to compete with the Labour Party, which also supported Scottish devolution.

With the Liberal parliamentary party dependent upon Scottish members of the House of Commons following the two 1910 elections, the Young Scots Society stepped up its demands for legislative devolution to Scotland as well as Ireland, something also supported by a majority of Scottish Liberal MPs. Increasingly, these demands were couched in terms of 'federal' Home Rule, a constitutional updating of what had been termed 'Home Rule all round' the previous century. Churchill even set out his 'federalist' thinking during a notable speech in his Dundee constituency.

In July 1911, the YSS published its *Manifesto and Appeal to the Scottish People on Scottish Home Rule*. The following year it produced a booklet, *Sixty Points for Scots Home Rule*, which became an important part of the YSS's propaganda work. There was also a lively internal debate as to how much emphasis should be placed on Home Rule, which James Kennedy believed underscored 'a key dilemma for Young Scots: a belief that liberalism should not be subordinate to nationalism; rather, that nationalism should be subsumed within liberalism'.[22]

A related concern among Young Scots was that the presence of so many Scottish Liberal MPs in the UK government represented an impediment to achieving Home Rule. Some also objected to the imposition of English candidates in Scottish constituencies, a view endorsed by Harry Watt, the MP for Glasgow College since 1906. His concern was that 'alien' candidates would lack 'local patriotism' and know nothing of Scotland's 'institutions . . . customs and law and methods':

> Scotland can derive not the smallest gain or benefit from representation from Englishmen . . . No sooner do these men get back to London elected than they forget that they are Scottish members . . . they never think how this legislation will suit the Scottish people who have sent them there. These men of course only make the necessity for Home Rule for Scotland all the more marked. But how is that goal ever to be reached if we continue to import freely from all sorts and sizes of Englishmen.

The Young Scots Society's *Manifesto* also argued that:

> For years and years Scotland has been clamouring for legislation on Land, Temperance, House-letting, Education, and Poor Law Reform, but to all these demands the Imperial Parliament turns a deaf ear – it has no time for Scottish affairs . . . Scotland's story since the Union is a story of legislative starvation . . . [it has] to submit to laws being imposed upon her in defiance of her wishes and desires.[23]

Young Scots did approve, however, of Lloyd George's concession of separate National Insurance commissioners for Scotland, Wales and Ireland, even if this reform undermined the arguments above.

In 1912, the Government of Ireland Bill sparked a constitutional crisis in both Ireland (where Ulster neared open revolt) and Great Britain (where the Unionists spoke of unconstitutional means to oppose it). Asquith immediately regretted a Commons resolution of 28 February 1912 which had stated:

That in the opinion of this House any measure providing for the delegation of Parliamentary powers to Ireland should be followed in this Parliament by the granting of similar powers of self government to Scotland, as part of a general scheme of devolution.

Two-hundred-and-twenty-six Liberal MPs, including 15 members of the government, backed the motion, but the Prime Minister appeared to backtrack in meetings with Scottish Liberal delegations, to whom he made sympathetic noises (saying, for example, that Home Rule for Ireland only would leave the constitution 'lop-sided'[24]) while protesting that 'sound statesmanship and sound business' made it impossible to commit fully. The satirical magazine *Punch* poked fun at the Prime Minister for telling one delegation that he 'would not let the grass grow under his feet'.[25]

Scottish Liberal Members produced a report on the Government of Ireland Bill which recommended that 'the delegation of legislative, executive, and judicial powers by the Imperial Parliament to each of the subordinate legislatures must be of the same nature and extent', while in May 1913 Sir Henry Cowan, the Liberal MP for Aberdeen East, introduced a Private Members' bill. This conflated party and nation, arguing that the Scottish Liberal Association was:

... so predominantly Liberal that, in the absence of a Scottish Parliament, that body can claim to be the most representative institution in the country [and] advocates without reserve Scottish Home Rule. At its annual meeting year after year it debates the question, and it passes resolutions, which become only more urgent as time goes by, calling upon the Government to introduce a measure giving self-government to Scotland. At Aberdeen last November this great body declared in its resolution the urgent need for a federal system of Home Rule and demanded that a measure granting Home Rule to Scotland should be introduced and passed through all its stages without delay. The Scottish Liberal Members to a man are declared and convinced Home Rulers.[26]

But few Scottish MPs turned up to support Sir Henry's Bill. Even Thomas McKinnon Wood, who like Lord Pentland had become increasingly unpopular with the Scottish Liberal grassroots,[27] did not rise to the occasion. 'Half an hour was left for the Secretary for Scotland,' observed the *Scotsman*, 'but twenty minutes sufficed for his perfunctory defence of the Bill.'[28]

The temperature increased a few months later. By November, McKinnon Wood was telling a 'National Conference and Demonstration' in Edinburgh that 'he had the authority of the Prime Minister for stating that the Government accepted Scottish Home Rule in principle and that a measure would be prepared to carry it into effect'.[29] A correspondent writing in the *Scottish Nation*, one of a plethora of journals sympathetic to the YSS, judged the statement to be for 'home consumption', the truth being that Home Rule was 'in the Government refrigerator at Westminster, and nothing will thaw it but public pressure from without'.[30] Indeed, it was 'cynically said that the English Liberals could not afford to set up a separate Scottish parliament and thereby deprive their party of the support of the Scottish Liberals, who had more than once put them into power at Westminster'.[31]

Presentation of a Government of Scotland Bill had become almost an annual event, with measures placed before Parliament in 1906, 1908, 1910, 1911, 1912, 1913 and 1914. That in May 1914 was moved by Ian Macpherson (who had served on the Scottish Land Enquiry) and although it had the distinction – unlike any other measure since the 1880s – of passing its second reading, this Bill, like its Irish equivalent, fell victim to the gathering storm in Europe.[32]

Even during the Great War, there was constant pressure on Scottish Liberal MPs to constitute themselves as a separate pro-Home Rule party in Parliament in a quixotic attempt to emulate the glamour and influence of the Irish Parliamentary Party. There existed a Scottish Liberal Members' Committee with its own secretary and chairman (which demanded, without success, its own meeting room in the Commons), but it never achieved the status enjoyed by the Welsh Liberal Members (who did possess a room). W. H. Cowan protested in October 1916 that his Home Rule Bill had managed a second reading while he had helped found a 'Scottish National Committee' of Liberal and Labour MPs. 'Had the Scottish Liberal Press given effective support to our propaganda', he added petulantly, 'the position of the movement would have been very different from what it is to-day.'[33]

EDUCATION

In one other area, meanwhile, the Liberals returned to the unfinished business of the 19th century. Scotland's voluntary schools – mostly Roman Catholic
   institutions – had long been a source of concern for educationalists. Although government grants were available, generally these schools were much worse off than those under state supervision. In 1917, Robert Munro, the Liberal Scottish Secretary, drafted a memo for the coalition War Cabinet in which he set out two possible remedies: that denominational schools receive fuller state aid than public schools (given the state of public opinion in Scotland this, observed Munro, was 'clearly out [of] the question'), or that:

> ... denominational schools providing elementary education should be compulsorily transferred to the local education authority and should be managed by them in all respects as public schools, but provision however being made for religious education according to the views of the former Managers, given by teachers who are acceptable to the representatives of these Managers, both as regards faith and character. This is the solution which I propose.

For a son of the manse, and a Free Church one at that, it was a remarkably far-sighted proposal. It was endorsed by the Cabinet, and the subsequent Education (Scotland) Bill also proposed raising the school leaving age to 15, removing the anachronistic term 'Scotch' from the Education Department, and creating directly-elected education authorities in place of school boards. In moving the second reading of the Bill, Munro was on eloquent form:

> What is the main object of the Bill? It is, in a sentence, the better education of the whole people of Scotland, irrespective of social class, age, sex, or place of residence ... Education shall become more and more a common possession, as befits a true democracy ... we shall mobilise the intellectual resources of the nation as against those arduous times which are in front of us, when brains developed by education will be of more and more account.

Not only was it an impeccably Liberal piece of legislation, but it neatly linked the past (the sectarian debates of the 1850s) to the future (in its use of PR to democratise education). Even the Vatican, which had initially reserved judgement on the Bill, was won over on being assured it would not prevent the building of new Catholic schools. Although not everything endured – the new elected authorities lasted only a decade – the Act's integration of Catholic schools with the existing state system survives to this day, albeit with occasional rumblings of discontent from Munro's Liberal Democrat successors.

These reforms inevitably upset the established Church of Scotland, which viewed such sops to Rome as potentially dangerous to its spiritual supremacy. As if to make amends, Munro also guided the Church of Scotland Bill through Parliament in 1921. As a young advocate, he had acted for the United Free Church in the property litigation arising from the church union of 1900. By the early 1900s the Presbyterian dissent which had driven a long-standing demand for disestablishment in Scotland had waned, as it had in Wales, although the Anglican church there was finally severed in 1920. Munro's Bill acknowledged the Kirk's independence in matters spiritual, healing the wounds of 1843 and thus helping clear the way for a merger between the Church of Scotland and United Free Church which took place in 1929. If the Scottish Liberal Party had once resembled the Free Church at prayer, then its congregation was less restless than in the late 19th century.

REACTION AND DECLINE

Although the 1906–10 Liberal government had many reforming measures to its credit, Michael Fry judged that such innovations did not belong to Scotland:

> The Scots Liberals were not so outstandingly innovative. True to their nineteenth-century principles, upheld stolidly against Rosebery, they regarded with suspicion ideas for an active welfare policy or for economic intervention. For no good reason, they did not attempt either to bring the lower classes into Parliament.[34]

In the view of W. H. Fraser, the Liberals of the early 20th century also remained wedded to an 'inherent belief that politics were about rational debate within an educated electorate'. They therefore 'frowned on oversimplifying political debate, on crude sloganising and on extensive canvassing. Even more critically, Liberal organisation was crumbling.'[35]

Between 1906 and 1922 there was also a 'rapid switch of

Catholic political allegiance from Liberalism to the Labour Movement',[36] while in 1907 Lord Rosebery ventured 'to predict that at no distant time the Liberal Party will find itself squeezed out between Socialists and Conservatives'. Socialism, he added with obvious distaste, 'can promise much more to the predatory element in politics'.[37] Rosebery denounced his own party's 1909 Budget as 'inquisitorial, tyrannical, and socialistic'.[38]

Although James Kellas has argued that Scottish Liberals viewed National Insurance, pensions and a minimum wage as 'much too Socialist',[39] Liberal espousal of social reform after around 1908 helped keep hold of voters who would otherwise have switched to Labour, its intertwined preoccupations of religion, free trade, franchise reform and the land question having been grafted on to a new welfarist agenda. A good example were free school meals. Having overwhelmingly backed a Great Britain-wide measure sponsored by Labour MPs in 1906, Scottish Liberals turned the House of Lords' exclusion of Scotland from its scope into an opportunity. Two years later, they introduced a more comprehensive and specifically Scottish measure which had secured Royal Assent by the end of 1908.[40]

So, despite various splits and setbacks, Liberals remained the dominant political force in Scotland at the end of 1910. As *Blackwood's Magazine* put it, 'the spirit of Mr. Gladstone still walks on Scottish soil, and the echoes of Midlothian have not died away'.[41] John Buchan also caught something of the hubris that surrounded the party in 1911:

> Its dogmas were so completely taken for granted that their presentation partook less of argument than of a tribal incantation. Mr. Gladstone had given it an aura of earnest morality, so that its platforms were also pulpits and its harangues had the weight of sermons. Its members seemed to assume that their opponents must be lacking either in morals or mind. The Tories were the "stupid" party; Liberals alone understood and sympathized with the poor; a working man who was not a Liberal was inaccessible to reason, or morally corrupt, of intimated by laird or employer. I remember a lady summing up the attitude thus: Tories may think they are better born, but Liberals know that they are born better.[42]

Born to some privilege was Arthur Ponsonby, the son of Queen Victoria's private secretary, who had succeeded Campbell-Bannerman as the MP for Stirling Burghs in 1908.

Demographically, Scottish Liberal MPs now included fewer landowners and more Scottish-educated lawyers. Liberal dominance was thereafter sustained, perhaps superficially, by the First World War and the 1915 coalition. In 1916 Asquith was ousted as premier by Lloyd George, beginning a Liberal fissure every bit as traumatic as that in 1886. In broad terms, those on the right of the party looked to Lloyd George while those on the left turned to Asquith, which included a majority of Scottish Liberal MPs. And Asquith, for the time being, maintained control of Liberal Party machinery.

The wartime coalition, meanwhile, confirmed suspicions in some sections of the electorate that Liberals were an establishment party aligned to industrialists (and now, in government, Conservatives) and therefore unconcerned with workers' rights. The government's heavy-handed response to the 1916 Easter Rising also alienated Scottish Catholics. Liberals such as James Barr, J. L. Kinloch, Rosslyn Mitchell and Roland Muirhead all defected to Labour. The Liberals 'were caught between the rock of acting as an anti-socialist bulwark and the hard place of advancing progressive social policies of their own,' judged the historian Richard Finlay. 'On both counts they were outbid by their respective competitors.'[43]

At a meeting of the Scottish Liberal Federation (as the SLA had become) following the November 1918 armistice, its chairman Sir William Robertson said he believed there:

> . . . was no reason why there should [be] any division in the party and that so far as the rank and file were concerned, there was none. He favoured a Coalition Government with Mr. Lloyd George as prime minister, being supported until the terms of peace were finally adjusted.

The SLA did not like the idea of 'labelling' candidates and resolved to protest to the Prime Minister about government leaders having issued 'a letter to certain Scottish Candidates in Scotland which recognised them as the only candidates in the various constituencies, of whom they approved'.[44] This was known as the 'coupon' and, significantly, only 150 Liberal candidates were to be so favoured.

Although 19th-century franchise reforms had benefitted the Scottish Liberals, the *Representation of the People Act 1918* ended up working against them. This added 8.4 million women and 5.6 million men to the UK electorate, and while overall Scottish representation increased from 70 to 71 seats, there was a significant redistribution from the rural areas of the north and south to the industrial areas of west central Scotland and the city of Glasgow, which was awarded a further eight seats. As Ewen Cameron has concluded, these changes 'disadvantaged the Liberal Party, as almost all of the 13 seats which were abolished had a Liberal history, and favoured Labour'.[45]

Glasgow had once been a Liberal city. In 1885 Scottish Liberals had taken all seven constituencies in the city, performing strongly thereafter even as Liberal Unionists became a significant force in the west of Scotland. But by the 1922 general election, the Liberals found themselves 'pushed to the geographical peripheries of Scotland in the Highlands and other rural areas'. Thus, many of the features of a distinct Scottish political landscape, those which had helped sustain Liberal dominance of Scottish politics since the Great Reform Act, were swept away.

As were many Scottish Liberal MPs. Of Glasgow's 15 parliamentary constituencies, 10 fell to the Unionists in 1918, three were secured by Coalition Liberals and two by Labour. No independent Liberals were elected. Thomas McKinnon Wood, the erstwhile Scottish Secretary, personally blamed Lloyd George for his humiliation at St Rollox. He gained just 8 per cent of the vote and lost his deposit. 'Almost daily', wrote the journalist and MP T. P. O'Connor, he 'could be seen at the Reform Club fighting the old battles over again and haunting the place where in the days of his glory he represented the prosperous, steady, and consistent members of the old Radical creed.'[46]

More traumatically, Asquith lost in East Fife, his parliamentary home since 1886. The *Representation of the People Act 1918* meant that the constituency now included the hitherto separate St Andrews Burghs (which had voted Tory even in 1906), more than doubling the local electorate and altering its demographic composition. The former premier had also neglected his seat, appearing only three times in as many years. De-mobbed soldiers were especially hostile due to Asquith's wartime record. On polling day, he lost by more than 2,000 votes, but refused to resign as leader of the Independent Liberals despite no longer being an MP.

The historian Stuart Ball painted a picture of Asquith in December 1918 as:

> . . . a politician out of his depth, ageing but arrogant, with an exces-
> sive assurance of his own indispensability; a leader with little of
> relevance with which to counter his critics, inspire his followers, or
> contribute to government, save the memory of earlier achievements
> and the symbol of his name.

Asquith later admitted that 'the disintegration of the Liberal
Party began with the Coupon Election of December 1918 . . .
a blow from which it has never since recovered'.[47] Thereafter,
remaining Scottish Liberals overwhelmingly sided with Lloyd
George, the 'heart of the ancient Liberal creed of fierce individualism' having come 'to rest in Scotland'.[48]

There was also a perception that Asquith's long-standing
opposition to women's suffrage had counted against him,
and indeed he and his party had failed to organise Scottish
Liberal women effectively. In the December 1910 Parliament,
43 Scottish Liberal MPs had supported votes for women and
female Liberals had been prominent in the campaign. By
1914 the Scottish Women's Liberal Federation (SWLF) had
25,000 members in 174 mainly urban branches. But when
this was merged with the male-only Scottish Liberal Association
to form the Scottish Liberal Federation in 1918, the SWLF
leadership argued against maintaining a separate organisation,
believing gender equality to have been achieved. This appears
to have been regretted, for in 1925 a Scottish Women's Council
was established, although this was moribund by the late 1930s.
And while three female Scottish Liberal candidates contested
seats in 1922, it took until 1987 for the party to elect a female
MP.[49]

In early 1920, the death of soap manufacturer Sir John
McCallum, the Liberal MP for Paisley, provided Asquith with
a route back into Parliament. The seat was now marginal
and considered a likely Labour gain, something bolstered by
R. B. Haldane's recent call for the Liberals to fuse with what he
regarded as the progressive party of the future. The *Guardian*
observed that local Liberals were hoping for a campaign which
'might be a respectable counterpart to the one begun in this same
land by his great forerunner and political sponsor'.[50] Initially
this allusion to Gladstone's Midlothian campaign weighed
heavily on Asquith (a protégé of the Grand Old Man), although
he embraced it as he got into his stride.

Basing himself in Glasgow, Asquith sought to re-define Liberalism for a radically altered domestic and international scene. The economic content of the 'Paisley Policy' was classically liberal: cut spending on armaments but maintain or even increase on social services; direct taxation of the rich; no borrowing to avoid inflation; no tariffs because of likely retaliation abroad. Competition was key, as was freedom from state intervention (especially nationalisation) and private monopolies. While this channeled Rosebery's old argument for 'efficiency' in government, Asquith's remarks on foreign policy showed that 'the whole world-view associated with Liberal-Imperialism was gone'.

In this, Paisley most strongly echoed Midlothian. Asquith stressed global interdependency, the rights of small nations and the folly of Lloyd George's policy of German reparations. His constitutional platform, meanwhile, 'showed the extent to which the Liberals were forced to rely more heavily than ever upon the Celtic fringe for their voting strength as other sources of support dropped away'.[51] Gone was the Liberal equivocation of old, with firm commitments to proportional representation, Lords reform and a move to a federal state with legislatures for England, Scotland and Wales. Asquith was particularly far-sighted when it came to Ireland, advocating dominion status rather than more half-measures (the Coalition government was shortly to announce its new policy of devolution and partition).

Asquith triumphed, and in the resulting melee his wife Margot was knocked on to the railway line at St Enoch's Station by the rush of her husband's admirers seeing him off.[52] An aide to Lloyd George had remarked during the campaign that Coalition Liberals remained Liberals, with 'old associations, friendships, business, trade and church connections . . . all based upon the habits of mind of Scottish Radicalism'.[53] Independent Liberals were not inclined to agree, and the Scottish Liberal split crystallised a few months after Asquith's by-election victory.

The Scottish Liberal Federation's annual report said a lot about Asquith and Paisley but very little about Lloyd George. Sir William Sutherland and other Coalition-supporting Liberals demanded a right of reply. The Prime Minister's Liberal supporters in Edinburgh had already formed the Edinburgh National Liberal Council, something *The Times* predicted 'may possibly be the beginning of a general cleavage'.[54] That newspaper even dispatched a special correspondent to cover a large SLF gathering at which both camps – MPs and their supporters – were out in force. When the chairman moved adoption of the executive's report, Coalition supporters asked for it to be referred back for reconsideration.

Robert Munro, the Secretary for Scotland, moved this amendment as 'a Liberal who deplored the schism which obtained in Liberal ranks to-day'. Ian Macpherson, who seconded it, was also heckled and barracked as he spoke. John Gordon, meanwhile, refought the 1918 election:

> The same election, too, which killed Independent Liberalism in Scotland killed constitutional Nationalism in Ireland … Scottish Liberals were anxious that there should be concord within the party, but they were not prepared to give up, as the price of that concord, the right to a free and unfettered expression of their opinions.

Another delegate called Lloyd George 'the wrecker of Liberalism'. Winston Churchill spoke last, earning 'a burst of derisive laughter' on claiming that 'he and his friends had come to Glasgow as a mark of respect to the Scottish Liberal Federation'. The Coalition amendment was not carried. A delegate from the East Fife Liberal association then asked the Federation to record:

> … its strong opposition to any policy that involves the fusion of Liberal and Unionist associations, and declares that it is essential to the continued existence and usefulness of the Liberal Party and Liberal associations that Liberals should give full and unfettered expression to Liberal principles and ideals, and avoid all entangling and compromising alliances with other political parties in the State.

The proposer was implored to withdraw his resolution, which he did, although some irreconcilable 'Wee Frees'[55] objected. When they were defeated in another vote, Churchill waved his hat and exalted 'Hurrah! Hurrah!' before leaving the hall.[56]

These events left a lingering hostility. Nearly a quarter of associations disaffiliated from the Scottish Liberal Federation out of loyalty to Lloyd George, who also poached the best organisers, including former SLA president Sir William Robertson (he described the Liberal Party as an organisation composed of 'men who held advanced views, moderate views, and what may be described as Conservative–Liberal views'). Robertson's resignation left an organisation 'nominally opposed to the coalition government but unable to retain a unity with which to confront it'.[57] The Anglo-Scottish MP Sir Donald Maclean became the new SLF chairman.[58] Coalition Liberals did not bother to nominate a candidate of their own.

The SLF, meanwhile, expelled branches which did not renounce the Coalition. Both wings of the party suffered as it proved difficult to build local party apparatus in seats where the opposing Liberal faction was in control. At a 1921 by-election, the Argyll MP and Lloyd George lieutenant Sir William Sutherland ranted that there was 'No organisation. Nobody knows anything about electioneering. The outlying parts quite neglected. You give orders and nothing happens.'

As Hutchison has observed of the Scottish Liberals, 'they had little to offer the working class and social progressives after 1918'.[59] Liberal members of the post-war Coalition also did not help themselves with their reactionary instincts. Despite his progressive work on education, Robert Munro's conservatism had come to the fore when industrial unrest brewed in Glasgow in 1919. A War Cabinet minute recorded Munro's (over)reaction:

> The Secretary for Scotland said that, in his opinion, it was more clear than ever that it was a misnomer to call the situation in Glasgow a strike – it was a Bolshevist rising. It was, he thought, of limited dimensions in numbers, if not in effect.[60]

Three years later, Liberals in Roxburgh and Selkirk resolved not to support a Coalition candidate (i.e. the incumbent) at the 1922 general election, effectively deselecting Munro. He lived to fight another day as a Scottish judge, UK Law Lord and peer.[61] Before 1918, Scots Law had been as Liberal as it later was Tory. Scottish Liberalism produced two Lord Chancellors (Haldane and Loreburn) while 11 advocates served as Liberal MPs between 1892 and 1914; *after* 1918, however, not a single advocate was elected under a Liberal banner while 24 Scottish Tories were prior to the Second World War.

When the Liberal–Conservative Coalition finally broke up in 1922, it lived on with the bizarre appointment of Viscount Novar, a former Liberal Imperialist and associate of Rosebery, as Scottish Secretary in a Unionist government led by the Canadian-Ulster Scot Andrew Bonar Law.[62] At a decisive Carlton Club meeting, Scottish Unionist MPs had overwhelmingly opposed ending the Coalition, and there remained greater co-operation between Unionists and Liberals in Scotland than in England.

At the general election that followed, 23 per cent of Scottish constituencies saw Asquithians fight National Liberals, a bigger proportion than in England. The speed with which Bonar Law had called the election had given the Liberals little time to heal their divisions.

Winston Churchill complained that an Asquithian candidate stood in Dundee simply to make it unwinnable for him. It worked. Churchill was not just defeated, but defeated heavily, coming fourth in a crowded field. Upon his election in 1908, the future premier had regarded Dundee as a 'life seat and cheap and easy beyond all experience'. Fourteen years later and several sections of the local electorate had cooled on Churchill, chiefly trade unionists and Irish migrants. The First World War, concluded William Walker, had been 'a major factor in Dundee's disenchantment with Churchill'.[63]

The long coalition, however, had served to erode Liberal organisation north of the border. Following each election setback, the SLF executive would discuss party organisation but little else. This was true in 1922 and again on 19 December 1923, when a report 'made reference to the result of the General Election in Scotland and while that of the Party point of view for the country was satisfactory, it was not so in Scotland'.[64] The SLF also discussed campaigning for the Alternative Vote (a form of PR), which was, of course, a loser's argument.

At the 1923 election, the SLF proved incapable of nominating more than a handful of candidates. In Edinburgh East, the (not so) 'Young Scot' J. M. Hogge was opposed by a former vice-president of the local Liberal association turned Tory, C. J. M. Mancor, who described his erstwhile friends as having 'a soul . . . so dead that they prefer their Association before the interests of their country'. Hogge held on, but in 1924 Dr T. Drummond Shiels stood on a progressive platform and won. Asquith fought Paisley again in 1922, 1923 and 1924, and although his vote held steady, Labour's rose at each election. Even faced with the clear rise of Labour, Liberal associations in many areas continued to retain men and women keen to believe that the 'continued existence of an organised Liberal Party is of vital importance to the country'.[65]

Meanwhile, Young Scots found other outlets for their Radical Liberalism, either joining the revived Scottish Home Rule Association or the Scottish Labour movement, which could be seen as 'an outgrowth of radical Liberalism, rather than an alternative to it'. Perhaps the most successful of the ex-Liberals was the Rev. James Barr, who joined the Independent Labour Party in 1920 and was elected the MP for Motherwell four years later (after which he unsuccessfully steered another Home Rule Bill through the House of Commons). Only J. M. Hogge, unable to reconcile himself with socialism, continued to press for Home Rule via the Scottish Liberal Party.

Scottish Liberal influence could even be detected in the moderate ideology of the Scottish Unionist Party, which came to dominate inter-war Scottish politics; this owed something to the Liberal Unionists the party had absorbed in 1912. As Peter Lynch has argued, hitherto the Scottish Liberals had gained much success from their ability to 'reflect and promote Scottish values and myths'.[66] But this was subject to the law of diminishing returns when challenged by both Labour and a 'new' Unionism which reduced Scottish Liberalism's appeal among both working and middle-class voters.[67]

NOTES

1. C. W. Hill (1976), *Edwardian Scotland*, Edinburgh & London: Scottish Academic Press, 78–9.
2. Scottish Liberal Association meeting, 7 February 1906, Scottish Liberal Association Papers Acc 11765/9. Alexander Murray, the Master of Elibank, complained to *The Times* 'that the Scottish Liberal Association is not a "caucus" in the usual acceptance of the term . . . It is an organization representative of the associations which are largely responsible for the return of 58 Liberal members to Parliament. It is supported by working-men subscribers throughout Scotland' (*The Times*, 27 December 1907).
3. J. Kennedy (2015), *Liberal Nationalisms: Empire, State, and Civil Society in Scotland and Quebec*, Montreal: McGill-Queen's University Press, 10.
4. Sinclair was a product of London's Toynbee Hall and a former progressive member of the London County Council. He was concerned with welfare and very much in the 'New' Liberal mould.
5. J. Kennedy, 124.
6. I. G. C. Hutchison (2001), *Scottish Politics in the Twentieth Century*, Basingstoke: Palgrave, 6.
7. J. Brown (1968), 'Scottish and English Land Legislation 1905–11', *Scottish Historical Review* 47:143, 72–85.

8. D. Torrance (2006), *The Scottish Secretaries*, Edinburgh: Birlinn, 62. The SLA also supported Sinclair, including at a 600-strong gathering in June 1907.
9. At CB's funeral, the SLA's wreath bore the inscription in gold letters 'In loving memory of our dear leader' (*The Times*, 29 April 1908).
10. D. Torrance, 63.
11. E. A. Cameron (1993), 'Politics, Ideology and the Highland Land Issue, 1886 to the 1920s', *Scottish Historical Review* 72:193, 60–79.
12. In December 1910 more than 20 per cent of Liberal MPs sat for Scottish seats, including major figures like Asquith, Churchill and Haldane.
13. See Lady Pentland (1928), *Memoir of Lord Pentland*, London: Methuen.
14. I. G. C. Hutchinson, 10–11.
15. Speech by David Lloyd George, Scottish Liberal Party Papers Acc 11765/77.
16. Scottish Land Enquiry Committee (1914), *Scottish Land: Rural and Urban*, London.
17. A. C. Murray later published a book about his and his brother's careers, *Master and Brother: Murrays of Elibank*, London: John Murray, 1945.
18. I. Packer (1996), 'The Land Issue and the Future of Scottish Liberalism in 1914', *Scottish Historical Review* 75:199, 52–71.
19. D. Torrance, 72.
20. T. C. Smout (1986), *A Century of the Scottish People 1830–1950*, London: Collins, 146.
21. The SLA hosted the Irish Nationalist leader John Redmond at a Home Rule demonstration in Glasgow on 12 October 1911.
22. J. Kennedy, 129.
23. YSS (1911), *Manifesto and Appeal to the Scottish People on Scottish Home Rule*, Glasgow: Young Scots Society, 2–3.
24. HC Debs 30 May 1913 Vol 53 c472.
25. *Punch*, 15 May 1912. A cartoon depicted Asquith surrounded by tall blades saying: 'Well, you know what grass is.'
26. HC Debs 30 May 1913 Vol 53 cc474–75; 480. A. J. Balfour later mocked Cowan for beginning his speech by quoting 'the [Scottish] Liberal Association as the great national authority proving how much this Bill is desired' and ending it by saying 'This is no party matter' (c530).
27. A newspaper correspondent in 1913 noted the 'frequency of contention between the Secretary for Scotland and certain Scottish Liberal members. No other Minister was so much troubled by

members on his own side' (Scottish Liberal Association Papers Acc 11765/88).

28. D. Torrance, 75.
29. SLP (1949), *Scottish Self Government*, Edinburgh: Scottish Liberal Party, 1–3. McKinnon Wood's pledge was still being quoted in Scottish Liberal Party literature in the late 1940s.
30. J. Kennedy, 146.
31. T. C. Smout, 9.
32. Now in his late 60s, Lord Rosebery spent the autumn of 1914 making 'A Martial Call to the Scots' in a series of speeches, later published in English and Gaelic, an indication that the uncrowned King of Scotland still possessed a degree of popular appeal.
33. *The People's Journal*, 21 October 1916.
34. M. Fry (1987), *Patronage and Principle*, Aberdeen: Aberdeen University Press, 129.
35. W. H. Fraser (2000), *Scottish Popular Politics: From Radicalism to Labour*, Edinburgh: Polygon, 158.
36. A. Dickson & J. H. Treble (eds) (1992), *People and Society in Scotland Volume III, 1914–1990*, Edinburgh: John Donald, 70.
37. R. Rhodes James, *Rosebery*, London: Orion, 562.
38. M. Dyer (1996), *Capable Citizens and Improvident Democrats*, Aberdeen: Scottish Cultural Press, 35.
39. J. G. Kellas (1968), *Modern Scotland: The Nation since 1780*, London: Pall Mall Press, 184.
40. See J. Stewart (1999), '"This Injurious Measure": Scotland and the 1906 Education (Provision of Meals) Act', *Scottish Historical Review* 78:205, 76–94.
41. S. J. Brown (1992), '"Echoes of Midlothian": Scottish Liberalism and the South African War, 1899–1902', *Scottish Historical Review* 71:191/92, 181.
42. J. Buchan (1940), *Memory Hold the Door. The Autobiography of John Buchan*, London: Hodder and Stoughton, 146. Buchan was referring to Liberals in generally but 'especially in Scotland'. His critique could be applied to the SNP of a century later.
43. R. J. Finlay (2004), *Scotland 1914–2000*, London: Profile, 61.
44. Meeting on 22 November 1918, Scottish Liberal Association Papers Acc 11765/10. The reorganised Liberal associations in Scotland had met for the first time in Glasgow on 1 and 2 November 1918. Asquith made an address as the guest of the Glasgow Liberal Club.
45. E. A. Cameron (2018), 'The 1918 Reform Act, Redistribution and Scottish Politics', *Parliamentary History* 37:1, 101–15.
46. D. Torrance, 77.
47. S. R. Ball (1982), 'Asquith's Decline and the General Election of 1918', *Scottish Historical Review* 61:171, 44; 51 & 61.

48. I. McLeod (1978), 'Scotland and the Liberal Party, 1880–1900: Church, Ireland and Empire – A Family Affair', M. Litt. thesis: University of Glasgow, 25.
49. K. Baxter (2013), '"The advent of a woman candidate was seen . . . as outrageous": Women, party politics and elections in inter-war Scotland and England', *Journal of Scottish Historical Studies* 33:2, 260–83.
50. *Guardian*, 27 January 1920.
51. R. Kelley (1964), 'Asquith at Paisley: the Content of British Liberalism at the End of Its Era', *Journal of British Studies* 4:1, 151–5.
52. See R. Jenkins (1994), *Asquith*, London: Papermac, 484–9; S. Koss (1976), *Asquith*, London: Allen Lane. For the Paisley Policy, see H. H. Asquith (1920), *The Paisley Policy*, London: Cassell; R. Kelley (1964), 'Asquith at Paisley: the Content of British Liberalism at the End of Its Era', *Journal of British Studies* 4:1, 133–59
53. I. G. C. Hutchison (1986), *A Political History of Scotland*, Edinburgh: John Donald, 322.
54. *The Times*, 26 April 1920.
55. This alluded to a minority group known as the 'Wee Frees' who stood apart from the Free Church of Scotland when it amalgamated with the United Presbyterian Church to form the United Free Church in 1900.
56. *The Times*, 1 May 1920.
57. S. Ball, A. Thorpe and M. Worley (2005), 'Elections, Leaflets and Whist Drives: Constituency Party Members in Britain between the Wars' in M. Worley (ed), *Labour's Grass Roots: Essays on the Activities of Local Labour Parties and Members, 1918–45*, London: Routledge, 24.
58. Sir Donald had served since 1918 as parliamentary leader of the Liberals pending Asquith's presumed return to the Commons.
59. I. G. C. Hutchinson (1986), 311.
60. D. Torrance, 83.
61. See R. Munro (1930), *Looking Back: Fugitive Writings and Sayings*, London: Thomas Nelson.
62. See D. Torrance, 94–101.
63. W. M. Walker (1970), 'Dundee's Disenchantment with Churchill: A Comment upon the Downfall of the Liberal Party', *Scottish Historical Review* 49:147, 91 & 108.
64. I. G. C. Hutchinson (1986), 313.
65. I. G. C. Hutchinson (1986), 315.
66. P. Lynch (1998), 'Third Party Politics in a Four Party System: The Liberal Democrats in Scotland', *Scottish Affairs* 22:1, 17.
67. See J. Kellas, 179–87.

4

The 'Strange Death' of Liberal Scotland:
1922–1946

For the next few decades, the once-dominant Scottish Liberals experienced a long decline which mirrored what George Dangerfield called the 'strange death' of the party in England. At the 1918 election the party had managed to elect 25 Coalition Liberals and 8 Independent Liberals; in 1922, 12 'National' Liberals and 15 regular Liberals; in 1923, 22 'Reunited' Liberals; and in 1924, just 8 Liberals.

The ideological bent of this dwindling band of Scottish Liberal MPs moved increasingly rightward. In 1923, the eight Scottish burgh Liberals were led by H. H. Asquith, now the MP for Paisley, and they had a strong publishing/media background. The 14 county Liberals were more conservative, and included a few London lawyers. Only two landowners remained, Archibald Sinclair in Caithness and Sutherland and Cecil Dudgeon in Galloway.[1] Asquith proved ineffective in opposing Lloyd George between 1920 and 1922, and little better against Bonar Law and Stanley Baldwin thereafter. The Asquithian court resembled 'an extra-parliamentary conclave of the elder venerated, meeting in spacious drawing-rooms to await the second coming.'[2]

Asquith's decision to prop up a minority Labour administration in 1924, meanwhile, 'evoked a wave of shocked hostility in Scotland'. In Paisley, Unionist and Liberal businessmen implored Asquith not to support Labour. The hitherto Liberal-supporting *Daily Record* switched to the Unionists while Liberals flocked to the Unionists in order to keep Labour out of office. 'It was appropriate', judged I. G. C. Hutchison, 'that the most spectacular casualty of the Liberal rout in that year's general election was Asquith himself.'[3] He was defeated by an unknown young Labour solicitor called Rosslyn Mitchell (who later led a Commons rebellion against the revised Anglican prayer book). 'Keep your eye on Paisley', Asquith had once declared. 'The country did just that,' observed the writer James McMillan, 'And witnessed the end both of Asquith and the Liberal Party.'[4]

Asquith's message to a Scottish Liberal Federation council meeting in October 1924 was to 'Let Scottish Liberalism stand firm'.[5] But the 1924 election was no 1900; there would be no 1906-style bounce back, in Scotland or anywhere else. 'People and politicians alike found Liberal ethics impossible of application to the immense social and economic problems of the post-war period,' judged T. C. Smout. 'Reduced to a tiny faction at Westminster, the Liberals could offer no hope of fulfilling anyone's moral imperatives or political aspirations.'[6] While middle-class Liberals fearful of socialism sought refuge with Unionists, working-class Liberals found a new home in the Labour Party. When Lloyd George returned as UK Liberal leader in 1926, the Leith MP William Wedgwood Benn (father of Anthony) defected to Labour.

While the Scottish party organisation was often more preoccupied with survival rather than constitutional matters, support for Home Rule remained, at least on paper. At its annual gathering in 1924, the SLF reaffirmed support for Scottish devolution within a federal framework, while the following year Scottish Liberal conventions in Edinburgh and Inverness declared that the 'case for Scottish Home Rule is overwhelming, both on Imperial and National grounds'.[7]

By the mid 1920s, all the Liberal Associations in Scotland, including the Scottish League of Young Liberals, were affiliated to the SLF. Chairman of its general council was Sir John Anthony (vice-chairs included Lady Pentland, wife of the former Scottish Secretary). It had offices in Edinburgh and Glasgow and held an annual meeting alternately in Glasgow and Edinburgh, much as the SLA had done since the 1880s.

Its president was the Earl of Oxford and Asquith, who – seatless since 1924 – finally resigned as Liberal leader in 1926. Echoing Rosebery in 1896, Asquith considered Scotland an apt setting for his farewell, for he had 'passed his whole House of Commons career as a Scottish member . . . and he owed to the "Kingdom" of Fife and to Scotland the avenue which led to the leadership'. He closed a celebrated speech in Greenock by imploring Liberals to look neither to the right nor the left but to 'keep straight on'.[8]

The SLF, meanwhile, threw itself into detailed policy work. The report of another Scottish Liberal Land Inquiry chaired by Sir Archibald Sinclair clocked in at nearly 400 pages,[9] while a Committee of Inquiry into the Scottish Fishing Industry was similarly detailed.[10] Both reports signalled the party's retreat into rural parts of Scotland, chiefly the Highlands and Islands. There were also policy tensions between London and Scotland. In October 1926, Sir Archibald contrasted the 'concrete proposals' of Lloyd George's 'Green Book' with an SLF programme containing 'nothing but pious resolutions'.[11] Parts of the later 'Yellow Book', which had special application to Scotland, became known collectively as 'The Tartan Book'.

The 1928 SLF conference expressed unhappiness at a proposed consolidation of local government in Scotland. 'We may as well give up calling ourselves Scotsmen,' fumed A. P. Laurie, the Liberal candidate in South Edinburgh, 'and regard ourselves as a mere province under the rule of bureaucrats in London.' Not only was it regarded as undermining the Acts of Union (which had preserved the royal burghs), but there was resentment at the measure being carried by English MPs and it not having been referred to the Scottish Grand Committee.[12]

Speaking in Dalkeith in January 1929, the former Liberal leader Sir Herbert Samuel claimed the 'spirit of British Liberalism had always included the ideals of nationalism'. Having consulted with David Lloyd George, he warmly supported Home Rule for Scotland, arguing that it would revive the Scottish spirit and address Scottish problems while also serving England and the Empire: 'What had been done for Ireland by Gladstone and afterwards by Sir Henry Campbell-Bannermen and Mr. Asquith – all of them returned to Parliament by the South-East of Scotland – should now be accomplished by their successors for Scotland herself.'[13]

At a general election later that year, the Scottish Liberals managed a modest revival – winning five more seats than in 1924 – but they were now Scotland's third party, behind Labour and the Unionists and far from their glory days with just 13 MPs (as if to symbolise this retreat, Lord Rosebery died during the election campaign on 21 May 1929). The party also enjoyed a degree of (indirect) success in Glasgow, where Unionist and

Liberal-backed 'Moderates' controlled the city 'corporation' (or council) until 1933.[14] Unionists remained keen to maintain the 1916–22 alliance in spite of Liberal decline.

Tales of woe were never far from minutes of SLF executive meetings. At a meeting in Edinburgh on 31 January 1930, it was observed that a 'grant' from the London-based party had come to an end, making it essential for the Federation to become 'self-supporting'. A sub-committee was formed to figure out how. Staffing, meanwhile, was reduced to a secretary and typist in Glasgow and Edinburgh. Two members of staff even volunteered to be paid less, quite a sacrifice in 1930. Others were given notice of redundancy.[15] Many prominent Liberal activists defected to the Unionists. In April 1930, Major Edwin Donaldson resigned from the SLF in protest at the party's partial dependence on the Lloyd George Fund and its 'mute subservience to the insincere and disastrous leadership of Mr. Lloyd George'.[16]

The Scottish Liberals, judged T. C. Smout, 'had been reduced to a bunch of squabbling factions united only by a name and its memories'.[17] The squabbles were about to get much worse. In August 1931, the SLF emphatically supported the formation of a 'National' government, by which point the Liberal Party had split into two groups. The Simonites, led by Sir John Simon, favoured outright opposition to Labour in alliance with the Conservatives, while the Samuelites, led by Sir Herbert Samuel, were prepared to support the National government while fighting for 'free trade' from within. Sir Archibald, a leading Samuelite, became Secretary of State for Scotland and fought the October 1931 election as a member of the government.

The National government won an overwhelming majority with 554 seats (470 of which were Conservative), but it left Ramsay MacDonald, the Prime Minister, as a prisoner of the Conservatives (led by Stanley Baldwin). In Scotland, 'National Liberal and Conservative' (or simply 'Liberal-National') candidates won eight seats and the dissenting Liberals seven. There were soon tensions. In December 1931, the Scottish Liberal Federation, alarmed by Lord Stonehaven saying that the National government had 'a mandate to carry out Tory policy',[18] held an emergency meeting, which earned a reassurance from Ramsay MacDonald that this was not so: 'I am the head of a Government which was elected on a national issue embodied in a national appeal, and so long as I remain in the Government that will be its policy.'

Then, on 18 January 1932, the National government proposed a 10 per cent general tariff, prompting Sir Archibald Sinclair to urge Samuel and his followers to cross the floor. They were persuaded to stay on the basis that they would be free to vote against and publicly condemn the policy from the government benches, something endorsed by an emergency meeting of the SLF.[19] This proved unsustainable and the Samuelites thereafter split into three factions: those supporting the National government; those who did not but supported the Samuelite ministers; and those who condemned both.

The Imperial Economic Conference which opened in Ottawa on 21 July 1932 proved the final straw. Conservative leader Stanley Baldwin excluded free traders from the British delegation and used the conference as an opportunity to introduce a system of imperial preference (once advocated by Joseph Chamberlain). Senior Samuelite Liberals met at Sir Archibald's Caithness home over the summer and resolved to resign from the government. 'Well anyhow you will be Liberal leader in Scotland,' wrote Churchill to Sinclair, 'and there is nothing like having an official dunghill of one's own to crow from, however small and redolent it may be.'[20]

The National government endured and Sir Godfrey Collins, a publisher and Greenock Liberal,[21] succeeded Sinclair at the Scottish Office. Like his predecessor, he regarded Home Rule for Scotland as 'an academic question' given the international situation (clearly SLF resolutions held little sway in Whitehall),[22] although he did begin moves to consolidate Scottish administration in what would become St Andrew's House in Edinburgh. Sir Godfrey also preached 'social justice' as he attempted to improve inter-war Scotland's health, housing and heavy manufacturing.

By October 1933, the Scottish Liberal Federation was demanding that Liberal MPs go fully into opposition. Although Sinclair responded that the SLF 'should put its own house in order first',[23] Sir Herbert Samuel and his followers finally quit the government benches (although J. P. Maclay, the Liberal MP for Paisley, refused to join them). After a period of relative calm, the April 1935 SLF conference witnessed a split over whether its annual report should express support for the

National government. A few months later, SLF chairman Sir William Baird circulated a private memo expressing support for the government and recommending an arrangement with the Simonites at the forthcoming general election.

An emergency meeting of the SLF's general council censured Baird by a majority, after which Sir William and other office holders left the meeting in Glasgow, some later joining the Simonite Liberal-National Organisation in Scotland. *The Times* noted that the SLF's 'unhappy week' had left its 'Glasgow head-quarters in charge of a solitary typist'.[24] Sir Archibald Sinclair found himself leading Scotland's remaining opposition (or independent) Liberals, while the 11th Marquess of Lothian succeeded Baird as SLF chairman. Both published an 'open letter' to the 'Liberals of Scotland' as the National government sought re-election in November 1935:

> Never, perhaps, has the world stood in greater need of the Liberal spirit, and Scottish Liberals can make a great contribution towards that end. The present office bearers desire the cooperation of all Scottish Liberals in restoring the party in Scotland to a position which will enable it to insist upon Liberal remedies being applied to the disorders of our times ... To vote for the so-called National Government is to vote for a party which is mainly preoccupied with protectionism and armaments, the basic cause of the present international poverty, unemployment, and drift towards war ... We, therefore, urge you at this General Election to give your unreserved support to the Scottish Liberal Federation in fighting for the great Liberal causes of peace, free trade, social justice, and Scottish Home Rule, and to vote only for candidates pledged to support them.[25]

Another document signed by Sir William Baird, Lord Maclay and Lord Rosebery (the 6th Earl) urged a different course:

> In a large number of Scottish constituencies there are no Liberal candidates standing at this General Election, and in these cases we who have had a lifelong connexion with Liberalism strongly recommend our fellow-Liberals to give their support to candidates of the National Government.[26]

The Scottish Liberal Federation rather feebly protested at an election being held at all, it being an attempt, it fumed, 'by an incompetent Government to secure on a false issue a further lease of power ... exploitation by the Tory Party for their own advantage'.[27] On polling day, the Liberal-Nationals – still led by Sir John Simon – won 33 seats, of which 7 were in Scotland, while the Independent Liberals secured 21 MPs, just 3 of whom hailed from north of the border. Thereafter, Liberal-Nationals would be gradually absorbed by the Conservatives, just as the Liberal Unionists had been half a century before. 'Not only have we lost our trusted and influential leaders,' Sir Archibald Sinclair lamented, 'but we could not make our free-trade case. Nobody would listen to it or think about it'.[28]

Even so, what Churchill had termed a 'dunghill' proved fertile when Sir Archibald replaced Sir Herbert Samuel (who had lost his seat) as leader of the Independent Liberals. Michael Dyer considered Sinclair something of a Whig throwback, his castle dominating Thurso and his 'vast estate fill[ing] the surrounding horizon'.[29] Such was Sir Archibald's authority that as late as 1966 some could still recall 'how people were astonished by the lack of respect when somebody had the temerity to question him at a political meeting in Bettyhill'.[30]

This aristocratic authority could not prevent an increasingly dysfunctional relationship between the SLF and local associations. The Ross and Cromarty by-election of February 1936, meanwhile, further highlighted Liberal marginalisation when the party struggled even to find a candidate for a seat the party had held since 1832. It was called when the incumbent MP, Ian Macpherson, was elevated to the peerage as Lord Strathcarron. As Ewen Cameron has observed, Ross and Cromarty represented a microcosm of Liberal divisions in the inter-war period:

Macpherson had been a Coalition Liberal in 1918 and a National Liberal in 1922, on each occasion with a Liberal opponent; in 1923, 1924 and 1931 he was unopposed. In 1929 and 1935, however, he had Labour opponents; on the latter occasion Macpherson scored his best result with more than three-quarters of the votes and a majority of over 7,500.[31]

After a couple of false starts, Samuelites eventually settled on William Russell Thomas as their candidate, a Welsh doctor based in London, while the National Liberals chose Malcolm MacDonald, son of the former Prime Minister Ramsay. But Thomas was condemned by the chairman of the local Samuelite association for having been a supporter of the National government. Thomas told Sinclair he was:

... sure it is essential to fight Ross and Cromarty. I am convinced, for many reasons, that the country districts of Scotland and Wales are the places to revive Liberalism; and Ross and Cromarty could well be the opening stage of a campaign in that region. The people are imbued with Liberalism, and do not want Socialism, and trust in the National Government is but a temporary error of mental vision which, I believe, can soon be brought back to its normal Liberal focus.

Sir Archibald's speeches in support of Thomas stressed familiar themes:

Liberal policy, the development of which was stopped by the war, rests on the historic right of the highland people to the land upon which the clans lived. We want greatly to modify the number of family farms and give enlargements on an adequate scale to hold-ings which are now too small to support a family, and in doing so to make sure that land which is capable of supporting a man should not merely be used to feed deer.

On polling day, Thomas lost his deposit and won just 738 votes. An understandably depressed Sir Archibald called it 'the most melancholy episode in the whole history of the Liberal party'. The National Liberals also had their woes. A few months later Sir Godfrey Collins, the Scottish Secretary, died in office and the National Liberals put forward two nominees for the by-election, both of which were rejected by the Unionists, who ran their own candidate under the 'National' banner deployed by Malcolm MacDonald in Ross and Cromarty. The result was a Labour victory in another hitherto Liberal stronghold.

'While at the centre the federation is doing what it can,' wrote Sinclair a little while later, 'most of the associations throughout the country are simply dead.'[32] In June 1936, the SLF approved proposals for a closer relationship with the Liberal Party in England and Wales, part of a reorganisation scheme recom-mended by the Meston Commission. 'While representation on the Council and Executive of the party will make for greater unity and influence,' judged *The Times*, 'the Scottish Liberal Federation will retain its identity, and its application of Liberal policy to Scottish conditions will not be subject to veto or amendment.'[33]

This rather assumed that Liberal policy in Scotland had any purchase or prospect of success. The SLF's annual report for

1938 could only take comfort from Sir Archibald's success in the Glasgow University rectorial contest, although even that harked back to the glory days of the late 19th century when such contests had broader significance. Otherwise, the minutes record grimly, the Federation 'lost many good friends by death during the year, and the financial position suffered as a result'.[34]

It was perhaps understandable that some Liberals looked elsewhere for advancement. A prominent example was Sir Alexander MacEwen, an Indian-born solicitor who had served as the Liberal provost of Inverness between 1925 and 1931. Although a founder member of the SNP in 1934 (and its first leader until 1936), he remained a Liberal, and was even quoted approvingly in the Scottish Liberal Federation's industrial policy of 1937.

This observed that while Liberals had advocated 'self-government' in the 19th century 'principally on the grounds that it would make for greater administrative efficiency and would relieve the congestion at Westminster', a Scottish Parliament was 'nowadays advocated, not merely as an administrative convenience, nor even as a concession to nationalist theory, but rather as an instrument which will enable Scotland to save herself by her exertions'.[35] This echoed the utilitarian arguments in MacEwen's book, *The Thistle and the Rose*. As I. G. C. Hutchison put it:

> The older nationalistic right to self-determination was now almost subsumed by the argument that urgent and radical action was needed if the social ills afflicting Scotland – notably rural decline and urban squalor – were to be redressed. A Westminster parliament was too clogged up with imperial business to handle competently Scotland's peculiar problems. National regeneration, a key social radical concept, was thus explicitly conjoined with Home Rule in the propaganda material produced by left Liberals in the last few years of peace.[36]

In May 1935 the Duke of Montrose, the SNP's president, resigned the Conservative whip in the House of Lords and joined the Liberals. He later announced a merger of the SNP and Liberals in a letter to the *Glasgow Herald*, although this came to nothing. Sir Alexander MacEwen, meanwhile, considered re-joining the Liberals in 1936. A special SNP conference in October 1936 paved the way for John MacCormick, a Scottish lawyer and prominent Home Ruler, to open negotiations with the Scottish Liberals, but the only product of this was a joint candidate in a Glasgow rectorial contest.[37]

MacCormick made contact with Lady Glen-Coats (the SLP's 'most active member') in 1937. Although Glen-Coats has gone largely unacknowledged in the male-heavy history of Scottish politics, she was the dominant personality in Scottish Liberal politics during this period.[38] She invited MacCormick for dinner along with Archibald Sinclair and the former Liberal chief whip Sir Robert Hamilton. After some momentary social awkwardness, MacCormick 'found that both the Liberal leaders were genuinely interested in the possibility of some kind of working arrangement with the Scottish National Party' (which at this time did not support full independence). At a second meeting they reached a 'tentative agreement' that at the next general election the Liberals would not field candidates in 12 seats chosen by the SNP. They would also put their local organisations at the SNP's disposal and urge their backers to support SNP candidates. In 1938 there was a third meeting with Andrew Dewar Gibb, by now chairman of the SNP. The previous agreement was confirmed, but all this was to be overtaken by wartime events.[39]

Writing in 1938, C. de B. Murray observed that the 1906 landslide seemed a distant memory, 'the Liberal Party with difficulty maintain[ing] a precarious foothold in the Western Isles and in a few scattered divisions beyond the Highland Line'. The party, he added, 'which led Scotland in the nineteenth century and the first decade of the twentieth has disappeared, and a new Progressive Party [Labour] has taken its place'. Murray also lamented a related decline in 'intellectual vigour':

> Except Sir Archibald Sinclair, there is not a first-rank man in the Party. Asquith, Haldane, Campbell-Bannerman and all the others, including, prematurely, Sir Donald Maclean, have gone; and no one has taken their place . . . Ask . . . for the name of a prominent Scottish Liberal still in the Party, and it is hard to get an answer. It is harder still to get an explanation for what has happened. A partial explanation may perhaps be found in the Party's refusal to adapt itself to new conditions.

Latter-day Liberals, continued Murray, chattered about the 'eternal principles of Liberalism', a phrase to which 'no meaning can be attached': 'All along the front line the red lights are going up, indicating attack, calling for help. In the face of such a spectacle no one has time to bother about a small band of dis-gruntled Liberals, and so they are left to hawk their shop-soiled wares in deserted markets.' Scotland, he concluded, had 'gone Labour for good: a wise statesmanship, accepting the inevitable, would try to make the best of a fait accompli.'[40] In local government, there was an occasional bright spot, with the Liberals providing one of Dundee's most respected Lord Provosts between 1940 and 1946, the retailer Sir Garnet Wilson.

By the outbreak of war, the Scottish Liberal Federation was reliant upon voluntary contributions and had become little more than a middle-class debating society. At an emergency meeting of office bearers on 6 September 1939, the party learned that it was to function under Ministry of Information guidelines and sent a supportive message to Sir Archibald Sinclair: 'In the part which organised Liberalism is going to play in the national emergency, the Scottish Liberal Federation will, we feel sure, contribute its share in full and generous measure.'[41] Sinclair joined the wartime coalition as Secretary of State for Air, while Ernest Brown, a Torquay-born Baptist preacher and Simonite 'Liberal-National' went to the Scottish Office.[42]

Even during the war, the Scottish Liberals managed to fall out with one another. At the 1941 Scottish Liberal conference, Lady Glen-Coats' resolution calling for a Scottish parliament and associated plebiscite was opposed by the Aberdeen Liberal Association, which believed Scotland was 'not geographically suited for a Legislature of its own', fearing it would increase bureaucracy and what it called 'sectional interests'. Devolution, it added, could be 'attained by Parliament through other effective means'.[43] There had been discussions in 1940 with a view to John Bannerman contesting the Argyll by-election as an SNP candidate, and again in 1941 regarding the idea of a plebiscite on Home Rule.[44] Neither came to fruition.

Conscious that the SLF was 'well in its decline', John MacCormick decided it might offer 'an open platform on which I would be free to speak my mind both on political questions in general and on Scottish Home Rule in particular'. Having first checked there was no objection to turning the SLF 'into an independent Scottish Liberal Party', he threw in his 'lot with the Liberals and bent myself to the task of helping to frame a new constitution for Liberalism in Scotland'. MacCormick – who had left the SNP in 1942 – subsequently became vice-chairman and stood in Inverness-shire in 1945. His Liberal election address was little different to that he had previously issued as an SNP candidate.[45]

Churchill, meanwhile, had appointed the 6th Earl of Rosebery as a caretaker Secretary of State for Scotland, who went to considerable lengths to argue that Churchill's re-election agenda was essentially a Liberal platform. He also stated with 'absolute confidence' that if his father were still alive, he 'would have been the leader of the National Liberals, and would have lashed the Sinclairites with a scorn of which he was a past-master'.

While Liberal-Nationals and Independent Liberals retained three seats each in Scotland, not a single official Liberal was elected. Lady Glen-Coats even earned the dubious honour of being the first Liberal candidate to lose her deposit in Paisley. Sir Archibald Sinclair lost Caithness and Sutherland in a three-way contest in which only 61 votes divided the candidates. At an SLF executive meeting in Glasgow on 5 September 1945, only 14 out of 23 candidates who had fought the recent election indicated a willingness to be re-adopted. Mr Fothergill of the general election committee said that 'real, active, intellectual and spiritual enthusiasm must accompany all our efforts to carry on the fight for what we believe to be political truth'.[46] But party subscriptions had dried up and by the following month there 'was not sufficient money in the Bank to pay the [party's] salaries'.[47]

The party's general election committee also called on the SLF to reorganise because of the need for 'real live Liberals organised in active associations all over the country putting in the maximum amount of hard work for the Liberal cause'. At the SLF's annual meeting on 15 March 1946 there was extensive discussion as to what the name of the new organisation ought to be. Eventually two young Liberals from Edinburgh University suggested 'The Scottish Liberal Party', which was agreed. This, it was optimistically recorded, would take over the functions of the Scottish Liberal Federation 'as an active organisation to bring about a Liberal revolution in Scotland'.[48]

NOTES

1. Dudgeon stood for Mosley's New Party in 1931, unsuccessfully.
2. Quoted in D. Dutton (2004), *A History of the Liberal Party*, Basingstoke: Palgrave Macmillan, 81.

3. I. G. C. Hutchison (1986), *A Political History of Scotland 1832–1924*, Edinburgh: John Donald, 328.
4. J. McMillan (1969), *Anatomy of Scotland*, London: Leslie Frewin, 101.
5. *The Times*, 11 October 1924.
6. T. C. Smout (1986), *A Century of the Scottish People 1830–1950*, London: Collins, 148.
7. SLF (1925), *Liberal Principles and Aims adopted by the Scottish Convention of Liberals*, Edinburgh and Glasgow: Scottish Liberal Federation, 13.
8. *The Times*, 16 October 1926.
9. SLF (1928), *The Scottish Countryside*, Glasgow: Scottish Liberal Federation.
10. SLF (1929), *Our Scottish Sea Fisheries: Their Present Plight, and the Liberal Remedy*, Edinburgh & Glasgow: Scottish Liberal Federation.
11. *The Times*, 15 October 1926.
12. *The Times*, 15 October 1928.
13. *The Times*, 18 January 1929.
14. See J. J. Smyth (2003), 'Resisting Labour: Unionists, Liberals, and Moderates in Glasgow between the wars', *Historical Journal* 46:2, 375–401.
15. SLF executive meeting, 31 January 1930, Scottish Liberal Association Papers Acc 11765/13.
16. *The Times*, 14 April 1930.
17. T. C. Smout, 178.
18. *The Times*, 5 December 1931.
19. *Glasgow Herald*, 2 February 1932.
20. D. Torrance (2006), *The Scottish Secretaries*, Edinburgh: Birlinn, 124. See also G. J. De Groot (1993), *Liberal Crusader: The Life of Sir Archibald Sinclair*, London: C. Hurst & Co.
21. Collins began his career as a supporter of Lloyd George's 'New Liberalism' but later joined Asquith's faction on quitting the Coalition government in 1920.
22. At the October 1932 SLF conference, there was a clear split on Home Rule, with some Liberals proposing an investigatory commission rather than immediate devolution.
23. *The Times*, 21 October 1933.
24. *The Times*, 26 October 1935.
25. *The Times*, 5 November 1935.
26. *The Times*, 13 November 1935.
27. SLF executive meeting, 21 October 1935, Scottish Liberal Papers Acc 11765/16.
28. G. J. De Groot, 98.

29. M. Dyer (1996), *Capable Citizens and Improvident Democrats*, Aberdeen: Scottish Cultural Press, 160.
30. D. E. Butler & R. Rose (1966), *The British General Election of 1966*, London: Macmillan, 229.
31. E. A. Cameron (2008), '"Rival foundlings": the Ross and Cromarty by-election, 10 February 1936', *Historical Research* 81:213, 507–30.
32. T. C. Smout, 179.
33. *The Times*, 2 June 1936.
34. Scottish Liberal Papers Acc 11765/45.
35. SLF (1937), *A Policy for Scotland: Interim Report of the Industrial Policy Committee*, Edinburgh & Glasgow: Scottish Liberal Federation. Dingle Foot, brother of Michael and a Dundee Liberal MP, served on the Industrial Policy Committee.
36. I. G. C. Hutchison (2001), *Scottish Politics in the Twentieth Century*, Basingstoke: Palgrave, 7.
37. R. J. Finlay (1994), *Independent and Free: Scottish Politics and the Origins of the Scottish National Party 1918–1945*, Edinburgh: John Donald, 194.
38. The otherwise comprehensive *Biographical Dictionary of Scottish Women* (2006, EUP) ignores Lady Glen-Coats, as do other works on women in Scottish politics.
39. J. MacCormick (1955), *The Flag in the Wind: The Story of the National Movement in Scotland*, London: Victor Gollancz, 93–4.
40. C. de B. Murray (1938), *How Scotland is Governed*, Edinburgh & London: The Moray Press, 47–9. Sir Donald Maclean was a second-generation Scot who served as Liberal Leader of the Opposition between 1918 and 1920.
41. SLF executive meeting, 6 September 1939, Scottish Liberal Papers Acc 11765/14.
42. D. Torrance, 153–6.
43. SLF annual conference, 12 September 1941, Scottish Liberal Papers Acc 11765/15.
44. R. J. Finlay, 218.
45. J. MacCormick, 112.
46. SLF executive meeting, 5 September 1945, Scottish Liberal Papers Acc 11765/14.
47. Joint Finance Committee meeting, 15 November 1945, Scottish Liberal Papers Acc 11765/14.
48. SLF annual meeting, 15 March 1946, Scottish Liberal Papers Acc 11765/14.

5

'Intransigence and Domestic Strife': 1946–1964

As a Scottish Liberal Party (SLP) publication later observed: 'Partly because of distance, partly because of national feeling, Liberals in Scotland felt they could run their own affairs better as an independent Party, rather than as a unit of a U.K. Party, directed from London.'[1] At this point the SLP was not, as activist Sandra Grieve observed, 'a mass membership party, it had virtually no money, no external sponsorship and little prospect of electoral success'.[2] It was headed by a president, initially 'titular, rather than active', beneath which sat a chairman, 'the organisational head' and 'political leader', three vice-chairmen and one or two treasurers. Finally, there was a small executive to which all specialist committees reported.

Lady Glen-Coats was the first chair (1946), succeeded by John G. Wilson in 1952, both of whom had the job of leading the SLP 'through the especially difficult days of the late 40s and early 50s'.[3] Glen-Coats in particular kept the show on the road when the party could easily have ceased to exist. The daughter-in-law of Sir Thomas Glen-Coats, the Liberal MP for West Renfrewshire 1906–1910 and a prominent industrialist in Paisley,[4] she became something of a Liberal talent spotter, encouraging Sir William Beveridge to stand for Parliament during the war and recommending a young Jo Grimond to the electors of Orkney & Shetland in 1945 (she had been due to stand herself).[5] Sandra Grieve reckoned Glen-Coats 'set the tone for women in the party', with those prominent 'well educated, well connected, articulate and confident, in fact not so different from the men'.[6]

Despite the reforms of 1946, there remained a rather 'uneasy' and 'ill-defined' relationship between the SLP and the Liberal

Party Organisation (LPO) in London.[7] The Scottish Liberal Federation had been part of the LPO but the SLP considered itself 'wholly independent, running its own organisation, raising its own money, selected its own Candidates, determining its own priorities and campaigns'. In practice, however, it accepted the leadership of the UK Parliamentary Liberal Party, from whom the national leader was drawn, while also tending 'to follow policy leads from its larger English partner'.[8] Early meetings of the new party were dominated by the precise nature of the relationship between the parties in Edinburgh and London. On 20 June 1946 it was agreed (on the motion of John MacCormick) that this would function 'on the basis of political co-equals with the same ideals and objectives working for a common cause'.[9]

But what did political co-equality look like? Representation had previously been agreed between the Aberdonian president of the LPO, Lord Meston, and the SLF; 'our people going to their meetings and their people coming to ours', was how Lady Glen-Coats put it, 'thus maintaining a friendly liaison'.[10] This arrangement, whereby the LPO appointed representatives to the SLP's general council and vice versa, was maintained after 1946. At the same time, Scottish Liberals could not help thinking that the LPO looked on them as 'a splinter party' rather than an 'Independent Organisation' (and indeed on Scotland as 'a splinter of England').[11]

The LPO constitution did not accord the SLP any special status, and therefore it was in the curious position of being formally non-affiliated. Lady Glen-Coats observed that the SLP's position vis-à-vis the LPO 'was unconstitutional but it was never questioned. Their position was challengeable but no one challenged it'.[12] In June 1947, the LPO informed the SLP that if it wanted to affiliate then it would have to pay, quite an ask of a cash-strapped party. But while unaffiliated, all officers and members of the SLP executive were ex-officio members of the UK Liberal Assembly and had the right to submit one resolution for inclusion in its agenda.[13] The LPO also offered that one of six peers on the Liberal Council 'shall be representative of Liberalism in Scotland', as would one of its six MPs, although this was rather academic.[14]

And despite the SLP's 'independent' status, the LPO was still able to by-pass Edinburgh and supervise candidate selection and financial arrangements in several Scottish constituencies until the 1960s. In 1946, for example, the Eastern Committee of the old Scottish Liberal Federation had declared that, in the event of a by-election in Caithness and Sutherland, all arrangements should be made from London, such interventions being more common in constituencies where the party actually had a chance of success. For this reason, Mark Egan judged that it was 'more convenient to consider the SLP as the equivalent of an English federation rather than as a separate party'.[15]

Funding remained a perennial problem. At another meeting in September, it was agreed to move away from reliance upon 'generous subscribers' and 'special appeals' (usually to the same people) and 'be a democratic Party, each of us paying for our politics'. Instead, the SLP moved to an LPO-type 'covenant' system, set at £20 a year for five years. The LPO had also agreed to give the SLP 60 per cent of the profits from Scottish subscriptions to the *Liberal News*, with half going to SLP HQ and the other half to constituency associations (this, however, proved quixotic). Indeed, the lack of finances was already 'retarding' efforts to such an extent that Covenant forms were handed out to Council members at the end of the same meeting.[16] The following year, Sir Thomas Glen-Coats agreed to lend the party £600 (interest free) in order to pay an assistant organiser for a year.[17] In December 1946 a 30-seater coach was hired to take delegates from the east of Scotland to the meeting of the General Council of the party in Perth. The booking had to be cancelled as only 8 seats were reserved.[18]

During 1947 Lady Glen-Coats bemoaned the lack of 'new enthusiasm' arising from these organisational changes. She criticised the Glasgow Liberal Council (GLC), arguing that 'caucus domination . . . within the Party [was] not in accordance with democratic principle' and was having a 'disrupting' influence on the SLP. As a consequence, she resigned as chairman, effective at the end of the following month. Members of the GLC walked out in protest, and a motion begged Lady Glen-Coats to reconsider in view of her 'services to the Party'.[19] She explained on 25 June 1947 that she felt something 'to be fundamentally wrong in the Party':

> She said she had always felt a tremendous urge of duty. Many a time she had sacrificed her own inclinations, her own real interests too, to march on with it. As circumstances were, she did not feel that

sense of duty to be quite so strong . . . She felt it was wrong that the Party should be dependent on one person alone.[20]

The party's age-old image problem also stood unresolved. An executive report in late 1947 admitted that the adoption of working-class candidates had been 'entirely neglected', and that the party risked being seen to 'represent only the middle-class of bourgeoisie'.[21] Relations between (largely middle-class) Liberals in London and Edinburgh had at least improved by 1948, when the executive boasted of 'exceptionally close liaison between the Scottish Liberal Party and the Liberal Party Organisation'. The SLP had increased its representatives on the Liberal Council to 14, while a Liberal Society was formed at Aberdeen University in early 1949. A windfall from the Trustees of the Helensburgh Liberal Club had even allowed the party to balance its budget.[22]

REUNIFICATION

There was also the matter of the Liberal-Nationals (or National Liberals, both labels were used), who had remained affiliated to various coalition – and Conservative dominated – governments since the early 1930s. The June 1946 SLP conference had resolved to approach the Liberal-National Party 'with a view to exploring the grounds for a Liberal Reunion'. A meeting duly took place on 26 July at the Edinburgh Chambers of Commerce. Lady Glen-Coats (whose resignation had not lasted long) said there ought to be 'no post-mortems', a stipulation immediately broken by Sir James Henderson-Stewart, the Liberal-National MP for East Fife, who evoked Asquith and Lloyd George, 'not altogether to the credit of the departed'. Lady Glen-Coats also feared that a press campaign was setting out to put the Liberals 'in the wrong'.[23] She reported:

> I am glad to report that the majority of our opposite number appeared sincerely wishful for Reunion, and were not prepared to be exacting as to conditions, and I have no fear that, if left to themselves, we should have it almost immediately . . . most of the answers on political issues as such came from the two M.P.s and it was obvious . . . none of our opposite number had any very concrete political opinions. They were the views of the man in the street – nothing more. There was also some question about adding the word "United" to S.L.P. Our difficulty is going to be just with the M.P.s where direct Reunion is concerned.

Those were prescient words. Lady Glen-Coats said she was 'not disappointed, or over-optimistic – just hopeful' but said the SLP had to be 'steady, and not allow ourselves, by impulsive action and too much outside talk, to be jockeyed into a position where the Press can pin any future failure to unite on the Scottish Liberal Party and on them alone'.[24]

An early test of these negotiations did not augur well. A by-election was pending for the Combined Scottish Universities constituency (this elected three MPs via the single transferable vote). In October 1946 the Liberal-Nationals nominated a candidate, Major Scott Stevenson, without consulting the SLP, who wanted John Bannerman to stand as a joint candidate. The SLP agreed to support Major Stevenson if he stood as an Independent Liberal, but he refused, saying he already had more than 100 graduates pledged to support him as a Liberal-National. Bannerman said if he stood it would be as a 'pure Liberal . . . diametrically opposed to Liberal-Nationalism and all it stands for'.[25]

Reunion negotiations, meanwhile, got under way at the Scottish Liberal Club in a 'strained atmosphere' given the knowledge that parallel talks between the LPO and Liberal-Nationals in England had recently broken down. Reporting back to the SLP executive, Lady Glen-Coats was of the view that 'if public opinion among Liberals here in Scotland is not to be further puzzled and alienated by the recurring impression of intransigence and domestic strife, then some hope of ultimate Reunion, however remote, had to go to the Press'. She remained concerned that the media would depict the Scottish Liberals who, after all, had no MPs, as 'incorrigible diehards whom the country need no longer continue to take seriously'. She noted that other 'forces' within the Liberal-Nationals were striving 'for full co-operation with the Conservative Party if they will have them'.[26]

The draft terms were 'to form a United Scottish Liberal Party, enjoying complete independence as a political organisation'. Its object would be to 'advocate the practical application of Liberal principles in Scotland, and to develop a social economic and foreign policy designed to create a free, peaceful and prosperous society at home', the 'fundamental cleavage' being between 'those who believe in State socialism' and those who believe that 'individual enterprise and individual ownership of property are essential to the maintenance of the democratic form of government'. Point 5 was a fudge, stating merely that 'a measure of devolution of Scottish Government is necessary in the interests of Scotland's welfare'. John MacCormick observed that it was 'obviously a compromise document', but one that appears to have exhausted Lady Glen-Coats, who had been advised by her doctor to go abroad for three months' rest.[27] MacCormick stood in as party chairman.

On 8 March 1947, a rested Lady Glen-Coats intimated that the Scottish Liberal-National Association had broken off negotiations for reunion, despite tentative agreements having been reached at a second joint meeting with the SLP. 'The onus,' she said with a degree of relief, 'therefore ... rested with the Liberal-National Association.'[28] Later, Glen-Coats concluded that the Liberal-Nationals' 'aim and object was merely to gain Liberal support for the Conservative Party, to which they are tied, and on which they are dependent for the retention of their Parliamentary Seats'.[29]

In late 1947, Sir James Henderson-Stewart, the Liberal-National MP for East Fife, wrote to *The Times* suggesting a merger with the Conservatives. He went on to serve as a Scottish Office minister in the Conservative governments of Churchill and Eden, as did Niall Macpherson in Dumfriesshire. As Malcolm Petrie has observed, in Scotland, National Liberalism 'enjoyed a long afterlife', especially potent in areas of historic Conservative weakness, and therefore relative Liberal strength.[30] Between 1947 and 1964, the position of National Liberal chairman (or UK leader) was held exclusively by Scottish MPs, while John Maclay, the National Liberal MP for West Renfrewshire, served as Secretary of State for Scotland between 1957 and 1962.[31] The Woolton-Teviot pact of 1947 was intended to presage a wider pact between Conservatives and Liberals as well as the National Liberals – Churchill even offered to make Clement Davies (the UK Liberal leader) education minister in his 1951 government.

DEVOLUTION AND PAISLEY

Although the Scottish Liberal Party generally took its policy lead from London, a major exception was its stance on the government of Scotland, on which 'it took a strongly independent federal line and [led] U.K. Liberal thinking'.[32] This had already proved a stumbling block in negotiations with the Liberal-Nationals and Lady Glen-Coats was obsessed with reaffirming the Scottish Liberal commitment to what it now called 'devolution' rather than Home Rule. She even set out a comprehensive scheme of constitutional reform to journalists in October 1946.[33] Opinion polls in 1945 and 1947 suggested that around 70 per cent of Liberal supporters in Scotland also backed devolution.

When John MacCormick's 'Scottish Convention' (a cross-party Home Rule group) held a National Assembly during 1947, the Scottish Liberal Party sent five delegates, with the Duke of Montrose (a founder member of the SNP) intending to 'propound' Scottish Liberal views, although he ended up being too ill to attend.[34] During a House of Lords debate on Scottish Affairs in November that year, Montrose presented Home Rule as 'the foremost principle on our Liberal platform in Scotland', taking care to protest that the party had 'never dreamed of separation or the breaking up of the United Kingdom'. Responding as a Liberal-National, the Earl of Rosebery reminded Montrose that:

> if the Scottish Liberal Party at the last Election did have Home Rule for Scotland as the main plank of their platform not only did they not win a single seat in Scotland but they did not even retain any of the seats they held before. Therefore, it is perfectly fair for those of us not in favour of Home Rule for Scotland to point out to the noble Duke and his supporters that there does not seem to be a general wish in Scotland for Home Rule, let alone for separation.[35]

There were tensions with the Liberal Party Organisation in London, whose recent policy statement had included a paragraph on devolution MacCormick considered 'vague, weak and uninspiring', representing a watering-down of a 1945 Liberal Assembly resolution.[36] He demanded that in future any 'major pronouncements on Liberal Policy should be accepted both in England and in Scotland as statements of British Liberal Policy' and urged 'a policy of federalism for Great Britain as a central feature in its programme'.[37]

MacCormick must have been reassured when Clement Davies spoke at a Scottish Liberal rally in Glasgow on 11 April, the first time he had addressed an audience north of the border. He flattered them with talk of Scotland as the 'nursery of Liberalism', evoking Gladstone, Rosebery, Campbell-Bannerman and even Asquith. He regretted Sir Archibald Sinclair's recent failure to

recapture Caithness and Sutherland at a by-election and asked
rhetorically what the remedy was for an overworked Parliament
at Westminster:

> Obviously Devolution. Devolution for Scotland, for Wales and I
> would advocate also Devolution for Greater London with its 10
> or 11 million inhabitants, and for such other regions in England as
> can only be fairly worked under a system of Devolution. This is in
> accordance with the true Liberal principles, for we not only believe
> in democracy but we believe that the institutions should be working
> institutions ... [it was] high time that the system of Home Rule
> should be extended so that Scotland can deal with Scottish affairs
> and Wales with Welsh affairs and England with English affairs.[38]

In October 1947, John MacCormick reported back from the
National Assembly, saying that its proposals for a Scottish
Parliament 'were to a very large extent the proposals adopted by
the Liberal Party in 1924, brought up to date'. 'We as Liberals
can support these proposals not merely because we are Scots,'
he added, 'but because we are Liberals and because they express
the fundamental principles of Liberal policy.' This was unanimously accepted.[39]

A pending by-election in Paisley, meanwhile, represented
an opportunity for the party to test popular support for this
nationalist-unionist agenda. Lady Glen-Coats had been due to
stand as the Scottish Liberal candidate but had resigned, and
so her place was taken by MacCormick. Although the party's
performance in the recent Edinburgh East by-election had been
disappointing due to the weakness of Liberal organisation and
the 'specious claims of the Liberal-National-Tory Candidate to
represent Liberals',[40] the SLP had high hopes for Paisley.[41]

Matters were complicated when the Conservatives approached
MacCormick and asked him to stand as a Liberal-National
instead. Even after a Unionist candidate had been selected they
tried again, suggesting he stand as a 'Liberal and Unionist' candidate and 'pipe down on Scottish Devolution'. MacCormick,
who nursed a quixotic goal of merging the SLP, National Liberal
Party and Scottish Unionists, agreed to stand as a 'National'
candidate but told the SLP executive he had 'every intention
of saying that he is a Liberal and if returned would sit on the
Liberal benches in the House of Commons'. Despite considerable unhappiness, the prospect 'of seeing a Scottish Liberal

spokesman returned to Westminster, someone who could stand up for Scottish Liberalism and who could stand up for Scottish interests' won out against those who feared pacts with the Tories 'would eventually lead to the loss of our independence and the end of the Scottish Liberal Party'.[42]

Lady Glen-Coats wobbled, refusing to carry out the executive's decision at the Scottish Liberal Council, and resigned a week later, citing 'her own personal principles', i.e. the potential loss of Scottish Liberal independence. Sure enough, the Council resolved that it could not 'support the Paisley pact on the grounds that it is in conflict with the declared policy of the Party',[43] even though MacCormick had convinced the Conservatives to agree what was essentially a 10-point Liberal policy grandiosely dubbed the 'Paisley Declaration'. Basically, the split came down to those who believed pragmatic pacts would help increase Liberal influence and those who wanted to maintain ideological purity, which would remain a familiar Liberal theme for the remainder of the 20th century. In his memoirs, MacCormick protested that he had kept Sinclair and Glen-Coats informed of the Declaration so was 'surprised' at the rows which followed its publication.[44]

In a straight fight with Labour's Douglas Johnston on 18 February 1948, MacCormick lost the by-election by more than 6,500 votes. He resigned as SLP vice-chairman two months later. Attempts at local alliances did not end there. Throughout 1948 and 1949 the Dundee Unionist Association, now incorporating the National Liberals, encouraged local Liberals to agree to another pact which would include support for a National Liberal candidate in both the city's constituencies. Initially, the Liberals refused and selected the journalist John Junor (a future newspaper editor cultivated by Lady Glen-Coats) to fight Dundee West. Eventually, he stood down with the proviso that the seat would be left to the Liberals should the Unionist be unsuccessful.[45]

Scottish affairs, meanwhile, remained very much on the party's mind. It looked into adopting the Lion Rampant as its party logo, while a special conference of the SLP in Dundee adopted a resolution later issued as a leaflet entitled 'Liberal Scotland: Our Own Country'. This stated that:

We Scots know our own troubles, but we could solve them. We must have our own Parliament in Scotland, dealing with Scottish affairs. At the same time we must continue to be represented in the British Parliament, which would deal with matters that concern all Britain, such as foreign relations. Northern Ireland has an arrangement like this.

The publication also fleshed out the party's hitherto rather thin policy agenda, including the first mention of a 'Special Development Area' administered by a Highland Development Board.[46]

Scottish Liberals also prepared a pamphlet on what some still called 'Home Rule for Scotland'. One executive member feared the 'understanding of this term in Scotland would be a breaking away from England and that was not their intention'. He suggested 'Scottish Devolution', but after much discussion the party settled on 'Scottish Self-Government',[47] a form of words which remained in use until the 1980s. When this publication finally appeared, it spoke of the SLP having played 'its full share' in the 1947 Scottish National Assembly, and its proposals for a Scottish Parliament being 'based upon the resolutions adopted by the Scottish National Assembly and represent[ing], we believe, the demands of a great majority of the people of Scotland'. The arguments were both technical (an 'overburdened' Parliament) and sentimental: 'Without self-government a nation can have no adequate focus for the expression of its spiritual, cultural and economic life.'[48]

Feebly, the party executive was still invoking Thomas McKinnon Wood's 1913 commitment (undelivered) to legislate for Scottish Home Rule. In March 1949, meanwhile, the annual Liberal Assembly in Hastings endorsed this 'long-standing' policy 'with only half a dozen dissentients'.[49] Yet the party struggled with a question of priorities. When the SNP wrote to the SLP asking it 'to state that it gives priority to self-government for Scotland', Andrew McFadyean responded that it was 'asking the impossible'. 'A Liberal government coming to office would depend upon "the national situation",' he explained. 'If . . . a Liberal Government attained power at a moment of grave international tension, or even of threatened war, it is equally plain that Scotland would have to wait.'[50]

The subsequent *Manifesto of the Scottish Liberal Party: The Scottish Party of Progress* nevertheless declared:

... as its first goal the attainment of such a measure of self-government in Scotland as will enable the Scottish people, while retaining their place in the United Kingdom and Commonwealth, to translate their Liberal aspirations into the actual structure of a free community of men and women.

The manifesto carried a now boilerplate statement of the party's independence, the SLP being 'freely associated' with the LPO and PLP 'for the attainment of common ends'. 'It is as a Scottish Party, free from any external control, that it appeals to the people of Scotland,' it added. 'It believes that Liberalism is the natural political expression of the Scottish genius.'[51]

When the Scottish National Assembly launched a 'National Covenant' demanding a devolved Scottish Parliament at the end of 1949, Liberal associations were active in acquiring signatures. Scottish Liberals, therefore, looked ahead to an election in 1950 in surprisingly good spirits for a party without any MPs. Attendance at its conference at the end of 1949 was larger than it had been in many years, while there had been a number of well-attended rallies. At a special conference in January 1950, the SLP and Liberal Party of Wales proposed a motion saying the Liberal Party would give high priority to parliaments for Scotland and Wales.

The party's main irritation remained the Conservatives, who had spent the past year making 'impertinent' attempts to form 'Liberal-Unionist' Associations, which the SLP condemned as 'a barefaced attempt to deceive the voters'.[52] H. G. Rae, the SLP's secretary, said the party had to 'make it plain that these movements had nothing to do with Liberalism'.[53]

1950 AND 1951 GENERAL ELECTIONS

The general election on 23 February 1950 meant an end to the Scottish Liberal Party's electoral wilderness, for it now had two MPs: Jo Grimond in Orkney & Shetland and Archie Macdonald in Roxburgh & Selkirk, the latter a surprise victory.[54] But a post-mortem meeting of the SLP executive the following month found most of those present in a gloomy mood, obviously having hoped for greater success at the polls, not to mention 28 lost deposits (from among 41 candidates). Resources, as ever, had been few. A study of the campaign in Glasgow noted that Liberal candidates had been 'themselves responsible for the production of their own posters'.[55] Some members blamed the London leadership, others an eve-of-poll statement from the LPO and even Winston Churchill, who had called Liberal intervention in the election 'malicious and wanton'.

Tony Stodart, a party vice-chairman, was especially pessimistic, saying 'it was very difficult to produce a leaflet stating how a vote for the Liberal was not a vote wasted. He did not see how they were going to make headway in fighting three-cornered fights.' G. M. Johnston said the Scottish Liberal position – as distinct from that of London – should have been clearer. Dr L. T. M. Gray, meanwhile, declared that he, Lady Glen-Coats, Stodart and John Bannerman 'must be looked upon as the leaders of the Scottish Liberal Party'.[56] However Stodart, who had fought Berwick and East Lothian, followed his own logic and shortly thereafter defected to the Scottish Unionists, presumably believing a Liberal revival to be all but impossible.[57] As *The Times* observed, throughout the past 20 years 'the cold light of remorseless reason has slowly hastened Scottish Liberal thought into channels of practical expression, and the process continues'.[58]

The party's two new MPs, Grimond and Macdonald, both made their maiden speeches on self-government for Scotland. Macdonald was on the right of the party and was married to the daughter of Lord Craigmyle, who had held ministerial office under Rosebery, Campbell-Bannerman and Asquith. Grimond was similarly steeped in Liberal heritage, his wife Laura (nee Bonham Carter) being Asquith's grand-daughter. Macdonald's business background meant he became the party's economic spokesman at Westminster, and he became a strong supporter of co-partnership in industry.[59] Clement Davies appointed Grimond chief whip.

Macdonald was present at a meeting of the Scottish Liberal Council in Galashiels that October, predicting that 'the day was not far off when the Socialist Party could be "Liberalised"'. The meeting considered future general election strategy given the narrowness of Labour premier Clement Attlee's majority. Ideally, a Scottish Liberal candidate would contest every seat but, realistically, 'at the time of a General Election the fight would clearly have to be concentrated on those constituencies where Associations were strong enough in organisation and funds'.[60] The February election had drained the party's coffers, and the SLP considered asking constituency associations to contribute funds without which party HQ, 'the political heart of the Scottish Liberal Party . . . will be unable to carry on'.[61]

Although its quarterly report for October 1951 recorded 'a much more cheerful atmosphere' in the constituencies, the disappointments of the last election having worn off,[62] the second election in as many years saw the Scottish Liberals lose one of its 1950 gains, Archie Macdonald in the Borders, despite having increased his number of votes (the party fought nine seats in all). Indeed, the Liberals performed marginally better in Scotland than in England. The existence of several 'anti-socialist' pacts with Unionists in certain constituencies had done the party little good,[63] although in Dundee West, the Liberal candidate secured 45.7 per cent of the vote thanks to the absence of a Scottish Unionist candidate. John Bannerman also believed that the Scottish Convention had 'usurped' the SLP's unique selling point, therefore it was up to them 'to put it before the public that they – not [the] Convention – were the constitutional Party for Home Rule for Scotland'. Maitland Mackie suggested changing the name of the party; one executive member suggested 'The Scottish Radical Party'.[64]

In March 1952 the SLP urged a commission to 'investigate the factors attendant on the Scottish demand for Home Rule',[65] an idea borrowed from the Scottish Unionists and a clear attempt to regain the constitutional initiative from both Conservatives and the Convention. The party chairman also referred to the 'fettered' (and recently stolen) Stone of Destiny as being 'symptomatic of the Scottish people who were struggling in chains in this so-called Elizabethan age of freedom and liberty to gain even the bare bones of their freedom'.[66]

Otherwise, the SLP spent the early 1950s issuing rather pompous resolutions to the press on international affairs. Relations with London were also tense. Lady Glen-Coats secured an agreement to alter the UK party constitution so as to include a reference to the SLP, but when she requested 'constitutional representation' on the Liberal Party Committee (LPC) 'it was almost brutally turned down', the excuse being that this committee was a 'Shadow Cabinet' and 'that if Scotland were given representation on it Wales and others might also demand it'. Typically, Lady Glen-Coats promptly resigned from the LPC.

The SLP considered sending 'a very strongly worded protest' to London but, conscious of its reduced status, agreed this would 'not be immediately effective'.[67]

In August 1952 D. S. Macdonald, the party's organisation convener, reported having visited 16 constituencies with Lady Glen-Coats 'to find that little or nothing had been done', with a recent financial plan having 'been almost completely ignored'. Glen-Coats added that her constituency visits 'had in many cases revealed too much apathy, too much sitting back and waiting for the "other fellow" to do the work'. Liberalism was there, she said, 'if only it could be co-ordinated and brought to life'.[68] By the end of that year, there had been 'no response from Associations' in relation to yet another financial appeal from SLP HQ.[69] Jo Grimond annoyed the SLP by refusing invitations to speak and help out, even in northern constituencies. He later asked to be counted out from addressing meetings, although he made time to stand as the 'Scottish and Highland Candidate' for the rectorship of Glasgow University in the autumn of 1953.

At another party meeting in December 1952, Colin Kemp, the treasurer, warned that 'organisation over the whole country was lamentably weak and so badly run that they had not a hope of improving their position at another Election unless they did something now and quickly'. He paid tribute to Lady Glen-Coats, saying that without her 'tremendous amount of time and energy . . . they would not have a Scottish Liberal Party to-day'.[70] She had indicated her intention to stand down as party chairman in May 1953. Only Orkney & Shetland and Roxburgh & Selkirk had any local organisation to speak of. Some members thought Scotland should become a federated part of the Liberal Party Organisation in London and 'cease to call ourselves the Scottish Liberal Party'. Kemp said this would 'be an admission of defeat and incompetence'.[71]

D. S. Macdonald, the party organiser, believed such a move would give the impression the SLP was 'drifting away from Scottish self-government'.[72] Lady Glen-Coats thought that was already happening, having observed upon her pre-announced resignation that the Scottish Liberal Party was 'wavering in its adherence to Home Rule for Scotland'. The apparent cause of this was a resolution from Perthshire Liberals which had caused 'a good deal of misunderstanding among Covenant supporters' in the area.[73] In August 1953, Macdonald also resigned over an incorrectly recorded minute. In a letter addressed to 'Fellow Liberals' on 18 August 1953, he said:

> The plight of the Party is desperate, and yet the Executive have shown themselves unwilling to make such self sacrifice as would be involved in having an occasional Saturday afternoon meeting of the Executive in order that a man of the caliber of Colonel William Scott of South Angus could join in their deliberation. And there are others in a similar position to Colonel Scott. It will be a great disservice to Liberalism if Colonel Scott's wise and wide experience is lost to the Executive Committee.[74]

The SLP executive acceded to this request for Saturday afternoon meetings, but Macdonald did not withdraw his resignation. 'Our affairs had reached a crisis now,' declared Colin Kemp. 'Either we applied ourselves and did a great deal more than we have been doing or it would be far better to stop fooling ourselves and call it a day.'[75] The party now had only two full-time workers, both women who then quit or retired shortly after Kemp's ultimatum. The treasurer placed before the Council 'continual and persistent pleas to raise money for Headquarters and none of them had done so'. The chairman of the Galloway Liberals bluntly admitted that he could not possibly read such pleas to his committee, 'otherwise they would pack up immediately'.[76]

By June 1954, the Scottish Liberal Party had pulled back from the brink. Its finances had stabilised, and the party was to be reorganised into five areas. Executive meetings were to be quarterly rather than monthly, with general council meetings to be held once a year mid-way between annual conferences. Officers were now expected to carry out correspondence personally, 'with the aid of part-time clerical assistance which might conveniently be provided by a lawyer's firm'.[77] What an SLP party publication later called an 'effective fight back' began when John Bannerman came within 1,331 votes of success in the December 1954 Inverness by-election.

At the end of 1952, representatives from 24 constituencies had also ranked policy priorities, the result being:

Home Rule for Scotland;
Co-ownership;
Electoral Reform;
Free Trade;
Human Rights.[78]

This was to remain a fairly accurate summary of the party's agenda for the next few decades, while in 1950 the SLP had become an early proponent of what later became known as 'right to buy', a policy considered by Labour in the 1970s and legislated for by the Thatcher government of the early 1980s.[79]

But with an election expected now that Sir Anthony Eden had succeeded the ageing Churchill as Prime Minister, the Scottish Liberals failed to formulate any detailed policy. The SLP also struggled to find candidates and contemplated asking the LPO to lend it a full-time organiser, which it now lacked. On 26 March 1955 the party executive decided to 'fight on a limited front', contesting only winnable seats such as Orkney & Shetland, Roxburgh, Selkirk & Peebles, and Inverness-shire, adding the caveat that 'if any other Association insisted upon fighting, every assistance would be offered'.[80] On polling day the SLP went into the election with one seat and came out with one, Jo Grimond in Orkney & Shetland. The party had lost nearly 30,000 votes since the last election in 1951.

LIBERAL FORTUNES

Addressing Scottish Liberals after that election, John Bannerman (who had come within 966 votes of winning Inverness) warned of the effect on Liberal 'fortunes' from the presence of a 'large number of Scottish-Nationalist candidates'.[81] Given that the SNP had fielded only a few candidates and won fewer votes than the Scottish Liberals (though the Nationalist vote share had risen), this appeared curious, but Bannerman had warned before about competition from the SNP, not least because it too advocated 'self-government' for Scotland.

A few months later, the SLP met representatives of the SNP and Scottish Covenant Association to explore 'liaison with these bodies on Scottish affairs',[82] while in May 1956 it was agreed 'that no objection would be made to collaboration and help being given at constituency level'.[83] Three months later, the Glasgow University Liberal Club joined forces with GUSNA to sponsor Ernest Hemingway in its forthcoming rectorial election. This debate regarding degrees of co-operation with the SNP would become a fixture of the next decade.

In September 1956, Clement Davies retired as Liberal leader. He was succeeded by Jo Grimond, although as a brief party history acknowledged decades later, he 'could give only limited attention to Scotland'. Responsibility instead fell upon John Bannerman, who had become something of a folk hero in the party, largely due to his two near victories in Inverness. 'He was a man of great kindness, warmth and vision,' gushed the same history. 'He laid the basis of the modern Scottish Liberal Party.'[84] *The Times* later hailed Bannerman as 'a character':

> He is Scottish through and through, was once a great sportsman, is a Gaelic authority and is at all times a stirring orator of the old kind. It is hardly possible to doubt that in some sense Liberalism must have been only an incidental element in his success.[85]

The presence of Scotland's only Liberal MP as the new party chief also had little immediate effect on its fortunes or morale north of the border. Executive meetings in early 1957 were often consumed by petty infighting between executive members and organisers. Better news came with the revival of the Scottish League of Young Liberals (which had been disbanded in 1954) and the candidacy of William Douglas-Home, brother of the Tory grandee Lord Home, at the Edinburgh South by-election, at which he polled a respectable quarter of the vote (a Unionist post-mortem attributed this to 'disgruntlement' among 'middle-class voters'). In Torrington, meanwhile, Mark Bonham Carter (Laura Grimond's brother) won a significant by-election on a Liberal ticket.

At the same time, the once-dominant Scottish Unionist Party was beginning to experience Liberal-like indications of decline. Its vote fell by more than 20 percentage points at a series of by-elections between 1957 and 1959, each time as the consequence of Liberal interventions in seats the party had not fought since 1950. At contests in Aberdeen East, the Liberal candidate won 24 per cent of the vote, and in Argyllshire 28 per cent.

In that latter contest, Liberal candidate William McKean's platform had been significant. He presented himself as taking a stand for 'the individual' against Labour and the Unionists, also supporting tax cuts and restrictions on monopolies. Echoing this, SLP chairman John Bannerman declared that his party would always 'look to the individual's interest'. This echoed Jo Grimond's 'New Liberalism', which repositioned the Liberals as a progressive alternative to Labour's state socialism, preaching individual freedom, reductions in personal taxation and critiques of nationalisation and the Welfare State. As Malcolm Petrie concluded, it was this 'fragmenting' of the Unionist vote which created the opportunity for the Liberals (and indeed the SNP) 'to present alternative renderings of this individualist appeal' to voters.[86]

The March 1958 Kelvingrove by-election was a special case, where an industrial journalist called David Murray chose to stand as a 'Liberal Home Rule' candidate. He claimed to have the support of local Liberals and Scottish Nationalists, but the Scottish Liberal Party denied he was an official Liberal. As polling day approached, John Bannerman announced his intention to speak on Murray's behalf, but as a 'Liberal individual' rather than party chairman. 'My presence will be an indication to Kelvingrove Liberals that they should vote for Mr. Murray,' explained Bannerman. But the SLP's secretary R. T. McPake was not amused: 'I am surprised that Mr. Bannerman has adopted this attitude, of which we had no indication.'[87] Murray came a poor third. The only bright spot that year was the SLP's purchase of 2 Atholl Place in Edinburgh, its home until the early 1980s.

In Dumfriesshire, where the Unionist MP Niall Macpherson claimed to represent both Conservatives and Liberals, Glasgow University Liberals responded by spending a summer campaigning in Dumfries, where a Liberal association had been established in 1957. 'The Liberals – straight Liberals,' reported the *Manchester Guardian*, 'not what Mr John G. Wilson [the SLP treasurer] called "hyphenated abominations" – met to form a town branch.' A Dumfriesshire Liberal Association affiliated with the SLP was also set up in May 1959, with its Conservative rival forced to change its name to 'National Liberal'.[88]

There were also signs of policy life. Unhappy with John MacCormick's work on a 'Scottish Policy' pamphlet, the SLP executive believed that Home Rule 'was sufficiently dealt with in existing pamphlets'.[89] The party's policy on a Scottish Parliament had been re-affirmed at its Arbroath conference in 1957 as well as in Jo Grimond's 1958 publication, *The New Liberal Democracy*. But while the party believed 'Scotland must have answers for her own problems', it also resolved 'in matters of principle, rather than detail, [to] try to integrate our policies with those of the Liberal Party Organisation wherever possible'. Looking ahead to the next election, party secretary

R. T. McPake said: 'We will go forward only where there is a good Liberal vote. There will be no lost deposits this time.'[90]

At the October 1959 general election, the Scottish Liberals fielded 16 candidates and more than doubled their share of the vote but emerged once again with a solitary MP. Jo Grimond's appeal proved a slow burner, but he did come to inspire a generation of Liberals across the UK. As president of the Scottish Liberal Club at Edinburgh University, a young David Steel persuaded Grimond to stand as Rector, setting the 'boy David' on his own path to the UK party leadership. At around the same time, Grimond appealed to all constituency associations in Scotland to contribute financially to party HQ. Amid a broader Liberal revival in England, there was a sense in the early 1960s that the Scottish Liberal Party was over its worst. In 1961, for example, it hosted the first ever Joint Assembly with the English and Welsh Liberal parties in Edinburgh. In April that year, John Bannerman had come a close second in another Paisley by-election, capturing more than 41 per cent of the vote. The party chose, however, not to contest Glasgow Bridgeton in November, something Bill Miller considered 'a tactical blunder' in that it allowed the SNP to capture valuable third-party votes.[91]

In March 1962 John Taylor, the Labour MP for West Lothian died. The Scottish Liberals got off to a bad start when David Steel, soon to become assistant general secretary of the Scottish party, invited Billy Wolfe, a local chartered accountant and prominent local Home Ruler, to stand as the Liberal candidate.[92] Wolfe stood instead as the SNP candidate, having joined the party three years earlier. He came second behind Tam Dalyell while the Liberal candidate came fourth, prompting a young activist called Michael Starforth to explore the old idea of an electoral pact between the SNP and Liberals in a draft pamphlet entitled 'A Scottish Government and Parliament'. The SLP executive refused to publish it, although it subsequently appeared in October 1962 as having 'been agreed by a panel of Scottish Liberals'.[93]

As Malcolm Petrie has argued, by the early 1960s individual liberty was 'beginning to be understood in constitutional rather than economic terms',[94] which represented an obvious electoral opportunity for both Liberals and Nationalists as the Unionist vote continued to decline. The Glasgow Woodside by-election of November 1962 neatly illustrated this when the incumbent

Conservatives lost to Labour and the Liberals' Jack House came a respectable third with 5,000 votes and 21.7 per cent of the vote – a swing of 14 per cent. Given the two-party system that still dominated Scotland and the UK at that time, it was considered something of a Scottish Liberal triumph. Usefully, the SNP had also been pushed back into fourth place.

Clearly of the view that its existing devolution literature was no longer fit for purpose, the SLP had published an update of its *Scottish Self Government* pamphlet to coincide with the Woodside by-election. This reheated long-standing arguments about the shortage of parliamentary time and Scotland's 'distinct' problems, but added a section on the European Economic Community (EEC), which the UK was to spend the rest of that decade attempting to join. It framed parliamentary devolution for Scotland and entry into the EEC as 'complimentary', and quoted Jo Grimond's call for Scotland to 'stake her claims to be represented on some European institutions'. Scottish Liberals still opposed the SNP's goal of 'Separation', instead promoting a 'moderate and Federal form of Home Rule'.[95]

In December 1962 the SLP executive gave 'sanction, but not approval' for talks between the SNP and Scottish Liberal chairmen. The SNP tried to make self-government a 'test' issue at a future election, demanding that the Scottish Liberals 'force' the matter should it and the SNP win a majority of Scottish constituencies, a quixotic scenario rejected by John Bannerman. Instead, the Scottish Liberals established their own study group to investigate measures that could hasten the achievement of self-government, although that did not preclude 'discussion with outside bodies'. The Liberal Alistair Duncan-Miller (son of a former Liberal MP for St Andrews), contested the Kinross and West Perthshire by-election in 1963 and came second with 20 per cent of the vote, 'a gratifying result in difficult circumstances', as John Bannerman described it. The SNP had refused to give him a free run.[96]

David Steel recalled Scottish Liberal organiser Arthur Purdom saying 'we need fewer brilliant second places and a few more mediocre firsts!'[97] Following a particularly disastrous by-election in Dumfriesshire in December 1963 (11 per cent), Steel also resolved that Liberals ought not waste time fighting seats that might produce the dreaded sentence: 'The Liberal candidate lost his deposit.' 'These six words,' wrote Steel in *Liberal News*, 'do the Liberal cause more damage than any six sentences uttered by Tory or Labour propagandists.'[98] It had chosen not to contest Dundee West in November 1963.

Political scientists have argued that an important factor in the Scottish revival of the Liberal party was its decentralising agenda as well as its campaign for a Scottish Parliament. Indeed, the party produced a number of regional plans in the early to mid-1960s, which came to be seen by activists as key, although Mark Egan has argued that early forms of 'community politics' by Liberal activists in Scottish towns and cities was also an under-appreciated factor, which led in turn to a local government revival in the early 1960s.

Before 1961, Liberals were almost completely absent from Scottish town halls despite the Scottish Liberal Party having called in 1952 for local elections to be fought more vigorously. Edinburgh had been the first to reverse this, although there and in a number of other burghs Liberals were rarely elected. The exception was Greenock, where Bill Riddell – who polled more than 10,000 votes at the 1959 general election – built up the local organisation, with an emphasis on recruiting well-known community leaders. The Greenock Liberals elected four councillors in 1961 and by 1967 controlled the burgh. In turn, Greenock activists assumed prominent positions within the SLP hierarchy (Riddell became convenor of its local election committee), although they remembered the party leaders' surprise 'that the Party was at all active in the town, never mind that it had fought and won local elections'.[99]

The results in 1964 were impossible to ignore. The Scottish Liberals, according to Graham Watson, entered that election campaign 'on a platform of federalist fervour'.[100] Even the *Daily Record* felt compelled to report on Liberal policy in a series of articles on the 'Liberal revival'. In a lively letter to the *Spectator*, Michael Starforth (joint honorary treasurer) set out the SLP platform: co-ownership in industry, 'a Scottish Parliament for all Scottish Affairs', membership of the EEC, support for NATO ('but not in retaining a separate British nuclear deterrent') and the continuance of private wealth, 'but only if it is spread as widely as possible throughout the community'.[101] George Mackie, party vice-chair and the prospective candidate for Caithness and Sutherland, had published a pamphlet on Scottish farming in 1963.[102] On education, although the party disapproved 'of the privileges and distinctions which result from Independent School education, it is felt that the total and immediate abolition of Independent Schools would be an illiberal action'.[103]

Although Mackie had played a vital role in building up party organisation since 1959, some candidates were still rather amateurish. Standing in Ross & Cromarty was Alasdair Mackenzie who, in David Steel's words, 'was an expert on sheep but not thought to be so on politics'. When challenged at a meeting in Dingwall as regards Liberal policy on defence, he simply declared: 'The Liberal Par-ty will de-fend Brit-ain, the commonwealth and the free world.' Mackenzie sat down to 'tumultuous applause' and went on to win the seat.[104]

As did George Mackie in Caithness & Sutherland and Russell Johnston in Inverness, with Jo Grimond holding on, as expected, in Orkney & Shetland. The campaign had been 'coherent' (the party's own adjective), focused on a clear 'regional strategy' – later taken up by Harold Wilson's governments – set out in pamphlets such as *A Plan for the North East* and *Highland Development*, the latter the work of Russell Johnston.[105] After polling day, George Mackie could 'exault' that everything 'from Muckle Flugga to Ballachulish was controlled' by Liberal MPs.[106]

NOTES

1. 'Note on the Scottish Liberal Party', in R. Johnston (1979), *Scottish Liberal Party Conference Speeches 1971–1978*, Edinburgh: Bookmag, 80.
2. S. Grieve (1991), 'Women in the Scottish Liberal Democrats', in *A Woman's Claim of Right in Scotland: Women, Representation and Politics*, Edinburgh: Polygon, 60–61.
3. 'Note on the Scottish Liberal Party', 80.
4. Sir Thomas had also been heavily involved in Rosebery's Liberal League.
5. 'It is to her' wrote Grimond, 'that I owe twenty-eight years as their Member.' J. Grimond (1979), *Memoirs*, London: Heinemann, 97.
6. S. Grieve, 60.
7. 'Note on the Scottish Liberal Party', 80.
8. Ibid. Unlike the LPO, the SLP executive was a policy-making body equivalent to the Liberal Policy Committee in England.

9. SLP meeting, 20 June 1946, Scottish Liberal Papers Acc 11765/56.
10. SLP meeting, 1 July 1946, Scottish Liberal Papers Acc 11765/56.
11. SLP meeting, 8 October 1946, Scottish Liberal Papers Acc 11765/56.
12. SLP meeting, 13 August 1947, Scottish Liberal Papers Acc 11765/56.
13. The Scottish Women's Council and Scottish Young Liberals were also ex-officio members of the UK Liberal Assembly.
14. SLP meeting, 25 June 1947, Scottish Liberal Papers Acc 11765/56.
15. M. Egan (2009), *Coming into Focus: The Transformation of the Liberal Party 1945–64*, Riga: VDM Verlag Dr Müller.
16. SLP meeting, 7 September 1946, Scottish Liberal Papers Acc 11765/53.
17. SLP meeting, 16 September 1947, Scottish Liberal Papers Acc 11765/56.
18. SLP General Council meeting, 7 December 1946, Scottish Liberal Papers Acc 11765/53.
19. SLP meeting, 14 June 1947, Scottish Liberal Papers Acc 11765/53.
20. SLP meeting, 25 June 1947, Scottish Liberal Papers Acc 11765/56.
21. SLP executive's quarterly report, December 1947, Scottish Liberal Papers Acc 11765/53.
22. SLP executive annual report 1948–49, Scottish Liberal Papers Acc 11765/45.
23. *Glasgow Herald*, 27 July 1946.
24. SLP meeting, 9 August 1946, Scottish Liberal Papers Acc 11765/56.
25. SLP meeting, 1 November 1946, Scottish Liberal Papers Acc 11765/56. In the event, both contested the by-election that November, which was won by the Unionist candidate Walter Elliot. Bannerman lost his deposit.
26. SLP meeting, 1 November 1946, Scottish Liberal Papers Acc 11765/56. Liberal voters in the December 1946 Kilmarnock and South Aberdeen by-elections were urged by Liberal-Nationals to vote Conservative, much to the irritation of the SLP.
27. SLP meeting, 1 November 1946, Scottish Liberal Papers Acc 11765/56. Glen-Coats went to the United States, where she broadcast 'twice to the American public on purely Scottish Affairs', addressed the Canadian Liberal Party conference and conveyed the fraternal greetings of the SLP to premier McKenzie King 'as a brother Scot' (Scottish Liberal Papers Acc 11765/45).
28. SLP meeting, 8 March 1947, Scottish Liberal Papers Acc 11765/53.
29. SLP executive annual report 1946–47, Scottish Liberal Papers Acc 11765/45.

30. See M. Petrie (2018), 'Anti-Socialism, Liberalism and Individualism: Rethinking the Realignment of Scottish Politics, 1945–1970', *Transactions of the Royal Historical Society* 28, 197–217.
31. See J. Maclay (1950), *Liberalism and the Present Situation*.
32. 'Note on the Scottish Liberal Party', 80.
33. SLP meeting, 8 October 1946, Scottish Liberal Papers Acc 11765/56. Glen-Coats' proposals included an Upper House comprising Scotland's Lord Provosts, representatives elected by Scottish county councils, representative Scottish peers and representatives of Scottish Universities elected by graduates. The Lower House, meanwhile, was to use Single Transferable Vote (STV) to elect two members for each current constituency.
34. SLP executive quarterly report, February 1947, Scottish Liberal Papers Acc 11765/53.
35. HC Debs 13 November 1947, Vol 152 c655 & c669.
36. SLP meeting, 8 March 1947, Scottish Liberal Papers Acc 11765/53.
37. SLP meeting, 2 April 1947, Scottish Liberal Papers Acc 11765/56.
38. Speech at Scottish Liberal rally in Glasgow, 11 April 1947, Clement Davies Papers K/1/35.
39. SLP meeting, 4 October 1947, Scottish Liberal Papers Acc 11765/53.
40. SLP executive quarterly report, December 1947, Scottish Liberal Papers Acc 11765/53.
41. For a comprehensive analysis of the by-election, see M. Dyer (2003), '"A Nationalist in the Churchillian Sense": John MacCormick, the Paisley by-election of 18 February 1948, Home Rule and the Crisis in Scottish Liberalism', *Parliamentary History* 22:3, 285–307.
42. SLP meeting, 14 January 1948, Scottish Liberal Papers Acc 11765/56.
43. SLP meeting, 7 February 1948, Scottish Liberal Papers Acc 11765/53.
44. J. MacCormick (1955), *The Flag in the Wind*, London: Victor Gollancz, 122.
45. M. Petrie.
46. 'Liberal Scotland' leaflet (1950).
47. SLP meeting, 5 March 1949, Scottish Liberal Papers Acc 11765/53.
48. SLP (1949), *Scottish Self Government*, Edinburgh: Scottish Liberal Party, 1–3.
49. SLP executive annual report 1948–49, Scottish Liberal Papers Acc 11765/45.

50. Andrew McFadyean to the SNP, Scottish Liberal Papers Acc 11765/53.
51. SLP (1950), *Manifesto of the Scottish Liberal Party: The Scottish Party of Progress*, Edinburgh: Scottish Liberal Party.
52. SLP executive annual report 1948–49, Scottish Liberal Papers Acc 11765/45.
53. SLP meeting, 18 December 1948, Scottish Liberal Papers Acc 11765/53.
54. See M. McManus (2001), *Jo Grimond: Towards the Sound of Gunfire*, Edinburgh: Birlinn, 77–82.
55. S. B. Chrimes (ed) (1950), *The General Election in Glasgow: February, 1950*, Glasgow: Jackson, 151.
56. SLP meeting, 25 March 1950, Scottish Liberal Papers Acc 11765/53.
57. Between 1959 and October 1974, Stodart was the Unionist/Conservative MP for Edinburgh West.
58. *The Times*, 23 February 1950.
59. *Journal of Liberal History* 41, Winter 2003.
60. 7 October 1950, Scottish Liberal Papers Acc 11765/53.
61. SLP quarterly report, October 1950, Scottish Liberal Papers Acc 11765/53.
62. SLP quarterly report, October 1951, Scottish Liberal Papers Acc 11765/54.
63. M. Petrie.
64. SLP meeting, 8 December 1951, Scottish Liberal Papers Acc 11765/54.
65. SLP meeting, 1 March 1952, Scottish Liberal Papers Acc 11765/53.
66. One of the Stone's captors had been Bill Craig, a member of the Scottish Liberal Party.
67. SLP meeting, 7 June 1952, Scottish Liberal Papers Acc 11765/53.
68. SLP meeting, 27 August 1952, Scottish Liberal Papers Acc 11765/56.
69. SLP meeting, 12 November 1952, Scottish Liberal Papers Acc 11765/56.
70. SLP meeting, 6 December 1952, Scottish Liberal Papers Acc 11765/53.
71. SLP meeting, 18 February 1953, Scottish Liberal Papers Acc 11765/56.
72. SLP meeting, 18 February 1953, Scottish Liberal Papers Acc 11765/56.
73. SLP meeting, 30 May 1953, Scottish Liberal Papers Acc 11765/53.
74. Scottish Liberal Papers Acc 11765/56.

75. SLP meeting, 3 October 1953, Scottish Liberal Papers Acc 11765/53.
76. SLP meeting, 5 December 1953, Scottish Liberal Papers Acc 11765/53.
77. SLP meeting, 5 June 1954, Scottish Liberal Papers Acc 11765/53.
78. SLP meeting, 6 December 1952, Scottish Liberal Papers Acc 11765/53.
79. SLP meeting, 17 June 1950, Scottish Liberal Papers Acc 11765/53.
80. SLP meeting, 26 March 1955, Scottish Liberal Papers Acc 11765/57. It fought five seats in all.
81. SLP meeting, 25 June 1955, Scottish Liberal Papers Acc 11765/53.
82. SLP meeting, 8 November 1955, Scottish Liberal Papers Acc 11765/57.
83. SLP meeting, 11 May 1956, Scottish Liberal Papers Acc 11765/57.
84. 'Note on the Scottish Liberal Party', 81.
85. *The Times*, 21 April 1961.
86. M. Petrie.
87. *The Times*, 11 March 1958.
88. *Journal of Liberal History* 76, Autumn 2012.
89. SLP meeting, 27 September 1958, Scottish Liberal Papers Acc 11765/55.
90. *The Times*, 12 April 1958. At an April 1959 Galloway by-election, Liberal candidate Simon Mackay secured more than a quarter of the vote.
91. W. L. Miller, 33.
92. The source for this invitation is Sir Graham Watson, although Lord Steel has no memory of it.
93. Derek Michael Henderson Starforth was from North Berwick, claimed to have fought in Oman and to have connections to Violet Bonham-Carter. He introduced himself either as Michael Starforth or as Derek Henderson, though there were other combinations. 'He was a man of immense energy,' recalled Sir Graham Watson, 'not all of it constructively employed' (Sir Graham Watson to the author, 13 February 2021).
94. M. Petrie.
95. SLP (1962), *Scottish Self Government*, Edinburgh: Scottish Liberal Party, 8–9.
96. G. Watson (1999), 'Scottish Liberals, Scottish Nationalists and Dreams of a Common Front', *Journal of Liberal History* 22, Spring 1999.
97. *Journal of Liberal History* 80, Autumn 2013.
98. D. Torrance (2012), *David Steel: Rising Hope to Elder Statesman*, London: Biteback, 25.
99. M. Egan.

100. M. Egan.
101. M. Starforth (1964), 'No Gunfire', *Spectator*, 10 January 1964.
102. G. Mackie (1963), *Policy for Scottish Farming*, Edinburgh: Scottish Liberal Party. Mackie had joined the SLP in 1949 but only decided to stand as a candidate following the 1956 Suez Crisis.
103. SLP meeting, 7 March 1964, Scottish Liberal Papers Acc 11765/55.
104. *Journal of Liberal History* 80, Autumn 2013.
105. Highland Development proved influential with the Labour MP Willie Ross, who was about to become Secretary of State for Scotland in Harold Wilson's government. The SLP pamphlet also built on earlier SLF proposals for a 'Highland Development Commission'.
106. 'Note on the Scottish Liberal Party', 82.

6

'Home Rule in a Federal Britain':
1964–1979

The Scottish Liberals now possessed that most valuable of political commodities: momentum. Just six weeks after the 1964 general election, the incumbent Unionist MP for Roxburgh, Selkirk and Peebles (a seat briefly held by a Liberal in the early 1950s), the elderly and ineffective Commander Charles Donaldson, died during surgery in London. *The Times* judged that the resulting by-election gave the Liberals a chance to further increase their representation in the Commons, noting that David Steel, 'a young and vigorous campaigner', had obtained the third-highest Liberal vote among the 54 Liberals who had achieved second place at the recent election.[1]

Steel had been what Jo Grimond's biographer called the 'beneficiary of considerable sponsorship' from the Liberal leader. Indeed, the two were close personally (Steel had been Grimond's bag carrier during the campaign) and ideologically. Russell Johnston, a university contemporary, later observed that 'David was always a Grimond Liberal', whereas he and Judy Steel, David's wife, were 'Bannerman Liberals', a reference to SLP folk hero John Bannerman, who had failed to take Paisley at the 1964 election.

Grimondites were, crudely speaking, less passionate about Scottish Home Rule than followers of John Bannerman who, according to H. J. Hanham, 'looked at times to be a Home Ruler who happened to be a Liberal rather than vice versa'.[2] George Mackie judged that Bannerman was 'never anti-Scottish Nationalism' but 'highly suspicious' of some in the SNP. Jo Grimond's 'heart', by contrast, was in Mackie's view 'unquestioningly in Westminster and in Orkney and Shetland'. 'It was very difficult to get Jo to talk about a Scottish Parliament,' Mackie added in his memoirs, 'although he would talk happily about devolution.'[3]

This division – or more accurately, difference of emphasis – informed ongoing talk of a Liberal-SNP pact, which loomed large for the remainder of the 1960s. The SNP's suggestion of a pact had been rebuffed on the grounds that the SLP, 'although autonomous, was part of the Great Britain Liberal Movement, and would not contemplate any unilateral action for Scottish self-government'.[4] David Steel, the Scottish Liberal Party's assistant general secretary, reckoned the pending Borders by-election could also be a 'test case' for Grimond's 'realignment' strategy of closer co-operation with the Labour Party. Peter Preston of the *Guardian* would later observe that Steel and his Labour opponent, Ronald King Murray, both sang 'diverting variations on the same theme so that the Lib-Lab duet is quite harmonious'. That did not prevent King Murray challenging Steel to say whether he was a genuine radical or a crypto-Tory, however, while the Conservative leader Edward Heath described the Liberals on a campaigning visit as 'a petty annexe to the Labour Government'.[5]

It was the first time professional politics had hit the normally sleepy and deferential Borders; Steel's campaign was energetic and meticulous, breaking new ground in how the game of politics was played in that part of the world. 'THIS TIME DAVID STEEL' was the legend on posters, tin badges and car stickers, as well as a glossy election address that still looked impressive nearly half a century later. It amounted to a mini manifesto, augmenting a pamphlet (co-authored by Steel) entitled *Boost for the Borders*, which continued the party's already successful regional strategy.

At Scottish Liberal HQ, party chairman and MP George Mackie rebuffed attempts by the London-based party to interfere, its habit since the Second World War, while Eric Lubbock headed north to spread a little Orpington magic on the third anniversary of his own by-election win, as did Jeremy Thorpe and Grimond, both of whom addressed large meetings in the major Borders towns. Llew Gardner of the *Scottish Daily Express* memorably dubbed Steel 'the Boy David' – an epithet that would remain with him even decades later – and cast the whole by-election in terms of David versus Goliath (Robert McEwen, the Tory candidate, being the giant). When the votes were counted on 24 March, Goliath had taken a direct hit. A 7.3 per cent swing to the Liberals had given Steel a decisive majority of more than 4,600 votes.

John Bannerman was at the count, as was Jeremy Thorpe, the latter persuading a local landlord to open up so that everybody could celebrate. 'It's a historical moment,' proclaimed Thorpe. 'We can't let the licensing laws get in the way on a night like this!' Then the new Member of Parliament was carried shoulder-high down the street and 'hundreds of Liberals,' recalled Liberal activist Tony Greaves, 'many for the first time in their lives, knew what it was like to win'. The following day's *Scottish Daily Express* carried news of what it called a '2 a.m. sensation', a banner headline announcing: 'IT'S THE BOY DAVID!'[6]

THE SCOTTISH QUESTION

Flush with this success, Steel urged Liberal associations in Scotland 'relentlessly to hammer home the Liberal view on all occasions', while George Mackie warned that 'the expansion of the Party solely depended on getting its finances in order'.[7] Ex-RAF squadron leader Arthur Purdom, the party's chief agent and secretary, 'introduced new, but simple systems' to professionalise campaigning.[8] Russell Johnston also stressed the 'importance of having an overall look at the functions and aims of the Scottish Liberal Party, with a view to plugging gaps in policy'. It was strong on devolution and the Highlands, but had nothing on transport, local government, housing or power. He also pushed to standardise the party's colours, a wide range having been deployed at the recent election.[9]

In the general election that followed just over a year later, Steel held his seat as did Russell Johnston in Inverness, Alasdair Mackenzie in Ross & Cromarty and, of course, Grimond in the Northern Isles (23 candidates stood in all, 3 fewer than in 1964). The loss of George Mackie's Caithness & Sutherland seat (to Labour's Robert Maclennan, who later became a Liberal Democrat) was compensated for by James Davidson's victory in West Aberdeenshire.[10]

In none of these five Liberal seats had there been an SNP challenger, the value of which was clear to the Scottish Liberal Party. Indeed, in their analysis of the 1964 general election, the political scientists David Butler and Anthony King described the

Nationalists' support in seats where there was no SLP candidate as a 'disguised Liberal vote'.[11] Although the SNP had managed just 2.4 per cent of the vote in 1964, this was on an upward trajectory and had more than doubled to 5 per cent in 1966 – not far off the SLP's 6.8 per cent. Conscious they were competing over the same modest third-party vote, the SNP and SLP turned their attention to what the political scientist Bill Miller called the 'chimera of a united home rule front', i.e. giving each other a 'clear run' in certain constituencies:

> They produced a bewildering variety of detailed proposals. Some were trying to give priority to an issue that transcended party politics: others were manoevring [*sic*] to expose the other party, to show the Liberals' frivolity or the SNP's extremism.[12]

A resolution from the Ross & Cromarty Liberal Association at the party's June 1966 national council again called for a formal Liberal-SNP pact, which was debated at length. The broadcaster Ludovic Kennedy, a constituent of Steel's and a recent convert to Liberalism, had grown frustrated that the SLP's policy of 'Home Rule in a federal Britain ... never seemed to get discussed'. He tabled a motion for it to become the 'principal aim and object of our policy'. To his 'great astonishment this resolution was carried unanimously, and thereafter, equally unanimously ignored'.[13]

Michael Starforth, who had annoyed the executive with such talk in 1962, also urged the party to:

> ... intensify its campaign for a Scottish Parliament for Scottish affairs and to strive for the day when 36 M.P.'s who support this policy, having been elected in Scottish seats, the Party can justifiably demand the immediate establishment of a Scottish Parliament.[14]

This was passed by the SLP's general council and, interestingly, later became the basis of long-standing SNP policy on independence. There were inevitable divisions, but renewed discussions on an informal basis were agreed 'to see what common basis there was for a joint effort to promote Scottish interests' between the Scottish Liberals and the SNP.

A joint meeting that summer between the Scottish and English Liberal parties had not reached agreement as to whether a pact would serve (Scottish) Liberal interests for, in Graham Watson's judgement, 'the vanity induced by its victories across Britain had fueled belief in a nation-wide revival and had drawn some of the fluid from the Scottish self-government boil'. The SNP then said it intended to fight all 71 Scottish constituencies at the next election, so there the matter rested. Russell Johnston, meanwhile, introduced a private member's bill to establish a Scottish Parliament in the Commons, reviving a Scottish Liberal tradition which reached back to the late 19th century.[15] There followed, however, a strong SNP showing in the March 1967 Pollok by-election, which served to convince Nationalists that a pact was not in *their* interests.

It had the opposite effect on the Scottish Liberals, whose candidate lost his deposit. There was an air of panic at a special executive meeting called shortly after the by-election. James Davidson said he would try another approach to the SNP, something supported by Jo Grimond, who had recently resigned as UK Liberal leader, thereafter spending most of time promoting Home Rule. Sensing an opportunity, Ludovic Kennedy and Michael Starforth distributed the text of a resolution they intended to bring before the SLP's annual conference in May 1967, seeking formal links with the SNP. The SLP executive, however, defeated this proposal by 16 votes to 2, a decisive result which was then released to the press. Graham Watson viewed this as a victory for the 'hard-liners' Mackie and Johnston, who were 'reasserting their distinctive Liberal identity'.

The Perth conference proved memorable. Russell Johnston accused Jo Grimond of lacking self-discipline, criticising in particular his visit to the SNP's headquarters on Ardmillan Terrace. Billy Wolfe later observed that 'Grimond is obviously very close to the SNP but I doubt if he is very close to the Scottish Liberal Party'.[16] In what the *Scotsman* described as 'the most lively and hackle-raising debate . . . in the steaming political cauldron of the Salutation Hotel', Kennedy and Starforth tabled their resolution on an electoral pact 'to avoid splitting the self-government vote and to join in achieving a Scottish parliament before Britain's entry into the Common Market'. After a number of close votes, the conference narrowly accepted a compromise amendment from James Davidson and David Steel, which said the conference:

> . . . would welcome any indication from the leaders of the Scottish National Party that they are willing, in recognition of the need for

both Parties to place the national interests of Scotland, before short term Party interests, to co-operate with the Scottish Liberal Party to achieve a Scottish Parliament.[17]

This was mutually assured constitutional destruction. The SNP demanded that the Liberals prioritise self-government, while the Liberals insisted the SNP abandon independence and support federalism as the basis of any pact. Pride also played a part, with both parties refusing to make the initial approach. Mackie and Johnston then put out a statement to all Liberal constituency associations outlining the SLP's opposition to co-operation with the Nationalists.

In July 1967, Plaid Cymru scored a by-election win in Carmarthen, while the SNP had started to pick up seats in council by-elections. The Hamilton by-election in November 1967 sealed the deal. Winnie Ewing swept to victory in a hitherto safe Labour seat while the Liberals did not even field a candidate, not because of any local pact but due to the complete absence of party organisation in the constituency.

The heady days of 1964–6 once again gave way to panic in the Liberal ranks. Ludovic Kennedy, who had spoken on Ewing's behalf during the by-election, resigned from the SLP,[18] while party chairman George Mackie also came close to walking away. Mackie believed Kennedy had caused 'great harm' by quitting the SLP without actually defecting to the SNP. 'I suppose we should have been able to harness the surge of Scottish feeling instead of the Nat[ionalist]s,' reflected Mackie in his memoirs.

> But the Nationalists did it really by appealing not to a desire for a centre of power and excellence to promote Scotland, but to the anti-English chip on the shoulder which I am afraid many Scots have. I do not regard this sort of campaign as suitable for any Party with the name of Liberal attached to it.[19]

Mackie persuaded the Scottish Liberal executive to state their 'unanimous agreement that 'the gulf between the separatist policy of the SNP and the federalist system of self-government proposed by the SLP shows no prospect of being bridged'. Jo Grimond, now on the back benches, also argued during a speech in Kirkwall that there had been no decline in the Liberal vote, the SNP taking votes mainly from Labour. The rest of 1967 brought the devaluation crisis, the death of Lady Glen-Coats and the elevation to the House of Lords of John Bannerman, further increasing the Scottish Liberals' parliamentary presence. He referenced Hamilton in his maiden speech, warning that it represented the culmination of two centuries in which Scotland had been a 'sleeping partner' in the Union.[20]

Michael Starforth, meanwhile, followed Ludovic Kennedy's lead at Hamilton and resigned from the SLP, although he actually followed through and joined the SNP. In a letter to SLP HQ, meanwhile, four of the five Scottish Liberal MPs argued that the party 'should cease passing resolutions or making statements hostile to the Nationalists since it is impossible to do this without giving the 'impression that . . . we are hostile to self-government itself'.[21]

Jeremy Thorpe, Grimond's successor as UK Liberal leader, made efforts to revamp the party's constitutional agenda, personally introducing a Federal Government Bill in the House of Commons on 21 February 1968. This was actually more devolutionary than federal in aim, proposing parliaments in Scotland and Wales in addition to that already in existence in Northern Ireland, together with a 'commission' to explore options for England. The West Aberdeenshire MP James Davidson also introduced another private member's bill, the Scotland and Wales (Referenda) Bill, which offered the people of Scotland and Wales four 'clear' choices: maintaining the status quo; devolving additional powers to the Secretaries of State for Scotland and Wales and Scottish and Welsh Grand Committees; establishing devolved parliaments within a federal UK; or, finally, 'complete independence within the British Commonwealth'. If a majority backed the fourth option, declared Davidson, 'then that is surely the will of the people'.[22] Elsewhere, Thorpe warned darkly that Scotland could, like Ireland, resort to violence if Westminster did not concede Home Rule.

Both Bills were attempts to neutralise the SNP while maintaining the Scottish Liberals' position as the principal 'carrier' of nationalist-unionism. As the writer James McMillan cynically observed:

> In the twenties the Liberals were outflanked by Labour. In the sixties they were being by-passed by the Scottish Nationalists and the Welsh Nationalists. Without Scotland and Wales the Liberals would vanish completely. And in these countries they no longer have any unique appeal. They are not as radical as Labour, as moderate as the Conservatives, or as romantic as the Nationalists.[23]

A 1968 leaflet entitled 'Self Government' made a point of distinguishing the party from the Conservatives, Labour and the SNP. Scotland, it claimed, was neglected, because 'London doesn't care and isn't interested in Scotland'. Heath's recently announced 'Scottish Assembly' would 'just tinker with the problem and still wouldn't bring decision to Scotland', while the SNP wanted 'complete separation' and were 'prepared to see customs posts on the Cheviots'.[24]

The 'pact' issue resurfaced during 1968, when the SNP stormed to success in local government elections, earning Nationalists so much press coverage that the SLP made a formal complaint.[25] On a visit to Edinburgh, Jeremy Thorpe advocated a common front between Liberals and Nationalists on limited home rule 'which could sweep Scotland and Wales at the next general election and bring about national parliaments within three or four years'. Scottish Liberal leaders had not been consulted and were understandably furious. George Mackie believed that while 'a magnificent campaigner', Thorpe 'was lightweight and too fond of the tinsel'.[26]

Matters came to a head at the September 1968 Liberal Assembly in Edinburgh, the second time that decade the English, Welsh and Scottish parties had gathered jointly. *The Times* reported that 'collaborators' (those who favoured a deal with the SNP) included Grimond, Steel, James Davidson and Alasdair Mackenzie, while the main opponents of any pact were George Mackie and Russell Johnston. Collaborators had a majority on the SLP executive. Indeed, almost everyone at the Assembly believed Grimond was 'busy creating an impression of his readiness – even eagerness – to be the figurehead and leader of some ill-defined Home Rule coalition'.

Such talk naturally irritated Jeremy Thorpe, who attempted to agree with Grimond the wording of a Home Rule motion due to be debated on the Friday. Agreement was reached after an hour of talks, but Grimond did not show up at the press conference at which it was to be announced, leaving Thorpe to set out the policy on his own. George Mackie later stormed through the conference back rooms 'boiling with suspicion that Mr. Thorpe had sold out to Mr. Grimond and the Scottish nationalists, or to both'. Grimond also failed to attend a joint executive meeting to settle the official line, or a breakfast meeting of the parliamentary group, though, noted *The*

Times, he 'unsparingly met demands for star appearances on television'.

When Grimond spoke in the Friday debate, he backed a West Aberdeenshire amendment in preference to the motion promoted by the joint English and Scottish executives. This would have granted a 'national' parliament to England as well as Scotland, Wales and Northern Ireland, with representatives of all four in a United Kingdom federal Parliament. The amendment was also backed by SLP president Lord Bannerman, who warned delegates from south of the border that if 'poor old England does not get a parliament of her own, she is finished. We are fed up with being sleeping partners in what you call Great Britain.' The joint executive motion instead envisaged provincial assemblies for the regions of England, which some felt implied that Scotland too was being relegated to a mere 'region'. Delegates backed this by an overwhelming majority and rejected the West Aberdeenshire amendment by 365 to 335.

Matters did not rest there. During a debate on the Liberal Commission, set up earlier that year to review the party's ideology, Russell Johnston audaciously attacked Grimond, viewing as 'unhelpful' the former leader's suggestion that the whole basis of a political party was somehow suspect. 'I want to know what he means', thundered Johnston, 'and I want to know what he will put in its place.'[27] Rebuking Grimond in this way was, remarked David Steel, 'the Liberal equivalent of swearing aloud in church',[28] but Johnston's cry of 'classical' Liberalism was met with a standing ovation from George Mackie and several others. If this Liberal Assembly was remembered for anything, noted the journalist Hugh Noyes, it would be as:

> . . . the occasion when Mr. Grimond ceased to be the prophet and oracle of the party and became just another, although still the most beloved, of its elder statesmen . . . Although there was all the old fire and ringing oratory, and although he was cheered and clapped to the rostrum just as in the old days, the party is clearly no longer in a mood to follow their former leader with blind devotion.[29]

Beyond the Scottish Question, which was in any case over-shadowed by UK-wide discussion of prices and incomes policy, industrial decline and membership of the Common Market, Scottish Liberals worked to plug holes in their policy platform. R. A. Robertson, the party's industrial adviser, published a

Report on Coal Mining and Shipbuilding in 1968, which was credited with responding 'more quickly and positively than anyone else to the oil finds in the North Sea'; Donald Leach looked at general industrial development in another pamphlet entitled *Opportunity for Scotland*; Sandy Waugh did 'pioneering work' on credit taxation; and vice-chairman Kenneth Guest, Liberal candidate in East Renfrewshire, published *Prescription for Poverty: A Plea for Action*, also in 1968.[30]

The rural emphasis of the party's parliamentary successes was also balanced in the late 1960s by a belated Scottish Liberal revival in local government. Bill Riddell became the first post-war Liberal provost of Greenock in 1966,[31] while in Edinburgh Robert L. Smith (a future SLP president) used the Merchiston ward in Edinburgh as a 'springboard for other limited but significant advances'.[32] A pre-1970 election statement of policy claimed Liberals 'would much prefer' if local government elections were not fought along political lines, but nevertheless trumpeted seizing control of Greenock in 1966 and increasing its majority in the burgh a year later.

The enthusiasm of younger Liberals was also important to the SLP during this period. Robert Brown, who would later serve as a councillor and MSP, recalled Liberalism feeling 'modern, relevant, switched on, exciting, able to change the world', an appeal fuelled by clear policies and a disproportionate number of charismatic leaders and MPs in Scotland. Between 1968 and 1969 Brown was president of the Aberdeen University Liberal Society, which had 72 members and played an important part in Jo Grimond's election as Rector in 1969 (together with the campus Nationalist, Shetland and Celtic Societies).[33] Although these Young Liberals were not as plentiful as the Young Scots earlier that century, they tussled with George Mackie at SLP Assemblies and maintained a valuable presence both in Scotland's universities and local associations.

They were also useful when it came to furthering the SLP's aim of replacing the Conservatives (who after 1966 had only 21 seats) 'as the main opposition Party in Scotland', by fielding 50 candidates across Scotland. 'If Liberalism is to be properly projected', it reasoned, 'this means insisting on Candidates of the right calibre unlike other Parties who insist on the right background – Public School or Trade Union'. But if implemented, 'Target '70' could make a 'real breakthrough' at Westminster, though the publication also frankly admitted that party HQ remained 'under-equipped for the task it is now doing'. It therefore made the usual appeal to Liberals to 'sign Bankers Orders or contribute regularly to the Party by some other means'.[34] The policy statement also declared that:

> A Scottish Parliament for Scottish Affairs within the framework of Britain is the first priority of our Scottish policy and we pride ourselves that the hard work and practical common sense of our Scottish MPs have brought its establishment much nearer. But the foundation and basis of all we do is the achievement of greater freedom and opportunity for the individual.[35]

In February 1970, the SLP re-published its 1962 pamphlet, *Scottish Self-Government*, which had originally appeared in 1949. This largely comprised the party's evidence to the Royal Commission on the Constitution, which had been established by Harold Wilson's government following the rise of the SNP in 1967–8, as well as Russell Johnston's Self-government Bill and an old pamphlet written by David Steel on the shortcomings of the Scottish Office.[36] Drafted by Willis Pickard, the party traced its support for 'Home Rule' back to 1908, a belief it claimed was based on two 'essential principles', the 'pride of belonging' and the 'tremendous stimulus' devolution would bring to Scotland and the rest of the UK.

Full sovereignty as proposed by the SNP, it argued, though possible and even 'attractive in moments of Westminster stupidity, is nowadays an illusion' and, besides, was not necessary, the SLP's Structure of Government Committee having drawn up a 'pure federal concept': a 'Federal Assembly' of 315 members and a representative Senate of 32. The Scottish Parliament, meanwhile, would have 'about' 142 members. If the Royal Commission was not willing to recommend such a model, then the SLP politely asked it to consider what it called 'phased federalism' instead.[37]

Contributing to a 1970 publication, *The Scottish Debate*, David Steel – who had successfully reformed Britain's abortion laws a few years earlier – traced the Liberal Party's 'commitment to federalism' to an 1888 Scottish Liberal Association resolution, which had been 'passed with monotonous regularity at almost every annual conference' since. The lack of agreement on provenance underlined that Liberals had rarely spoken with one voice on the constitution, either in Scotland or England. Steel at least admitted that it was a 'complicated' policy which was 'difficult to expound' on the doorstep, unlike independence.[38]

In September 1969, Jo Grimond had once again riled some in the Scottish party by telling the broadcaster (and former Liberal candidate) Robin Day that the SNP and SLP ought to pool their efforts. Russell Johnston retorted that there were 'some Liberals who would do well to study the nationalist parties they court, for they would find them far from liberal'. Earlier that year the party had toyed with creating a new position of 'leader' (as opposed to president or chairman), something they had asked Grimond to take on. This, however, died a quick death and the Scottish Liberals made use of their former (UK) leader by offering to make him president instead.

The SLP also ruled out a 'common front' with the SNP, something Grimond considered too unequivocal. Instead, he suggested giving the Nationalists a clear run in the forthcoming South Ayrshire by-election (won, ironically, by Labour's Jim Sillars, who would later join the SNP). There was also an internal row regarding Joseph Rowntree money Grimond had secured for a full-time researcher and press relations staffer at Scottish HQ. He had George Mackie's daughter in mind, but when she turned it down, Mackie suggested Donald Gorrie, a former schoolteacher. Grimond was not keen, but the party chairman got his way. Grimond was also unhappy about the Scottish party's evidence to the Royal Commission, indeed he believed the SLP was going too far in setting out a completely autonomous constitutional policy without aligning with the party in other parts of the UK.

Grimond then indicated that he did not want to be president after all, claiming he had been led to believe this would mean being 'political leader of the Scottish Liberal Party', at which Mackie, Gorrie and Russell Johnston closed ranks. 'The bad blood was beginning to run deeply between Grimond and his senior Scottish colleagues,' judged the biographer Michael McManus, 'who evidently felt that he was behaving like an over-indulged child, grown paranoid in his desperate quest for recognition and appreciation.' Grimond attempted to oust Mackie as chairman, and at a stormy executive meeting on 4 April 1970, matters were only resolved when it agreed to Jo's terms. This rancorous episode, noted McManus, confirmed to the SLP 'that Grimond missed being party leader'.[39]

ON TO THE 1970S

Scottish nationalism, however, was a fickle phenomenon. At the 1970 general election, both the SNP as an electoral force and the issue of 'self-government' (an ambiguous term used by both the SNP and Liberals) appeared less salient than they had been just a few years previously. Ahead of polling day, the SNP had adopted candidates in eight of the most promising Liberal territories. As Chris Baur reported in the *Scotsman*: 'The Scottish Liberals and the Nationalists have become so entrenched in their official attitudes towards cooperation with each other that . . . a pact between the two parties . . . to preserve and enhance the Home Rule vote is an almost hopeless proposition.'[40]

The presence of an SNP candidate in Ross & Cromarty, for example, contributed to the defeat of the incumbent Liberal MP, while another in Caithness & Sutherland made it impossible for George Mackie to regain the seat he had lost in 1966. Scottish Liberals did not reciprocate in the SNP's best prospective constituencies, but to little effect, for Winnie Ewing lost in Hamilton and Donald Stewart scored a surprise win in the Western Isles. In two other seats, Banff and East Aberdeenshire, the combined vote for the Liberal and SNP candidates was greater than that cast for the victor. Jo Grimond, of course, held on in Orkney & Shetland ('where the inhabitants cherish him', wrote Douglas Young, 'as much as birdwatchers guard the last representative of some rare species') but the election had left the Scottish Liberals as 'a middle-ground Home Rule party of the fringes . . . though still capable of winning outlying seats'.[41]

With both parties disappointed at their respective results, yet another attempt was made to agree terms. It helped that Billy Wolfe, an admirer of Jo Grimond, was now SNP convenor, and that David Steel was on friendly terms with the Nationalist leader. The parties' presidents corresponded and met in July 1970. But each side had their dissenters, and it was a terse statement that flowed from Atholl Place following the encounter: 'The SNP have asked for these talks, and as a matter of courtesy the SLP executive will hear what they have to say. But in the light of recent press statements from the SNP the Liberal executive have not seen any great change in their attitude.'

Three hours of talks achieved little beyond agreement to co-operate at Westminster, and by the time the next election approached, both sides had lost interest. In early 1973, 10 SNP members and four Liberals met in Perth to revive the idea of a limited non-aggression pact, but this was thrown out by the SNP's conference in May and met a similar fate at the Scottish Liberal conference later the same month. Why did such talks repeatedly fail? As Graham Watson has concluded, while both parties were unhappy with the constitutional status quo, 'one advocated home rule, the other – increasingly – independence', and while the former cause 'held an intellectual attraction', the latter had a more populist appeal.[42] Arguing for 'self-government' rather than either of those goals might help paper over the cracks, but it disguised deeper disagreements, which were philosophical as well as tactical.

The two parties had, since the late 1960s, also been competing over the same sort of votes, those of skilled and semi-skilled Scots, many of them middle class and, during the 1970s, increasingly younger. But while a portion of the SNP's vote developed into a modest 'core' vote, the Scottish Liberals lacked such stability in their voter base.[43]

The Scottish Liberal Assembly speeches of Russell Johnston, party leader since 1973, represented a sustained intellectual attempt to differentiate his party's 'good' nationalism from the SNP's 'bad'. In one peroration, Johnston said he understood the SNP's motivation in his 'gut', but his 'reason' rejected their proposed solution (independence), while in 1974 he said of the SNP:

Here one finds, in the main, not Liberals, but frustrated Tories and Socialists – and the areas of their electoral success demonstrate this – who give priority to the need for a national identity over the long established centrist view of the Parties with which they have been traditionally linked. For us this has never been an issue because we have always been a Home Rule Party. The recognition of national identity is a basic part of the whole Liberal ethos as spelt out by Gladstone and Asquith and Sinclair and MacCormick and Bannerman ... I see the SNP as a pressure group – a pressure group which is doing a good job, but a one-ticket movement notwithstanding.

This cast Gladstone et al. as more enthusiastic devolution-
ists than the historical record justified, but in another speech
Johnston said the fact the SNP might 'temporarily outstrip' the
Scottish Liberals did not 'worry' him because:

> ... while their leadership has a commitment to total independ-
> ence, I believe that given a Parliament controlling our own affairs,
> we would shed outright nationalism and turn back to the political
> options, right, left and centre, which the Nationalists now contain
> temporarily in their ranks ... Because Liberalism is bigger than
> Nationalism. It is a world philosophy.

It was an obvious attempt to contrast the moderate, achievable
aims of the Scottish Liberals (a devolved Scottish Parliament
with direct representation in Europe) with the SNP's then anti-
EEC vision of independence:

> Those who see the SNP as a vehicle for genuine change in our society
> should think very hard about this. Firstly, real, lasting change does
> not happen quickly. It is a foolish self delusion to believe it: it is a
> cruel deception to seek support by suggesting it. Secondly, a change
> which simply replaces one power grouping by another is no change
> at all. It is simply history repeating itself.[44]

Johnston did not much like the SNP. In another speech he
rebuked a banner at an SNP Conference which read: 'The
Oil is Ours.' 'It had the stench of greed about it', he stormed,
'which would have been repugnant to a great Scot like David
Livingstone.'[45] He helped develop a Scottish Liberal policy
which was less greedy, advocating a Scottish Oil Development
Corporation (and a connected Scottish Development Bank)
'which would receive a proportion of the oil revenues to spend
on regeneration of the Scottish economy, control negotiations
with the oil companies'.[46] Johnston had first raised Scotland
and oil in the House of Commons on 3 February 1971, and
on several occasions thereafter, as did Lord Tanlaw (an SLP
vice-chairman) in the House of Lords. On a visit to Aberdeen,
however, Jeremy Thorpe warned that North Sea oil was not a
'panacea' for Scotland's ills.

The two general elections of 1974 brutally settled the SNP-
Liberal debate, as well as supremacy in terms of third-party
support. While between 1970 and February 1974, the UK
Liberals more than doubled their vote share to 19.3 per cent,
the party in Scotland saw its support rise by only a quarter of

the national rate. And while the Liberal vote (north and south) stagnated at the October 1974 election, the SNP's momentum continued, rising from 11.4 per cent in 1970 to 21.9 per cent in February and 30.4 in October. Worse, 35 per cent of the 1970 Scottish Liberal vote had switched to the Nationalists by 1974.

While the SNP won seven and then 11 MPs, the Scottish Liberals remained static on three: Steel, Grimond and Johnston. Across Britain, by contrast, the Liberals appeared on the cusp of coalition government, but in Scotland the SNP, not the Scottish Liberals, had become the second party. The second of the two elections left what Menzies Campbell called 'a corrosive legacy in Scottish liberalism',[47] the party having fielded candidates in almost every constituency but without adequate resources for basics like campaign literature.

SNP advances had further eroded party morale. In an angry letter to *The Times* after the second election, Donald Gorrie (the SLP's 'administrative director') rebutted SNP suggestions that Liberal candidates should have stood aside in certain constituencies:

> The Liberals polled just the basic straight Liberal vote … many of these Liberals would regard the naked appeal to greed amid the racialist propaganda of some SNP candidates and the intimidation by some of their activists as an even greater threat to Liberal democracy than the two-party grip and selfish class-warfare of the Tory and Labour machines. Some SNP speeches and attitudes inculcating hatred of the English and urging people to be rich Scots, not poor Britons, are utterly illiberal … For a long time the Scottish Liberal Party went out of its way not to contest seats in which SNP seemed to have prospects. The SNP riposted by standing in Liberal-held and hopeful Liberal seats. They were in business to promote the SNP, not to build up a broad self-government movement. So Liberals naturally regard them as political opponents along with the Tories and Labour. Until the voting system is reformed, electoral cooperation is disastrous. Scottish Liberals oppose all their three opponents equally, following the adage "If you can't join them, beat them".[48]

The prospects of a formal SNP-Liberal alliance were further away than ever before. David Steel's energies, meanwhile, would soon be channeled into UK rather than Scottish pacts.

The 1975 referendum on continuing membership of the EEC provided a brief constitutional diversion. Since 1972, the SLP had been calling for 'direct [Scottish] representation at all levels in the Community', a policy aspiration it later ignored. Even more quixotically, the 1971 conference had also rejected terms of entry 'which do not ensure special arrangements' for Scottish fishing and agriculture, Commonwealth trade, food prices and the balance of payments'.[49] The party supported the 1973 Kilbrandon Commission's proposals for a Scottish Assembly as 'a first step towards a full democratic European Federation in which Scotland would be a unit'.[50] The Scottish Liberal Party advocated a referendum on EEC entry, the English party did not. Significantly, the referendum campaign brought Steel into close contact with senior Labour figures with whom he would become politically friendly, although academic analysis later suggested that most Scottish Liberals voted to leave the EEC, despite the Europhile implorations of Thorpe, Grimond et al.

David Steel viewed the EEC referendum and 1973 'Border Poll' on Northern Ireland as a strong basis for a referendum on the 'constitutional question of altering the terms of the 1707 union', something which 'could usefully clear this issue out of the way and let us concentrate on effective devolution, which is what the great majority of Scots . . . actually wants'. A referendum, he added, would constitute 'badly needed recognition of the sovereignty of the Scottish people', an early airing for an argument that would later dominate Scottish political discourse. Steel also despaired of the UK government's terminology, preferring Parliament to Assembly and Prime Minister to Chief Executive, which he said gave the impression 'the whole thing were nothing but a grandiose local authority'.[51]

Scottish Liberals had tweaked their own constitution by dividing the post of chairman in 1973, the organisational and political leadership roles going to different people for the first time since 1946. When Lady Bannerman (her husband John had died suddenly in 1969) stood down as president the year the Jeremy Thorpe scandal broke,[52] George Mackie attempted to succeed her, but was 'thoroughly beaten' by Robert L. Smith, a Liberal pioneer in Edinburgh local government. Mackie had stood down as chairman in 1970 and was given a peerage in 1974, signifying a return to active politics 'not altogether welcomed' by the Scottish Liberal Party.[53]

The local government reorganisation of 1975, meanwhile, led to the 'remarkable' election of seven Liberals to Aberdeen District Council and the 'breakthrough' election of Robert Brown (later a Member of the Scottish Parliament) in Rutherglen.[54] Greenock had reverted back to Liberal control in 1972, and was for a while the only local authority under Liberal leadership in Britain. The Scottish Liberal Party also adopted a new logo, a stylised 'S' and 'L' with a saltire.

Jo Grimond, who served as acting leader during the Thorpe affair, continued to depart from the Scottish Liberal script. At a Perth Assembly, he feared that regional local government would simply become an extension of central government, foreseeing a Scotland 'exclusively run by bureaucrats', with local life 'drained out of many parts of the country'. In a 1976 pamphlet entitled *A Roar for the Lion*, he even advocated abolishing Scotland's new regional authorities and introducing a Bill of Rights to protect both individuals and communities like the Highlands:

> The success of Scottish industry after the constitutional changes will depend upon enterprise, good management, less waste and a repudiation by the unions of their suicidal tendencies ... the Civil Service has now joined the ranks of the Trades Unions – the modern equivalent of the Feudal Barons, intent on increasing their perks and power, stamping out competition and oblivious to the general interest.

Competition, added Grimond, 'must be reinstated as the major control of the market'.[55] For this reason, one of his biographers cast what he called 'Grimondonian ad hoccery' as being closer to 'One Nation' Conservatism than classical Liberalism.[56]

In the mid-1970s a young lawyer and former Olympic athlete called Menzies Campbell became Scottish Liberal chairman in what he later called a 'palace revolution' or 'a Young – or Middle-Aged – Turks' revolution'. The party's 1975 spring conference in Ayr had 'boiled over' with resentment from the 1974 elections and the vote on a chairman initially saw a tie between him and Robert Smith, a first in Scottish Liberal history. Campbell attempted to withdraw but eventually won a re-run ballot by two votes.[57] 'I kept the ship afloat,' he later recalled:

> We had practically no money; we were bust until we developed an early form of the lottery. What I was doing was holding the damn thing together – with a very good man as Treasurer called John Lawrie, who was an actuary, terribly precise. So – survival ... Since we had very few MPs, as Chairman I did a lot of television and radio. We tried to put some meat on the bones of the federalist case.[58]

Campbell also helped launch a 'pools' fundraising scheme which got SLP finances back on track, while arguing for reform of divorce, licensing and homosexuality laws, including 'the removal of penalties for homosexual behaviour between consenting adult males in private', firm liberal territory which also drew support from the Conservative MP Malcolm Rifkind and Labour's Robin Cook.[59] Campbell, who was nevertheless regarded as being on the right of the SLP 'because my jacket and my trousers always matched', went on, like David Steel, to become an MP and UK party leader.[60] Curiously, within the SLP homosexual law reform had been 'seen as divisive and electorally damaging'. In 1972, Steel had not been convinced of the need to change the law in Scotland given that the 'law of evidence in Scotland prevent[ed] the prosecution of consenting adults'.[61]

Councillor Terry Grieve replaced Campbell as chairman in 1977. 'As a Councillor for urban Bothwell,' argued an SLP publication, 'he symbolises with Russell Johnston as Leader, [who represents] the largest rural constituency in the U.K., the clear coming of age of the Party as a balanced national force'.[62] Nevertheless, party HQ in Edinburgh possessed what even the party acknowledged was a 'tiny staff' limited by 'financial constraints'. For a time, the Edinburgh councillor Donald Gorrie fulfilled 'a crucial political advisory role'. An advocate of religious 'desegregation' in Scottish schools, Gorrie was committed to reversing Robert Munro's 1918 reforms.

Writing in 1977, the journalist (and SNP supporter) Colin Bell acidly observed that Scottish Liberals could not 'begin to challenge the other parties in any contest that requires sheer numbers, or sheer funds', although their three surviving seats were at least 'neatly spread along the length of Scotland'.[63] Another sign of the SLP's decline and financial difficulties was the sale that year of the Scottish Liberal Club on Edinburgh's Princes Street. Although this had sought to widen its appeal by allowing women to become members (quite an Asquithian time lag), by March 1977 its annual general meeting accepted the inevitable and put the building up for sale. The proceeds were originally to be distributed per capita to SLC members, but when members Alan Blair and John Lawrie raised an action in the Court of Session (aided by Menzies Campbell QC pro bono), the net proceeds ended up purchasing new club premises

at 4 Clifton Terrace, to which the Scottish Liberal Party would
also move a few years later.[64]

That year – 1977 – was otherwise dominated by the David
Steel-engineered Lib–Lab Pact with James Callaghan's Labour
government, one product of which was a fresh legislative
attempt to establish a devolved Scottish Assembly, the Scotland
and Wales Bill having been guillotined in February (the three
SLP MPs had contributed to its demise). Separate Bills for
Scotland and Wales were introduced in November. Usefully for
Steel, the 1978 Scottish Liberal conference voted 210 to 212 to
extend his pact when others doubted its usefulness.[65] Writing
in the *Spectator* that June, Jo Grimond poured scorn on the
SLP for having 'allowed the self-government ball to be wrested
from them by the Nats', a curious observation given that the
SNP were by that point in decline. Grimond also lamented that
Scottish Liberals had failed:

> . . . to develop policies which have a wide appeal in Scotland. The
> two possible leaders of the Scottish Liberal Party are too occupied
> elsewhere. David Steel in London and Russell Johnston in Brussels.
> During the course of the Scotland Bill they have failed to make
> a hard fight for federalism, for proportional representation, for
> taxing powers to the Assembly, or for giving the Scottish people
> control of their public services, nationalised industries and their
> economy.[66]

Callaghan had his own devolution woes. Labour was split over
devolution, and the Scotland Bill was heavily amended. Not
only did Jo Grimond secure a potential opt out for Orkney
and Shetland, but the Islington MP George Cunningham (a
Scot) won support for an electoral threshold which stipulated
that only if 40 per cent of the Scottish electorate (as opposed
to those voting) approved would the *Scotland Act 1978* be
enacted.

Pro-devolutionists, whether Liberal, Labour or SNP, found
it difficult to rally four-square behind the government's plans.
Although the three Scottish Liberal MPs were all pro-Assembly,
tactical considerations prevented them from adopting a common
position. Jo Grimond declined to join 'Yes for Scotland'; David
Steel expressed concern about parties all doing their own thing;
and Russell Johnston launched the 'Alliance for an Assembly'
with Conservative devolutionist Alick Buchanan-Smith. Scottish

Liberal campaigning was therefore patchy. In Edinburgh, some Liberals even decided not to campaign because they did not consider the proposed Assembly to be powerful enough.[67]

David Steel, meanwhile, was naturally more focused on the looming general election and the survival of his realignment strategy. The Labour MP John Smith later claimed 'the Liberals were more or less sitting out the process . . . They were not at all active or pushing. Steel himself had begun to run into resistance on the ground, in the Borders.'[68] Indeed, the political scientist James Kellas found that by 1979 Scottish Liberal voters had moved 'strongly to the status quo' in terms of constitutional preferences, suggesting the SLP leadership was at odds with much of its voter base.[69]

Steel's Borders fiefdom registered a strong 'no' vote while Orkney and Shetland both voted against an Assembly despite Grimond urging them not to. On 16 March 1979, Steel told the Scottish Liberal conference that a devolved Assembly was 'not going to happen', adding that he would settle for a Scottish Grand Committee meeting in Edinburgh. This riled the troops, who defied him to vote for implementation of the *Scotland Act 1978* regardless.[70]

Steel was simply being realistic, and indeed the 1979 election result confirmed that devolution was no longer a vote winner. The Scottish Conservatives recovered many of their earlier losses, the SNP fell from 11 to 2 MPs and the Liberals held their usual trio of seats. The third-party vote had been squeezed throughout Great Britain. Nevertheless, the major achievement of the Scottish Liberal Party between 1964 and 1979 was to have gradually rebuilt its organisation and finances. From only selecting 26 candidates in 1964, it managed 68 at the October 1974 election (although this increase had strained its finances). In 1979, this slipped back to 43, but the party, as Steel regularly observed, was in an immeasurably stronger – and more credible – position than it had been in several decades.

NOTES

1. Steel had been the prospective Liberal candidate in Edinburgh Pentlands before the 1964 general election, but was moved by George Mackie to the Borders. See J. Purvis, J. Steel & D. Torrance, eds, 2015, *Militant for the Reasonable Man: Celebrating David*

Steel's Fifty Years as a Parliamentarian, Edinburgh: Birlinn, 65–7, for an account of the switch.

2. H. J. Hanham (1969), *Scottish Nationalism*, Cambridge, MA: Harvard University Press, 119.
3. G. Mackie (2004), *Flying, Farming and Politics: a liberal life*, Stanhope: Memoir Club, 164–5.
4. D. Steel (1989), *Against Goliath: David Steel's Story*, London: Weidenfeld & Nicolson, 59.
5. D. Torrance (2012), *David Steel: Rising Hope to Elder Statesman*, London: Biteback, 26.
6. D. Torrance, 29.
7. SLP meeting, 10 April 1965, Scottish Liberal Papers Acc 11765/57.
8. G. Mackie, 154.
9. SLP meeting, 4 September 1965, Scottish Liberal Papers Acc 11765/57.
10. Davidson had served as naval attaché at the British Embassy in Moscow before establishing himself as an Aberdeenshire farmer.
11. D. E. Butler & A. King (1965), *The British General Election of 1964*, London: St Martin's Press, 356.
12. W. L. Miller (1981), *The End of British Politics? Scots and English Political Behaviour in the Seventies*, Oxford: Clarendon, 34.
13. L. Kennedy (1995), *In Bed with an Elephant: A Journey through Scotland's Past and Present*, London: Bantam Press, 347.
14. SLP meeting, 3 September 1966, Scottish Liberal Papers Acc 11765/57.
15. Johnston wore a kilt for the occasion, which was taken less than seriously by other MPs.
16. W. L. Miller, 44.
17. SLP annual conference, 18–20 May 1967, Lesser City Hall, Perth.
18. In a letter to Andrew Haddon, president of the Roxburgh, Selkirk and Peebles Liberal association, Kennedy said the Liberals 'have an excellent policy on self-government, but the party as a whole has not pursued it with unanimity and vigour' (*The Times*, 1 November 1967). Kennedy later rejoined the SLP.
19. G. Mackie, 164–5.
20. HL Debs 6 December 1967 Vol 287 c705
21. Author's collection.
22. HC Debs 14 February 1969 Vol 777 c1735.
23. J. McMillan (1969), *Anatomy of Scotland*, London: Leslie Frewin, 101. McMillan's prediction that the Liberal Party 'as a factor in Scottish affairs seems doomed' was less accurate.
24. H. J. Hanham, 190.
25. W. L. Miller, 45.
26. G. Mackie, 152.

27. *The Times*, 21 & 23 September 1968. Elsewhere, Johnston branded Grimond a 'dilettante revolutionary'.
28. Grimond, added Steel, 'had the cavalier habit of making delphic pronouncements while not actually coming to grips with the necessary negotiations' (D. Steel, 1989, *Against Goliath: David Steel's Story*, London: Weidenfeld & Nicolson, 59).
29. *The Times*, 21 & 23 September 1968.
30. R. Johnston (1979), *Scottish Liberal Party Conference Speeches 1971–1978*, Bookmag, 82.
31. The same year, Riddell published an SLP/Vanguard pamphlet entitled *The future of the territorial army. Towards Scottish home rule* followed under the same imprint in 1968.
32. R. Johnston, 82.
33. Cllr Robert Brown to the author, 14 February 2021.
34. J. Thorpe & G. Mackie (1967), *The Liberal Crusade – People Count: The Liberal Plan for Power*, Edinburgh: Scottish Liberal Party, 29–30.
35. Ibid, 32.
36. See D. Steel (1968), *Out of Control: A Critical Examination of the Government of Scotland*, Edinburgh: Scottish Liberal Party.
37. SLP (1970), *Scottish Self Government: The Views of the Scottish Liberal Party*, Edinburgh: Scottish Liberal Party, 14–19.
38. D. Steel (1970), 'Federalism' in N. MacCormick (ed.), *The Scottish Debate: Essays on Scottish Nationalism*, London: Oxford University Press, 81 & 85.
39. M. McManus (2001), *Jo Grimond: Towards the Sound of Gunfire*, Edinburgh: Birlinn, 307–11.
40. G. Watson (1999), 'Scottish Liberals, Scottish Nationalists and Dreams of a Common Front', *Journal of Liberal History* 22, Spring 1999.
41. D. Young (1971), *Scotland*, London: Cassell, 141.
42. G. Watson, *Journal of Liberal History* 22, Spring 1999.
43. W. L. Miller, 184.
44. R. Johnston, 15; 39–40; 57.
45. R. Johnston, 25.
46. Scottish Liberal Party Conference '72 Agenda, 1–3 June 1972. This policy was included in another SLP pamphlet entitled *Oil – The Key to Scotland's Future* (1972).
47. M. Campbell (2008), *Menzies Campbell: My Autobiography*, London: Hodder and Stoughton, 86.
48. *The Times*, 30 October 1974. The following year, Gorrie unsuccessfully challenged Russell Johnston as SLP leader.
49. SLP Conference '71, 11–12 June 1971.
50. SLP 1971–4.

51. *The Times*, 26 November 1975.
52. Scottish party chairman Menzies Campbell was tipped off by David Steel regarding Thorpe's resignation. Naively, he telephoned Radio Forth in Edinburgh to give them a recorded (but embargoed) reaction. Ignoring the embargo, commercial radio stations across the UK used Campbell's statement to break the news (M. Campbell, 90).
53. Mackie, 171.
54. R. Johnston, 82.
55. Quoted in J. Mercer (1978), *Scotland: The Devolution of Power*, London: John Calder, 182–4.
56. See M. McManus.
57. M. Campbell, 86–7.
58. *Journal of Liberal History* 60, Autumn 2008. The SLP's 'Federal Unit' published *Scottish self-government: a fresh start with federalism* during 1976.
59. Scottish Liberal Party Conference '75 Agenda, 12–14 June 1975.
60. *Journal of Liberal History* 60, Autumn 2008.
61. R. Davidson & G. Davis (2012), *The Sexual State: Sexuality and Scottish Governance, 1950–80*, Edinburgh: Edinburgh University Press, 60 & 70.
62. R. Johnston, 82.
63. Colin Bell (1977), 'Scotch myths', *Spectator*, 18 June 1977.
64. Interview with Alan Blair, 14 February 2021.
65. D. Steel, 140.
66. Jo Grimond (1978), 'Scottish complacency', *Spectator*, 10 June 1978.
67. J. Bochel, D. Denver & A. Macartney (eds) (1981), *The Referendum Experience: Scotland 1979*, Aberdeen: Aberdeen University Press, 88–9.
68. I. Paterson (1998), *A Diverse Assembly: The Debate on a Scottish Parliament*, Edinburgh: Edinburgh University Press, 139.
69. J. Kellas (1989), 150.
70. J. Bochel, D. Denver & A. Macartney, 148.

7

'Breaking the Mould' of Scottish Politics: 1979–1988

In a memorable speech during the 1979 no-confidence debate in James Callaghan's minority government, Michael Foot, the Leader of the House (whose brother Dingle had been a Scottish Liberal MP), spoke of the Conservative leader Margaret Thatcher leading 'her troops into battle snugly concealed behind a Scottish nationalist shield, with the boy David holding her hand'. The leader of the Liberal Party, he added with the 'utmost affection', had 'passed from rising hope to elder statesman without any intervening period whatsoever'.[1]

Following that election, the Scottish Nationalist shield was weakened to just two MPs, while the Boy David held steady with three in Scotland, including his own. This, given the chaotic circumstances of that election, was a good outcome. With Mrs Thatcher resolutely opposed to legislative devolution – the little loved *Scotland Act 1978* was swiftly expunged from the statute book – the Scottish Liberal Party was robbed of its Home Rule rallying cry, although the decline of the SNP at least allowed it to recover third-party votes from the Nationalists.

Further disappointment came in June 1979 when Scottish party leader Russell Johnston contested the first direct elections to the European Parliament, having served as an appointed member since earlier that decade. Johnston had become a passionate Europhile, but some of his colleagues believed he was taking on too much and might end up neglecting his Westminster seat. Although 'Russell's in Brussels' had a certain ring to it, he lost in the Highlands and Islands to Winnie Ewing, who went on to be lauded as 'Madame Ecosse'.[2] Johnston lost even more heavily in 1984. Given that Ewing's party remained equivocal on Scottish membership of the EEC, it must have been galling for the French-speaking, Paris-loving Johnston. He concentrated instead on the (relatively powerless) Council of Europe in Strasbourg.

Better news for the Scottish Liberals came following a long-anticipated split in the Labour Party, the consequence of hard-left infiltration and disagreements on the European question. The Social Democratic Party (SDP) was launched on 26 March 1981 under the collective leadership of Roy Jenkins (to whom Steel was already close), Shirley Williams, David Owen and Bill Rodgers. It formed a regional 'Council for Scotland', while an 'Alliance' with the Liberal Party soon followed.

Russell Johnston favoured co-operation with the SDP but refused to substitute, in the words of Ross Finnie, 'the great Liberal tradition for a mish-mash of unsalted social democratic porridge'.[3] Assured that it would only proceed on the basis of shared principles, he moved the resolution for the formation of a Scottish Alliance on 12 September 1981. The two parties met in December to discuss a 'division' of parliamentary seats. Although this proved easier than previous discussions with the SNP, it still proved hard to reach agreement. Both parties, for example, identified Rutherglen and Hillhead as potentially winnable constituencies.

Charles Brodie, a computer executive known as 'Chic', had already been selected by the Liberals to fight Glasgow Hillhead when the incumbent Conservative MP, Tam Galbraith, died on 2 January 1982. A week later Jenkins spent 'a tense and uncomfortable' two hours at his Kensington home with Brodie and Ken Wardrop, chairman of the Hillhead Liberal association. They laid down what the SDP regarded as 'impossible conditions' regarding a joint campaign in the constituency, but eventually Paul Medlicott, an aide to David Steel, 'laid down the law' (with Steel's authorisation) to Brodie and Wardrop, 'informing them bluntly that either Roy Jenkins fought Hillhead or that was the end of the SDP-Liberal Alliance'.[4]

In his memoirs, Jenkins praised Brodie as 'a major artificer of the Alliance'.[5] An unstated *quid pro quo* for Chic's sacrifice was that Jenkins, and by extension the SDP, were to commit unequivocally to support for a devolved Scottish Parliament.[6] Although Jenkins could point to a 1976 speech supporting a Scottish Assembly, devolution 'henceforth took a rather higher place in his programme for the renewal of British democracy',[7] with a major speech in Hillhead on 10 March.[8]

Russell Johnston, David Steel and Jo Grimond all helped with Jenkins' campaign. Grimond even reputedly observed that 'the strength of the Alliance rests on the fact that David Steel is really a Social Democrat and Roy Jenkins a Liberal'.[9] The pair had been close since working together on the 1975 EEC referendum. In the second week of the campaign, the constituency was swamped by Scottish Liberal activists, including a magnanimous Chic Brodie.

For once, a local pact had the desired effect and the former Chancellor and European Commission president stormed to victory on 25 March. It was the first parliamentary gain with which the Liberals had been associated in Scotland since the general election of 1966, and the first by-election victory since the 'boy David' had stormed to victory in the Borders in 1965.

Jenkins' win happened to coincide with the SLP conference in St Andrews, where David Steel issued a warning that no seat was safe for Labour or the Conservatives. Scottish Liberals were genuinely thrilled at the SDP's success and gave Jenkins, whose team had driven from Glasgow early that morning, a champion's welcome. Addressing delegates, Jenkins said the Alliance 'were the real possibility of an alternative government':

> We are a partnership of principles because we Liberals and Social Democrats agree with each other, not on every dot and comma, but on all the main issues of politics more spontaneously than the differing wings of either Labour or the Conservatives. At a time when everyone else is pulling in an extremist direction whether it be extreme monetarism or Marxism, we can offer a message of something unique, a new deal of sense and hope and moderation.[10]

In his memoirs, Jenkins recalled a 'high-pressure haze' in the aftermath of the by-election, 'and of accidental and almost excessive Asquith pietism':

> I was driven across central Scotland and the Kingdom of Fife to address the Scottish Liberal conference in St Andrews, the most notable town of his old constituency base of 1886–1918, took in on the way back an SDP dinner in Edinburgh (a city redolent with memories of Gladstone and Rosebery if not of Asquith himself), and finished the evening at another SDP celebration in Paisley, the burgh in which Asquith, by winning a famous 1920 bye-election, and heralded one of the greatest false dawns in twentieth-century politics.[11]

The political scientist Vernon Bogdanor wrote to tell the victor of Hillhead he was 'not Asquith at East Fife, but Gladstone at Midlothian in 1880',[12] his point being that the Grand Old Man had gone on to lead three administrations. David Steel shared in the hyperbole, saying that Jenkins' decision to fight Hillhead 'was as critical to our public life as was Gladstone's to fight Midlothian and Asquith's to fight Paisley'.[13]

All were guilty of misinterpreting, or perhaps simply forgetting, Scottish Liberal history. 'Paisley was a false dawn, both for Asquith and the Liberal Party,' was Jenkins own verdict in his admiring biography of the former Liberal premier:

> At best it was the equivalent of some late winter daybreak on the fringes of the Arctic Circle ... the post-war Liberal day never achieved more than a grey and short-lived light. By 1924 it was dusk again. By 1926, for Asquith at least, it was political night.[14]

Jenkins himself acknowledged that his Hillhead win 'heralded not so much a false dawn as an anticlimactic return to Parliament'.[15]

The journalist Allan Massie detected a rhetorical Scottish Liberal attempt to present the Alliance as the natural heir to the two great reforming governments of the 20th century (1906 and 1945). 'It is rhetoric', he judged, 'that has a powerful appeal.'[16] The Alliance love-in, meanwhile, was further strengthened when in Greenock and Port Glasgow J. Dickson Mabon, a former Labour MP and SDP defector, finally agreed to step aside for the Liberals, who found the idea of campaigning for Mabon intolerable. Besides, the constituency already possessed a sizeable Scottish Liberal vote.[17]

If there was tension, it was *within* the Liberal Party. At the 1982 Joint Liberal Assembly in Bournemouth, Geraint Howells, the MP for Cardigan, complained that an SLP motion moved by Jim Wallace prioritised devolution for Scotland without any mention of Wales or the English regions.[18] Russell Johnston was unapologetic, arguing that the 'political reality' was that such a demand had 'been expressed for far longer and with wider support in Scotland than in any other part of the UK'.[19] The SDP's first consultative assembly in Scotland, by contrast, embraced 'Home Rule all round'. In a 'personal manifesto' published in 1983, however, Jo Grimond doubted the Alliance had 'faced the consequences of Scottish and Welsh self-government';[20] he remained sceptical about federalising England.

Other policy commitments appeared under the auspices of the Scottish Liberal Club, whose 4 Clifton Terrace premises also came to house the SLP in April 1982.[21] These included *An alternative economic strategy* prepared by Ross Finnie, who also addressed the SDP's first Scottish Assembly in February 1983.[22] The Liberal-SDP Alliance was polling well and David Steel ranked as the UK's second most-popular politician. Yet this did not necessarily translate into electoral success. Although the Alliance achieved 18.1 per cent of the vote in the 1982 Scottish regional elections, it managed just 25 councillors out of 441.

The commentator Allan Massie had predicted following Hillhead that with the Conservatives and Alliance likely to 'be almost equal in strength' north of the border, Labour would likely maintain its position 'as by far the strongest party in Scotland'. 'The mould of Scottish politics', he concluded, 'is likely to remain unbroken.'[23] At the 1983 general election, scant Liberal resources appeared to support Massie's analysis. Ben Coutts, who stood against Conservative Nicholas Fairbairn in Perth, later recalled that the local Liberal association was 'pathetically thin on the ground' compared with the 'well-oiled' Tory machine and even the 'Scots Nats who had a committee room and . . . quite a bit of cash'. Coutts, by contrast, 'worked on a shoestring'.[24]

Even so, Coutts came a respectable third and attracted a quarter of the vote, as did the Alliance Scotland-wide. This translated into just eight MPs, five of whom were Liberals. As part of the Alliance, however, a long-standing gap between support in Scotland and England (as in February 1974) was closed for the first time, polling 24.5 per cent north of the border and 26.9 per cent south. This 'pact' therefore allowed the Liberals and SDP to mount a major third-party challenge across all of Scotland, which was thereafter maintained (though the gap between Scotland and England later reopened). For the first time since the 1920s, candidates with a Liberal association could contest every constituency in Scotland and gain a respectable share of the vote – and even win – although this remained true of areas with an historic record of voting Liberal.[25]

The SNP held its two MPs but continued its decline, its MEP Winnie Ewing lamenting that 'the Liberal/SDP Alliance stole our clothes' in a letter to party leader Gordon Wilson,[26] quite a turnaround from a decade earlier. A fifth of the SNP's already diminished 1979 vote had opted for the Alliance,[27] although 'the almost complete absence of Liberal activity' in Dundee meant Wilson and the SNP consolidated its status as the city's 'foremost third-party' well into the new decade.[28] There had even been a degree of media support for the Alliance six decades after its Liberal component had lost the support of the *Scotsman* and *Glasgow Herald*, with 5 out of 11 Scottish newspapers urging a vote for the Alliance.[29]

Russell Johnston, still Scottish party leader, was among the first Liberal MPs to advocate a full merger with the SDP following the disappointment of the election. David Owen had other ideas. Bob Sawyer, a member of the SDP's Scottish Council, wrote to Owen in August 1984 enclosing a *Glasgow Herald* cutting about the two parties apparently inching 'nearer to full merger'. Sawyer believed the SDP's image was 'weakened rather than strengthened by merger rumours', and that the prospect of a vastly increased vote for a single party was a 'myth'. He mentioned Bunty Urquhart, the party's first Scottish organiser, who 'honestly thinks that we will take over the Liberal Party in Scotland and use their resources for the aim of Social Democracy. In this I think her judgement is seriously at fault.'[30]

Urquhart would stick with the party until eventual merger later that decade, as would the SDP's Denis Robertson Sullivan and Bernard Ponsonby, although the latter would soon quit politics for a successful career in broadcasting. David Mundell, a member of the SDP's Scottish Council, by contrast, returned to the Conservative Party and ended up in the Cabinet as Secretary of State for Scotland between 2015 and 2019. Indeed, it was a curiosity of 1980s politics that the Scottish Liberals said its 'chief care' was for 'the rights and opportunities of the individual, and in all spheres it sets freedom first', while railing against Mrs Thatcher's neo-liberal brand of individualism and freedom, often in moral as well as political terms.

The preamble to the SLP constitution spoke of building 'a society in Scotland in which every individual shall possess liberty, privacy, prosperity and security, and none shall be enslaved by poverty, ignorance or unemployment'.[31] But in the high unemployment of the early to mid-1980s lay the distinction between Scottish Liberalism and Conservative neo-liberalism; in one speech, Russell Johnston spoke of the freedom of the poor 'to dine at the Ritz'.[32]

When a row over rating revaluation consumed the Scottish Conservative Party in Easter 1985, the Scottish Liberals convinced themselves that the Alliance was poised to overtake Labour as the second party in Scotland (a System Three poll had put the Alliance on 20 per cent, 1 point ahead of the Conservatives). But there was concern among Scottish Liberal activists about the structure of the Alliance, and what they regarded as the 'rightward' drift of Dr Owen. 'He seems to be trying to construct . . . differences between the two parties,' complained one official.[33]

At its March 1985 Inverness Assembly, the Scottish Liberals took a near-unilateralist stand against the advice of their leadership, voting for a phased withdrawal of US bases from Scotland as well as the 'phased banning of all nuclear weapons and their delivery systems from Scotland'. Ross Finnie, the party chairman, said the resolution breached a convention whereby Scottish Liberals could only take policy decisions on functions delivered by the Scottish Office and declared himself to be 'unhappy'.[34]

Finnie (alongside Jim Wallace) had also been responsible for a review of Scottish Liberal relations with the UK's other Liberal parties, a source of constitutional confusion since 1946. This they declared 'unsatisfactory and in need of reform'. The 1984 Bournemouth Assembly had set up a working party to consider a proper federal constitution, after which its 'Scottish mentors' (Wallace and Finnie) identified three key considerations:

1. The SLP considered that the status quo was 'really an English Liberal Constitution';
2. There existed those in England who felt the SLP and Welsh Liberal Party were not bearing their share of federal costs (such as a deficit arising from the ever-ailing *Liberal News*);
3. And, the clincher, that 'there are those in all parts of Britain who feel that if we advocate a federal system of government for the country, we should adopt a proper federal structure for the Party'.

A federal structure meant the SLP's autonomy would 'be substantially preserved' although there could be 'some implicit surrender of sovereignty', i.e. defence resolutions at SLP conferences would be secondary to those at the Joint Assembly. It would also cost the SLP more in terms of federal HQ staffing and other common expenditure.[35]

The March 1986 Rothesay Assembly, meanwhile, re-asserted its 1982 commitment to:

> ... a fairly elected Scottish Parliament with significant economic, industrial and fiscal powers: these powers to include the levying and collection of income tax in Scotland, with a transfer of funds between our Parliament and Westminster to correct any imbalance between the revenue collected by Westminster in Scotland and Scotland's share of central spending.[36]

At another Assembly shortly before the 1987 general election, Menzies Campbell, the prospective Liberal candidate in Asquith's former North East Fife constituency, proposed a 'Scottish Home Rule Declaration'. This asserted that 'the case for Scottish Home rule has never been stronger and again stresses the commitment of the Scottish Liberal Party to introduce legislation to set up a Scottish Parliament elected by proportional representation as a priority of any Government in which we participate'.[37] The political scientist Henry Drucker had suggested that rather than seeking an electoral pact with the SNP (as it had in the 1960s), the Alliance should instead woo Nationalist voters, with whom it could credibly compete with Labour.[38]

But only after the 1987 general election,[39] in which a Conservative government was once again returned with a minority of Scottish seats (the Alliance won nine, the SNP three, and Labour 50), did devolution become a salient issue once again. Russell Johnston even warned that Scottish resentment could 'boil over into [a] form of violence' if the UK government continued to ignore demands for a Scottish Assembly, with 'hotheads at the extremes of politics' pursuing civil disobedience.[40] Jeremy Thorpe had issued similar warnings two decades before.

The Alliance called for cross-party devolution legislation given that the overwhelming majority of Scottish MPs supported what was now routinely called a Scottish Parliament rather than an 'Assembly', but Scottish Labour was not keen, leading Ron Waddell, the political director of the Scottish Liberal Party, to call on Labour to 'stop acting as though it was the only party to represent Scotland'. The party had achieved, he added with a straight face, 'only 42 per cent of the votes in Scotland'.[41] The

Scottish Liberal Party had, of course, once behaved in exactly the same way with roughly the same proportion of the vote.

By this stage the SDP posed minimal threat, and renewed merger proposals gained an unstoppable momentum, not least because they were supported by Charles Kennedy and Robert Maclennan, Scotland's two SDP MPs. The Scottish Liberal Party (which claimed 10,000 members) insisted on being balloted separately, even though the SDP in Scotland did not have equivalent autonomy. The ballot, to be drafted by the 18-strong SLP executive and to be held in October 1987, contained two questions:

1. Do you agree that the Scottish Liberal Party should negotiate a merger with the SDP?
2. Do you agree that the negotiations should be on the basis of an autonomous Scottish party within a federal UK party structure?[42]

The early ballot underlined the SLP's determination to retain the independence it had enjoyed since 1946 as well as move towards the federal party structure supported by Messrs Finnie and Wallace in their 1985 document. The Welsh Liberal Party was also consulted separately, while delegates from across the UK were to vote on the merger proposals at the September Assembly in Harrogate. Only the draft constitution was to be submitted to a nationwide vote.

David Steel – who generally found SLP assemblies 'both sensible and supportive'[43] – later attributed the successful outcome in Harrogate to an 'inspirational speech' by Sir Russell Johnston (he had been knighted in 1985), now the party's longest-serving MP. His conference speeches, which were collected in two published volumes, had taken on a legendary quality, admired for their intellectual consistency and uplifting rhetoric. 'They fuelled,' recalled Robert Brown, 'most of us in our campaigning for months afterwards.'[44] Ross Finnie, a close friend, contrasted the 'consistently logical approach' of Johnston's speeches to his 'totally chaotic life style: constantly travelling; generously agreeing to speaking engagements; and, as a consequence, committing to near impossible schedules'.[45]

In characteristic fashion, Sir Russell invoked the memory of great Liberals from Lloyd George to Jo Grimond to press his case for the creation of a new party while insisting on the preservation of Liberal values. His warning that 'you do not change the taste of the whisky by changing the shape of the bottle' seemed personally as well as politically appropriate. He had supported the Alliance for having 'led the revolt of the reasonable' but now believed a unified party offered the best of both worlds, although he was equally determined to ensure that the interests of the Scottish party were protected and enhanced in any new political marriage.[46]

There was to be no place in the new relationship for the Scottish Women Liberals Council (SWLC) which, 'in spite of strenuous efforts to use it as a vehicle for feminism in the mid-eighties' had 'never became the politicised women's section that in another party it might have' become. As the SLP activist Sandra Grieve pointed out, it was 'the women themselves who refused to be seen as a separate grouping in the party', just as their predecessors had in the early 1920s:

> When women in the party were consulted about what they saw as the way forward there was a remarkable unanimity of view, they want support, training, recognition and a voice. They do not want any form of positive discrimination, quotas or women's sections.

Grieve believed that in the last decade of its life the Scottish Liberal Party 'was becoming much more women-friendly but it still had a long way to go'. By the late 1980s a slight majority of the SLD membership and executive were women, as were 40 per cent of its office bearers. In Gordon, where Nora Radcliffe was a prominent figure, 60 per cent of SLD councillors were female, something Malcolm Bruce had done his best to encourage. At the 1987 general election, almost a quarter of candidates in Liberal-led seats were women, although only Ray Michie (daughter of John Bannerman) managed to get elected.[47]

In October 1987, the Scottish Liberal Party voted overwhelmingly (by 92 per cent) in favour of merger with the SDP in Scotland, although the turnout was much lower than expected at 43.8 per cent. Johnston attributed this to the 'virtually non-existent' opposition to merger in Scotland, others to Scottish thrift in returning ballots by second-class post. There was a near identical level of support for an autonomous Scottish party within a federal UK party structure. Dick Mabon was to the lead the SDP's negotiation team and Sir Russell the Liberals'. The latter declared that:

We have had two absolutely clear and conclusive results today, which is as near unanimity as you could get outside Albania. Our members want merger and a strong, united party. The new party must have a full federal structure, which would give Scots full control over affairs in Scotland and at the same time give a clearly defined say in the forming of policy for the UK as a whole.[48]

One of the difficulties of the merger process was the reconciliation of a decentralised Scottish Liberal Party, in which funds, membership and policies were controlled in Edinburgh, with a highly centralised SDP, in which finance, membership and policies were run by its central organisation in London. Nevertheless, a draft constitution appeared in December 1987 with the unlovely name of 'The New Scottish Liberal & Social Democratic Party'.[49]

David Owen's SDP (continuing), meanwhile, had a sorry afterlife in Scotland. A memo dated January 1988 expressed concern about running its Scottish Council without a full-time organiser. As such, 'we would be regarded as an alien intruder . . . the SDP would become what the SNP has always claimed it was, an English party.'[50] The last meeting of the SDP Council for Scotland took place at the Terraces Hotel in Stirling on 20 January 1990.

Slightly trickier were negotiations regarding the Scottish party's place in the new federal structure. Although the leadership was prepared to sacrifice some autonomy in policy-making, some of the membership were concerned that the federal conference would end up dominating policy-making.[51] There was also concern that the Scottish party would lose its existing (and often troublesome) ability to adopt resolutions on non-Scottish issues such as defence and foreign affairs. Balancing these concerns were clear gains. Unlike the situation since 1946, the Scottish party would have formal representation on the federal party executive, finance and administration committees, at its conference and, perhaps most importantly, on its Federal Policy Committee.[52] Liberals might not have managed to federalise the United Kingdom, but they were at last federalising themselves.

NOTES

1. HC Debs 28 March 1979 vol 965 c577.
2. The Scottish Liberal Party had argued for a single Scottish Euro constituency returning eight members via proportional representation, rather than eight first-past-the-post constituencies.
3. *Journal of Liberal History* 71, Summer 2011.
4. I. Crewe & A. King (1995), *SDP: The Birth, Life and Death of the Social Democratic Party*, Oxford: Oxford University Press, 154. Not unreasonably, Brodie expected a preferential candidature in a future contest, and when this was not forthcoming, it fostered resentment which later led him to the SNP. He was a Surrey Heath district councillor between 1995 and 1999 but joined the SNP in 2010 and served one term as a list member of the Scottish Parliament.
5. R. Jenkins (1991), *A Life at the Centre*, London: Macmillan, 560.
6. Lord Wallace to the author, 13 February 2021.
7. J. Campbell (2014), *Roy Jenkins: A Well-Rounded Life*, London: Jonathan Cape, 592.
8. Also in 1982, the SLP republished its *Scottish self-government* pamphlet, as revised by Jenny Robinson and Margo Von Romberg.
9. A. Massie (1982), 'Bright, beautiful morning', *Spectator*, 3 April 1982.
10. *Financial Times*, 27 March 1982.
11. R. Jenkins (1991), 564.
12. J. Campbell, 597.
13. A. Massie.
14. R. Jenkins (1994), *Asquith*, London: Papermac, 489. Jenkins' biography was first published in 1964.
15. R. Jenkins (1991), 564. Jenkins held the seat at the 1983 general election, but lost it four years later.
16. A. Massie.
17. Liberals had a substantial local base in Greenock. Menzies Campbell had polled a respectable second place for the Liberals in the seat in February 1974, as had James Boyd in 1979. Liberals also controlled the local council between 1977 and 1980, largely on the basis of community-politics campaigning of the sort pioneered by Bill Riddell in the 1960s (see Chapter 5). At the 1983 general election, the Liberal candidate Alan Blair achieved more than a 9 per cent swing and came within 4,625 votes of winning.
18. Howells bet Steel £1 that the resolution would cost the Welsh Liberals every seat in Wales at the next election. 'In fairness,' recalled Wallace, 'when we met at the first Parliamentary Party meeting after the 1983 election, he duly paid me' (Lord Wallace

to the author, 13 February 2021). The Alliance won two seats in Wales, the Liberals having won only one in 1979.

19. *Financial Times*, 25 September 1982.
20. J. Grimond (1983), *A Personal Manifesto*, Oxford: Martin Robertson, 55.
21. The new HQ was formally opened by David Steel just before he caught a train to London for a Saturday sitting of the House of Commons on the Falklands crisis.
22. Other Scottish Liberal Club publications were *Energy and the economy: the way out of recession* (Ross Finnie and Malcolm Bruce); *The new technology and unemployment* (J. L. Whitehead); *Putting energy to work* (Malcolm Bruce); and *A New deal for rural Scotland* (Bruce, Mike Burnett and Jim Wallace).
23. A. Massie.
24. B. Coutts (1988), *Bothy to Big Ben: an autobiography*, Aberdeen: Aberdeen University Press, 155.
25. See J. G. Kellas (1968), *Modern Scotland: The Nation Since 1870*, London: Pall Mall Press, 183.
26. Winifred Ewing to Gordon Wilson, 22 June 1983, Gordon Wilson Papers Acc 13099/44, Edinburgh: National Library of Scotland.
27. P. Lynch, *The History of the Scottish National Party*, Cardiff: Welsh Academic Press, 178.
28. T. A. W. Stewart (2019), '"A disguised Liberal vote" – third-party voting and the SNP under Gordon Wilson in Dundee during the 1970s and 1980s', *Contemporary British History* 33:3, 366.
29. The Alliance also worked well on a social level. The newly-elected SDP MP Charles Kennedy shared a flat with his Scottish Liberal colleagues Jim Wallace and Malcolm Bruce in London. Kennedy also became close to Russell Johnston, the Liberal MP for his home town (G. Hurst, 2006, *Charles Kennedy: A Tragic Flaw*, London: Politico's, 52–3).
30. Bob Sawyer to David Owen, 22 August 1984, SDP Scotland Papers SDPAR 2/2.2.
31. The Scottish Liberals advocated a system of local income tax and single-tier local authorities. The SDP agreed on the second point.
32. Cllr Robert Brown to the author, 18 February 2021.
33. *Guardian*, 1 April 1985.
34. *Guardian*, 1 April 1985.
35. Document signed by Jim Wallace and Ross Finnie, 29 March 1985.
36. Scottish Liberal Party Conference, 20–22 March 1986.
37. Scottish Liberal Party 1987 Conference Agenda, St Andrews 26–28 March 1987. North East Fife District Council was only local authority in Scotland with an overall Liberal majority.

38. Henry Drucker (1985), 'A three-shade champion tartan', *The Times*, 16 September 1985.
39. See SDP/Liberal Alliance (1987), *The Alliance programme for Government: The Time Has Come For Scotland*, Edinburgh/ Glasgow: Scottish Liberal Party/SDP.
40. *Financial Times*, 16 June 1987.
41. *Guardian*, 16 June 1987.
42. *Guardian*, 26 August 1987.
43. D. Steel (1989), *Against Goliath: David Steel's Story*, London: Weidenfeld & Nicolson, 257.
44. Robert Brown to the author, 18 February 2021.
45. *Journal of Liberal History* 71, Summer 2011.
46. *Financial Times*, 19 September 1987.
47. S. Grieve (1991), "Women in the Scottish Liberal Democrats", in *A Woman's Claim of Right in Scotland: Women, Representation and Politics*, Edinburgh: Polygon, 62–4. Michie defeated the incumbent Conservative MP John J. Mackay, who had previously been a member of the SLP.
48. *Guardian*, 13 October 1987.
49. John Hein, an Edinburgh-based gay rights activist, refused to recognise the merger. He stood in successive council, Westminster and Scottish Parliament elections as the 'Liberal Party in Scotland' candidate.
50. Document signed by R. Leishman, J. McCall and R. Sawyer, January 1988, SDP Scotland Papers SDPAR 3/1.
51. *Scottish Liberal Bulletin*, November 1987.
52. See P. Lynch (1998), 'Third Party Politics in a Four Party System: The Liberal Democrats in Scotland', *Scottish Affairs* 22:1, 16–32.

8

'Guarantors of Home Rule': 1988–1999

The new entity formed as a result of the long-discussed merger of the SDP and Scottish Liberal Party (SLP) saw public support fall to just 3 per cent during 1988. Its nomenclature was also in flux. Initially, they were the 'Scottish Social and Liberal Democrats' (SLD); in September 1988 the short-form 'The Democrats' was adopted (the Govan by-election in November was fought as the 'Scottish Democrats'); and in the autumn of 1989 the party finally settled upon 'Scottish Liberal Democrats'.[1] Yet in the space of a few years, this new party managed to win a by-election in Kincardine and keep hold of all the Alliance's 1987 MP intake at the 1992 general election.

David Steel (SLP) and Robert Maclennan (SDP) served as interim joint leaders of the Social and Liberal Democrats and Sir Russell Johnston as interim leader of the Scottish SLD (he later became deputy leader of the federal SLD).[2] In organisational terms, the latter was to be very much 'a party within a party'. Much like the former Scottish Liberal Party, it had control over membership, finance and rules. It could hire its own staff, maintain a distinct membership list and set its own membership fee (in conjunction with the federal party) – indeed supporters joined the SLD directly rather than the UK party. As before, two annual conferences served an autonomous policy role alongside the Scottish Executive and Scottish Policy Committee, while the party elected its own leader and senior office-bearers via a postal ballot of Scottish party members. Compared with the Labour and Conservative parties in Scotland, the SLD enjoyed significant autonomy.[3]

The party was candid regarding membership levels. Before the

1988 merger, the Scottish Liberals had around 10,000 members (the SDP had only 2,000 in Scotland). Upon completion of the merger in November 1988, this had been revised down to 7,250, with the party setting a goal of 8,000 by 1989. There seemed to be further losses after 1989, something the political scientist Peter Lynch attributed to post-merger teething troubles and the party adopting a more 'formal' centralised approach to membership, in contrast to the 'looser' methods deployed by constituency parties, Liberal clubs and branches prior to 1988.[4]

At the Glasgow Central by-election in 1989, one opinion poll could not find any detectable support for the SLD candidate Robert McCreadie (an asterix appeared next to his name) while in early 1990, several members quit as a result of internecine warfare in the Hillhead and Garscadden branch, including the former SDP agent Bunty Urquhart and her husband.[5] Even a brand new party could not avoid the sort of spats familiar to any Scottish Liberal of a certain vintage.

SCOTTISH CONSTITUTIONAL CONVENTION

The new party's 'Pocket Guide to Policy' opened with a section on 'Constitutional Reform', a clear indication of its ideological priorities. This, particularly in a Scottish context, had been a long-standing aim, but rarely had the party possessed an opportunity to put its ideas into practice. Fortuitously, this changed a few months after the merger when the Scottish Constitutional Convention met for the first time in Edinburgh.

This had its origins in the 'Claim of Right', the product of a Constitutional Steering Committee of 'prominent Scots' – one of whom was Judy Steel – to make practical recommendations on persuading the UK government to devolve power. Published on 13 July 1988, the Claim was pungently nationalistic, referring to the Union as 'a glaring anomaly' and 'a threat to the survival of a distinctive culture in Scotland'. Yet as the cultural historian Scott Hames has observed, the Claim then veered away from 'the consequences of its central argument' (i.e. independence) and instead urged the creation of a constitutional convention 'to draw up a scheme for a Scottish Assembly'.[6]

Initially, it looked as if Scotland's three main non-unionist parties would participate in the Convention.[7] By the end of January 1989, however, the SNP had withdrawn from inter-party discussions. As Paul Henderson Scott reflected in 1998, the SNP could hardly be expected to help 'strengthen the Union' from which it 'wanted to escape'. A much-quoted line about the 'sovereign right' of the Scottish people to 'determine the form of Government best suited to their needs', meanwhile, formed part of another declaration signed at the first meeting of the SCC on 30 March 1989.

This sat more comfortably with Scottish Liberal thinking, as articulated by David (now Sir David) Steel in 1975, although as Professor James Mitchell later observed, such rhetoric embodied 'a political rather than justiciable claim' to the 'sovereignty of the Scottish people'. Nevertheless, every single SLD MP put their name to the March 1989 declaration. Press photographs showed the SCC's joint chairs, Lord Ewing (a former Labour MP) and Steel smiling broadly. The Liberal Democrats were therefore closely associated with this nationalist-unionist exercise from the start.

This was politically useful. The withdrawal of the SNP earlier in the year had worried leading Scottish Liberal Democrats, who were fearful that the much larger Scottish Labour party would end up dominating the Convention. They had intended to occupy the middle ground between its own minimalist and the SNP's maximalist approaches to constitutional reform. In fact, the absence of the Nationalists – intoxicated by victory at the recent Govan by-election – allowed the SLD to forge alliances with more pluralistic elements in the Labour movement, the Scottish Trades Union Congress, Scottish Labour Women's Caucus and the zealously pro-devolution Scottish Labour Action. This was to prove important in fashioning the sort of Scottish Parliament that would emerge, not least in terms of its electoral system.

As Peter Lynch has observed, the SLD's status as the only 'other major political party in the Convention gave its representatives considerable leverage over Labour and made the SLD politically relevant'.[8] This was also true behind the scenes. David Millar, a Borders-based SLD member and clerk in the European Parliament, drafted standing orders for the anticipated Scottish Parliament with the Edinburgh-based (Labour-supporting) academic Bernard Crick. These were published in 1991, and set out a Continental rather than Westminster-style rule book with a view to facilitating the sort of coalition arrangements likely to arise from a proportional electoral system.[9]

Such activity was the stuff of Scottish Liberal dreams, although it highlighted ambiguities familiar from Scottish Liberal discourse since the late 19th century. While SLD MPs such as Charles Kennedy took care to identify as 'a nationalistic Scot in politics', which he observed was 'not the same thing as being, politically, a Scottish Nationalist',[10] others went much further. Ray Michie came particularly close to crossing a fine line between support for devolution and full independence. 'Ray would have lain under a train for Home Rule,' recalled Sandra Grieve. 'She was a Bannerman Liberal determined to finish her father's unfinished business.'[11] Former SLD executive member Richard Mowbray poured scorn on what he called 'the crypto-nationalists who masquerade as Liberal Democrats in Scotland today'.[12]

Two current SLD executive members declared their support for independence just as the Scottish Constitutional Convention completed its work ahead of the 1992 general election. One of them, Bob McCreadie (a party vice-chairman) cited a 'growing convergence' between the goal of 'self-determination' and the SCC, while the other, Denis Robertson Sullivan, suggested that independence should become the party's long-term objective. 'There has always been a strong thread of independence running through the party,' explained Sullivan, although neither he nor McCreadie intended to join the SNP. Malcolm Bruce, Scottish Liberal Democrat leader since 1988, attempted to square the circle by arguing that the party had always maintained the right to self-determination, including independence if the people of Scotland so desired, a conveniently post-hoc inter-pretation of party policy from a party that had long opposed 'separation'.[13]

In an SLD publication entitled *Sovereignty & Integration: The Case for a Scottish Parliament* reissued in 1992, McCreadie had expanded upon his constitutional thinking. Attempting (unsuccessfully) to consign the term 'devolution' to 'the waste bin of history', he spoke of 'Home Rule' and 'the develop-ment of citizenship and democracy at every level of government, from the local to the European, with each level having its own guaranteed, or sovereign, part to play in the democracy of the whole'. The 'expanding power of Europe', added McCreadie, made 'it more and more imperative that Scotland should be able to speak with its own political voice in European affairs',[14] a long-standing Scottish Liberal aim. He also envisaged a Bill of Rights, enacted alongside legislation for a Scottish Parliament.

In November 1991, meanwhile, the SLD had been cheered by a decisive victory at the Kincardine & Deeside by-election, which had been caused by the death of the widely-respected (and once pro-devolution) Conservative MP Alick Buchanan-Smith. The Scottish Liberal Democrat candidate was 31-year-old Nicol Stephen, a future party leader.[15] Privately, leading members of the constituency association had agreed that Chris Rennard and Paul Jacobs ought to run the campaign, a federal party duo fresh from by-election success in Eastbourne the previous October. The local party wanted a much bigger campaign than any of those overseen by Clifton Terrace in recent years.

It was the first parliamentary by-election in which the Liberal Democrats had used extensive opinion polling. Initially, Rennard did not include much party branding in leaflets promoting Stephen, although this changed later in the campaign, to which concern about the future of the local Foresterhill hospitals was central. On polling day, Stephen captured 49 per cent of the vote and achieved a majority of nearly 8,000, quite a turnaround from the party's lost deposits and single-digit opinion polls of a few years earlier.

The result delighted the SLD, who found themselves displacing the Conservatives as Scotland's second party, with 10 MPs to the Tories' 9. But in a way the by-election highlighted that a lot, perhaps too much, of SLD support came at the expense of one party: the increasingly unpopular Scottish Conservatives. Not only did this make Scottish Liberal Democrats vulnerable to a Tory revival, but it emphasised their poor performance beyond historic rural heartlands. Indeed, until 1997 the Liberal Democrats had no urban seats in Scotland and was only a moderate force in the Central Belt, where the vast bulk of Scotland's voting population was located.[16]

Many, however, believed that the aftermath of the victory was badly handled. Having said 'very little' about the prospect of a Scottish Parliament during the campaign, the result was then 'used to advance demands for it'. The party's 10 MPs were gathered together for a photocall which suggested that the result constituted some sort of 'mandate' for devolution (to which many in the constituency at that time were resistant). This 'switch of emphasis to the constitutional issue', concluded

Rennard in his memoirs, 'was a significant factor in the reversal of the result in the general election five months later.'[17]

1992 GENERAL ELECTION

In his 1992 New Year message, Malcolm Bruce said the Kincardine result had 'faced the Scottish Tories with annihilation'.[18] This proved hubristic. At that year's general election, the SLD supported the idea of sustaining a minority Labour government at Westminster in order to legislate for devolution in Scotland,[19] while federal party leader Paddy Ashdown kept his coalition options more open. Malcolm Bruce was questioned constantly about Ashdown's policy of voting down a Queen's Speech which did not contain a commitment to proportional representation even if it *did* contain the promise of a Scottish Parliament. He said there was no insistency: 'You will not secure one without the other.'[20]

Paddy Ashdown still talked of a political realignment which could see the Liberal Democrats emerge as the main opposition to the Conservatives, an evidently unrealistic policy in a Scottish context given Labour's dominance. Were that election to produce a 'hung' Parliament, meanwhile, Ashdown planned to seek Cabinet posts for Sir David Steel and Menzies Campbell, as well as junior ministerial posts for Charles Kennedy, Jim Wallace and Malcolm Bruce.[21]

The SLD also had to contend with the SNP, with which it had long competed for third-party votes. During the campaign, Steel attacked the SNP's nationalism as 'an aggressively destructive force', going on to make a questionable distinction between 'negative nationalism' and 'positive patriotism'.[22] Voters seemed to disagree, for the SNP's vote share at the election almost doubled, although this produced just three MPs and much bitterness. The SLD, by contrast, won nine seats despite its vote share falling to 13.1 per cent from 19.2 per cent in 1987. The party was clearly benefitting from a geographical concentration of support, indeed its targeted campaigning strategy depended on it.

The 1992 result disguised some worrying results. Not only did Nicol Stephen lose Kincardine & Deeside just months after seizing it in a by-election, but Malcolm Bruce, the Scottish party leader, came within 274 votes of being toppled in the hitherto safe constituency of Gordon. They were both victims of a modest Tory revival as the economy recovered and some traditional Liberal areas proved less enthusiastic than the party leadership about devolution. Organisation in such areas was often weak and particularly bad in Gordon, where there was little canvassing. As the academic Mike Dyer observed:

> Bruce's large majority had introduced an air of complacency, and his leadership of the Scottish party had distracted his attention from constituency developments, particularly the need to mobilise 20,000 electors who had not been on the roll in 1987. Furthermore, squabbling within the controlling group of SLD councillors on Gordon District [Council] and a botched attempt to remove the chief executive, leading to the resignation of the provost from the caucus, compromised party morale and created an unfavourable image with the electorate.[23]

Bruce stood down as leader within days of the election, doubtless to concentrate on his constituency, which he held for another two decades. On the upside, an academic study of the 1992 election later indicated that public awareness of Scottish Liberal Democrat policies had improved among voters, with the party beginning to shed its reputation for being obsessed with obscure policies.[24]

There was also a perception among the SLD leadership that over-identification with Labour (via the Constitutional Convention) had caused electoral damage in rural areas and marginal seats while encouraging its voters to defect to the Conservatives. Even after the election, Paddy Ashdown continued for some time to pursue a strategy of 'equidistance', asserting his party's independence from both main UK parties, something that landed awkwardly in Scotland given the toxicity of the Scottish Conservatives and the SLD's established links with Labour.[25] Two months after the election, Bob McCreadie – the SLD's lead negotiator on the SCC executive – quit over his party's refusal to forge closer links with 'Scotland United', one of several post-election groups formed to force Westminster action on devolution.

SCOTTISH CONSTITUTIONAL CONVENTION REDUX

Patriots might have noticed that two successive Scottish Liberal Democrat leaders were named Bruce and Wallace. The Dumfriesshire-born Cambridge-educated Jim Wallace had succeeded Jo Grimond as the MP for Orkney & Shetland in 1983.[26] The *Sunday Times* called him a 'traditional Scots rural Liberal and dedicated home ruler'.[27] The liberalism of Wallace – who had served as his party's chief whip at Westminster – was both economic and welfarist. 'Liberal Democrats want to foster the entrepreneurial spirit,' he said a few years into his leadership, 'whilst at the same time providing a safety net for those who need it most.'[28] On becoming leader Wallace promised 'fresh thinking' on economic and industrial policy, also pledging a stronger voice on behalf of the 'dispossessed'. He said the party would no longer be relegated to what he called 'tailpiece quotes' in press coverage.[29]

Wallace also made clear his view that the Scottish Constitutional Convention had outlived its usefulness. He spoke of putting the Convention into 'cold storage', instead pursuing a 'Scottish parliamentary council' and a multi-option referendum, the latter an SNP hobby horse at that time.[30] Scottish Liberal Democrats also expressed frustration at 'holding the jackets' while the SNP and Labour squabbled over devolution.[31] But when inter-party talks were called off by Labour following a now-impenetrable row about Scottish representation on the European Committee of the Regions (an episode which momentarily threatened Alex Salmond's leadership of the SNP), the SCC was back up and running by November 1993.

The SLD began to make compromises, not the easiest thing for a party with its share of ideological purists. First, negotiations between Labour and the Liberal Democrats led to the adoption of a German-style additional member voting system rather than the single transferable vote favoured by the SLD.[32] Second, rather than promoting federalism or 'Home Rule all round', the Scottish Liberal Democrats ended up supporting asymmetric or unilateral devolution. Although it could be – and was – argued that devolution and federalism were complementary, both these stances to some degree contradicted long-standing SLD policy.

There also emerged a formal agreement between Scottish Labour and the Scottish Liberal Democrats to promote an equal number of male and female members of the first Scottish Parliament. But while Labour favoured a statutory obligation, the SLD did not.[33] Former party chair Sandra Grieve even threatened to quit the Convention over this issue. The old Scottish Liberal Party had a poor record when it came to women candidates and MPs (it had managed only one, Ray Michie in Argyll & Bute), although the academic Alice Brown noted that prospective female SLD candidates 'were largely of the view that they had not experienced problems or discrimination on grounds of their sex'.[34]

Sandra Grieve has observed that when Ray Michie won Argyll in 1987 'it didn't occur to anyone that her gender was of any significance and it took her by complete surprise when significance was, subsequently, attached'. She added:

> In a way Ray had been limited by her gender. She was reluctant to add 'women' to her portfolio. Her view of women was not politicised and she felt side-lined by it. She was a powerful force in the Convention and the Party, but it was her Liberalism rather than her gender which drove her.[35]

The 1998 Scottish Liberal Democrat conference later reneged on the deal with Labour, resolving that party lists should be drawn up 'irrespective of gender' and based purely on ability. Legal advice also suggested 'zipping' (as it was known) would be vulnerable to a tribunal appeal under the Sex Discrimination Act.[36] This did not, however, prevent the Liberal Democrats in England adopting 'zipping' for the 1999 European Parliament elections.

Labour had sought 112 Members of the Scottish Parliament (MSPs) while the Liberal Democrats argued for 145. On 13 September 1995, Labour's Shadow Scottish Secretary George Robertson met Jim Wallace at the Edinburgh home of Menzies Campbell and eventually settled on 129 seats, 73 to be elected by first-past-the-post in the existing Westminster constituencies (Orkney and Shetland were to be divided), and 7 elected from 8 party lists in each of Scotland's European constituencies.[37] The SLD also moved away from arguing for assigned revenues to finance the Scottish Parliament, and towards a financing system that more closely resembled the existing block grant.

Even so, there had always been some scepticism in the party as to the likelihood of these proposals – however detailed – actually being implemented, doubts expressed by the Scottish

Liberal Democrats at a one-day conference in Dunfermline in November 1995. This gathering nevertheless endorsed the final SCC proposals, *Scotland's Parliament: Scotland's Right*,[38] which were unveiled at a joint press conference fronted by Jim Wallace and Shadow Scottish Secretary George Robertson. Scottish Liberal voices had been instrumental in the document advocating a 'reserved powers' model of devolution, under which everything else was de facto devolved.

This joint working made autonomous SLD activity on the constitutional front difficult. In January 1995, Menzies Campbell sustained a Liberal tradition by introducing another doomed devolution bill at Westminster. Not only was it virtually ignored even by the Scottish media (the *Scotsman* was the friendliest to the SLD while Malcolm Bruce penned a column for *Sunday Times Scotland*), but Campbell was assailed by SNP leader Alex Salmond, who said the Liberals had achieved 'precisely nothing' in spite of its century-old commitment to 'Home Rule'. Campbell retorted that the SNP clearly regarded themselves as the 'exclusive brethren' of Scottish politics.[39] SNP-Liberal rivalry was alive and kicking.

Thereafter, the Scottish Liberal Democrats presented themselves as the 'guarantors of home rule' in response to an apparent cooling in Labour's devolution position. Jim Wallace argued that:

> No-one looking at Scottish political history can be in any doubt about the commitment of the [Scottish Liberal Democrats] to the Scottish Parliament, to home rule, and if there is any question or uncertainty about whether the Labour Party under Tony Blair will deliver, then what better guarantee than to ensure that there are a good number of Scottish Liberal Democrat MPs backed up by a solid number of SLD votes in the next UK Parliament?

Wallace acknowledged that a number of his party's supporters felt that when it came to devolution, there had been an element of 'me too-ism' between it and the Labour Party.[40] The Scottish Liberal Democrat leader also made a point of lowering expectations, conscious that a lot of devolution discourse was positively utopian. He warned of falling into the 'trap' of 'seeing home rule as an end in itself':

> It's not. Home rule is the means to better government of Scotland, to try to deliver better education, health service, transport arrangements

– a whole series of issues . . . I think there is a danger those of us who espouse the cause of a Scottish Parliament must watch out for and that is that we don't give the impression that with one bound everything will be coming up roses.[41]

INTO THE 1990S

Other electoral tests of Scottish Liberal Democrat support offered mixed results. Peter Lynch judged the party's performance at the 1989 European Parliament elections 'best forgotten', with it polling only 4 per cent of the vote. The 1994 election was little better. Amid rising Euro-scepticism, even the SLD played down its Euro credentials, something that had long distinguished it from other parties in Scotland. Whereas in 1992 Malcolm Bruce had spoken of securing 'a self-governing Scotland's place in an increasingly federal UK and an increasingly federal Europe',[42] the 1994 SLD European manifesto omitted any mention of federalism, opposed the creation of a European super-state and instead preached 'subsidiarity' and regional decentralisation.[43]

The SLD had three goals in 1994: recovering from an embarrassing result in 1989, winning the Highlands & Islands constituency from the SNP's Winnie Ewing, and beating the Conservatives to third place. All three proved overambitious. Its share of the vote did increase, but only to 7.2 per cent; Ewing increased her majority with the SLD candidate coming fourth; and across Scotland the party remained in fourth place behind the Conservatives.[44] Scotland's most pro-European party was not very good at winning pro-European votes, even in a region where it held five out of its seven Westminster constituencies.

Achieving third place in the European elections echoed an identical (and more successful) objective for the last regional council elections in Scotland, a move to single-tier unitary councils long having been supported by Scottish Liberal Democrats.[45] The party placed this reform within its broader constitutional goals, which envisaged that a devolved Scottish Parliament would assume certain functions hitherto discharged by the regional authorities.[46] At the final district council elections in 1992, meanwhile, the SLD had gained control of 2 out of 53 authorities in Scotland, while in 1994 it emerged with joint control of only one of nine regional councils.

Although all those were swept away in 1995, the unitary elections brought belated success for the party in town halls, with a large increase in councillors and a role in six different local administrations. The SLD also gained more seats than the Conservatives, who had unsuccessfully contrived many boundaries with electoral self-preservation in mind. Having long suffered in local elections due to a lack of candidates, the SLD managed to field an impressive 528, almost half the number of seats (1,161). Despite these successes, Scottish Liberal Democrat representation remained lower than it might have been, largely due to a strong tradition of non-affiliated councillors in the Highlands and in the Borders.[47]

Those 528 candidates were all the more impressive given the SLD's membership in late 1995 stood at just 6,000, a fall of several thousand since the late 1980s. The problems caused by this relatively small figure were hardly new. The Scottish Liberal Democrats were dependent on their members for finance and therefore their limited number placed considerable constraints on the party's budget. Even so, the party had managed to increase its staff from three to four full-time members at Clifton Terrace in Edinburgh, which doubled up as the Scottish Liberal Club. This was augmented by three part-time staff and a number of volunteers, partly funded by the federal party. Scottish conferences were well known for home-baking stalls and members knitting during keynote speeches. 'The wider membership contained polite and well-meaning people,' recalled Bernard Ponsonby, 'some radical, others quite conservative, but never, I thought, aggressively political.'[48]

Constitutional amendments in 1993 had resolved a degree of conflict over federal/state (i.e. Scotland or Wales) policy-making remits. SLD members were unhappy that the English party continued to treat the federal conference as if it were an English party conference rather than a UK-wide body. Indeed, the federal conference often debated England-only issues, and therefore was not federal at all, although the changes meant the conference agenda now distinguished between truly federal resolutions and those applying only to England and Wales. In September 1995 the federal Liberal Democrats held their conference in Glasgow, a rarity for a UK party.

In other respects, the federal Liberal Democrats had a strong Scottish tenor, not least because a disproportionate number of its MPs had constituencies north of the border (the Birkenhead-born Malcolm Bruce hardly resembled the carpet-baggers of a century before)[49]. Between 1992 and 1997 Charles Kennedy was spokesman on Europe; Menzies Campbell, David Steel and Russell Johnston on defence and foreign affairs; Malcolm Bruce on Treasury issues; and Bob Maclennan on arts and the constitution. Archy Kirkwood also served as chief whip.

This left only two SLD MPs, Ray Michie and Jim Wallace, dealing exclusively with Scottish affairs. Kennedy and Maclennan also served as successive federal party presidents during the same period, while both MPs and SLD office-bearers were often away from Scotland attending federal committees and other policy-making bodies in London. These factors, judged Peter Lynch, 'limited the MPs' ability to advance the party's identity in Scotland, with the SLD often unable to use its MPs to boost the party's presence in the Scottish media and help to build the party organisation'.[50]

The death of Labour leader John Smith in 1994, meanwhile, had not only deprived the Home Rule movement of a high-profile and articulate ally, but altered the dynamic between the party he had led and the Liberal Democrats at Westminster. While Bob Maclennan held a series of constructive and productive talks with Labour front-bencher Robin Cook on constitutional reform, tempers frayed when in 1996 Tony Blair, the new Labour leader and a devolution sceptic nevertheless committed to his predecessor's 'unfinished business', announced a pre-legislative referendum on the parliament and whether it ought to have tax-raising powers.

When Blair gave Paddy Ashdown advance notice of his referendum plan, he warned the Labour leader it would be seen as a 'betrayal'. 'Jim has been exceedingly courageous,' noted Ashdown in his diary. 'He has put his political career on the line and face down his own Party for the deal he struck on the Scottish Convention with George Robertson.'[51] Wallace was not amused, not least because the SCC had long ago debated and agreed to reject a referendum. He also worried that a planned second question on tax-varying powers had the potential (if opposed) to seriously dilute the Convention's proposals. John McAllion, a Labour constitutional spokesman, resigned on discovering the news from Wallace rather than George Robertson, while Sir David Steel, co-chair of the Convention, complained that the Shadow Scottish Secretary had not bothered to mention it to him on a shared flight to London.

The SLD, therefore, felt obliged to condemn Labour's about turn as 'a gross breach of trust'.[52] This was not altogether consistent. Malcolm Bruce and Jim Wallace had toyed with a multi-option referendum after the 1992 general election, while in 1994 Wallace had argued that the Strathclyde water referendum (the brainchild of Christopher Mason, SLD group leader on the regional council) had 'created a culture where a referendum might be used to test popular opinion on Scotland's constitutional future'.[53]

That a referendum would both consolidate support for the devolution project and bring the SLD and Scottish Labour closer together was not yet clear. Scottish Liberal Democrats had fewer difficulties, meanwhile, differentiating themselves from the Scottish National Party. While they respectfully acknowledged that 'independence is a perfectly legitimate aspiration', the party rejected 'claims that independence is risk free and a passport to instant success'.[54]

1997 GENERAL ELECTION

The Scottish Liberal Democrats were bullish as to their prospects at the 1997 general election, although this optimism was treated with scepticism by the media and academic commentators.[55] Determined not to repeat the mistakes of 1992, the party campaigned on the theme 'one vote for the Liberal Democrats is the one vote needed for a Scottish parliament', which distanced it from both Labour – who it was argued could not be trusted on devolution – and the SNP's goal of independence in Europe. More broadly, there was a general 'get rid of the Tories' mood; polls anticipated a Labour landslide, while boundary changes and the prospect of tactical voting all favoured Scotland's non-Conservative parties.

Although it polled just 13 per cent of the vote, the SLD won 10 seats, only one more than in 1992 but continuing evidence that targeted campaigning paid electoral dividends (the SNP won six seats based on a 22 per cent vote-share, and the Conservatives none on 17.5 per cent). Peter Lynch was among those who noted the irony of a party 'which knows how to play the first past the post system to best effect in Scotland' being committed to a fairer, more proportional voting system. Long-standing Edinburgh councillor Donald Gorrie was one benefi-ciary of tactical voting, finally gaining Edinburgh West after several attempts. He was the first Liberal to represent Edinburgh in Parliament since the Second World War.

The federal party's tally of 46 MPs, however, meant Scotland was proportionately less important to the UK party than it had once been. 'We have achieved the largest number of seats of any third force,' declared Jim Wallace triumphantly, 'or Liberal force, since 1929 and the days of Lloyd George.'[56] Wallace claimed his party was Scotland's official opposition based upon seats; Alex Salmond claimed the same of the SNP based on voteshare.

With more MPs to populate its front bench than ever before, the SLD was also able to appoint a full Scottish team that com-prised Jim Wallace, Ray Michie, Michael Moore (who had suc-ceeded Sir David Steel, now bound for the House of Lords) and Donald Gorrie. In the devolution referendum that followed the party finessed its opposition to the two-question ballot,[57] while Wallace worked closely with Donald Dewar, now Secretary of State for Scotland (an office the SLD wanted to abolish), and the SNP leader Alex Salmond. SLD chief executive Andy Myles was particularly keen to avoid the fragmentation of the 1979 campaign.

Ironically, and as in 1979, pre-referendum System Three polling suggested that Liberal Democrat supporters in Scotland were split 44–42 per cent against the Scottish Parliament (and 45–38 per cent on tax-varying powers).[58] Academic analysis later suggested that just over half SLD voters had voted yes/yes with a large minority voting no/no, proportions that reflected the protest-vote nature of the party.[59] Nevertheless, the 'Scotland Forward' umbrella had successfully brought together the Liberal Democrats, Labour and even the SNP for the first time after several decades' abortive discussion of such alliances.

No sooner was the referendum over, however, and Jim Wallace was presenting himself as a mediator between SNP and Labour tribalism. He kept up this theme a year later when both were accused of betraying the 'spirit of the referendum' by 'slugging it out' in scenes akin to the 'worst of Westminster'.[60] He also condemned the 'seediness' of Labour-run councils in Scotland.[61] Paddy Ashdown, meanwhile, was still pursuing his dream of co-operation with Labour, despite its landslide majority in the new Parliament. This provoked a furious row between Ashdown and Wallace in July 1997, largely because the SLD leader had discovered the plans for a Joint Cabinet Committee (JCC) and electoral reform from a Scottish colleague rather than Ashdown himself.[62] 'What's in it for me?' Wallace shouted. 'What's in it for Scotland?'[63] He was also upset on discovering that Donald Dewar and Menzies Campbell were to attend the first meeting of the JCC, but not him.[64]

Although on one level Wallace was guilty of inconsistency given his long association with Labour in Scotland, the dynamics at this stage were rather different. Labour had won a landslide that May, which meant Blair had no need of Liberal Democrat votes at Westminster. And at a UK level, Wallace feared blurring his party's distinctiveness 'in return for little or no leverage', while he was also concerned that 'appearing to be enfolded into the Labour tent' just as the SLD were about to confront Labour in elections to the Scottish Parliament would hamper both the outcome and subsequent coalition negotiations.[65] Ashdown later admitted his mistake in not having involved Wallace earlier, but by December 1997 opposition from most Scottish Liberal Democrat MPs had cooled. The SLD, meanwhile, attracted several refugees from the Scottish Conservatives, who had been wiped out at the recent general election. Arthur and Susan Bell joined in November, as did former MP Anna McCurley in February 1998.[66]

Another former Conservative MP, Keith Raffan, fought a European by-election for the Liberal Democrats in North-East Scotland that October, while Rhona Kemp, a former Liberal Democrat convenor of Grampian Regional Council and member of the party's Scottish executive moved in the opposite direction, defecting to the SNP. The Scottish leadership, she claimed, 'seems entirely in thrall to London, and entirely obsessed with the possibility of getting a seat at the Blair Cabinet table'.[67]

This highlighted long-standing problems with Scottish Liberal Democrat strategy and the party's precise position on the ideological spectrum. On the one hand, Tory defections (mostly from the wetter end of the Conservative Party) spoke to the party's individualism and economic liberalism, while Kemp's departure flagged up something that had long concerned Jim Wallace et al., a perceived – and damaging – closeness to Labour. In December

1998, there was a concerted effort to put distance between the SLD and Scottish Labour, with Liberal Democrat strategists fearful that voters perceived them as the latter's 'poodles' or 'lapdogs'. After all, there were not just Scottish Parliament elections to contest in 1999, but council and European ballots too.[68]

'Paddy Ashdown is responsible at a UK level and I am responsible at a Scottish level,' declared Jim Wallace. 'The Scottish party will be master in its own house as far as the Scottish parliament elections are concerned.'[69] These tensions were further exacerbated by a refusal to countenance a future coalition with the SNP if the Nationalists insisted upon an independence referendum. In March 1998, Wallace said Alex Salmond 'needn't make the phone call' if that point proved non-negotiable.[70] Undeterred, the SNP leader spoke a few days later of 'the beginnings of a realignment in Scotland, involving the SNP, Liberal Democrats and some in the Labour party'.[71]

Although some Scottish Liberal Democrats favoured an agreement with the SNP – chiefly party treasurer Denis Robertson Sullivan and Donald Gorrie – it was generally expected that it would form some sort of coalition with Labour, building on the relationship begun during the constitutional convention and continued during the referendum campaign. There were private discussions between SLD and SNP MPs at Westminster – Willie Rennie referred to 'talks about talks' – but Scottish Liberals remained officially neutral. The 1998 Aberdeen conference agreed that the party would talk to the party with the largest number of seats. In his 1999 New Year message, Jim Wallace even raised 'the possibility of refusing to enter government and allowing there to be a minority administration'.[72]

Wallace was one of the first Scottish MPs to pledge himself to a Scottish parliamentary career (Charles Kennedy, on the other hand, made it clear he would remain at Westminster), with Lord Steel following suit after months of speculation. Candidate selection rarely extended beyond the Liberal fraternity, although George Lyon, a recent president of the National Farmers Union Scotland, and veteran journalist Neal Ascherson, were both selected.[73] Internally, the otherwise sure-footed Wallace – spoken of in 1995 as a successor to Paddy Ashdown – came under fire in late 1998 for personally endorsing a new convenor (the MP Michael Moore) following the resignation of Stephen Gallagher; agreeing that the number of MSPs would be reduced alongside Scotland's Westminster representation;[74] failing to consult Glasgow members over the appointment of a regional team leader; and long-running concerns as to his closeness to the Scottish Labour Party.[75]

The proportional electoral system agreed for the new parliament, of course, was to reward broad levels of support in addition to geographical concentration, and so the SLD was required 'to reach out of its strongholds to build support in new areas'. If it succeeded in doing so, predicted the academic Peter Lynch, 'then the party might begin to see the rebirth of Liberal Scotland in a more significant way than achieved at the 1997 general election'.[76]

As the first Scottish Parliament elections approached, Jim Wallace worked on improving party organisation. Chris Rennard suggested that Willie Rennie, who had been his lieutenant in Devon & Cornwall in 1997, might return to Scotland as SLD chief executive. Wallace was keen and Rennie subsequently moved to Edinburgh to head up a much strengthened staff at Clifton Terrace. By the standards of previous Scottish elections, and most of those that followed, significant financial resources were also put in place. These came largely from funds raised by the federal party, including from major donors like the Joseph Rowntree Reform Trust, and were allocated by Rennard as part of a wider strategy to take the Liberal Democrats forward following its successes in 1997.

Scottish Liberal Democrats did their best not to commit to anything during the campaign,[77] although tuition fees and the prospect of an independence referendum both attracted comment. Just days before Scotland went to the polls, Lord Steel went off script in declaring: 'Whether it's a coalition or a minority government, tuition fees will go. Tuition fees are dead as of Friday.' This apparently 'astonished and infuriated party managers',[78] who had instructed candidates to avoid using terms like 'non-negotiable'.

When it came to the SNP's suggestion of a referendum, meanwhile, Paddy Ashdown said the SLD would never form a pact with 'any party which seeks the break-up of the United Kingdom', something Jim Wallace considered an 'over-enthusiastic interpretation' of SLD policy-making procedures.[79] The refusal to countenance a referendum was, in the words of academic Nicola McEwen, 'a difficult policy to sustain for a party whose name reflects a commitment to democracy', not to mention previous Scottish Liberal Party policy.[80]

More broadly, the *Herald*'s Murray Ritchie found SLD fence-sitting irritating: 'here we have a party which says it wants to be part of a coalition but won't say with whom, and that it wants to use the Tartan Tax to fund education, if necessary, but won't say if it believes it will be necessary'.[81] Interviewed during the campaign, Jim Wallace echoed David Steel's 1970s rhetoric in saying that the SLD should not 'be content to be a glorified national think tank, far better that we're actually in there in government implementing [Liberal policies] at the right time and in good measure.'[82]

In a neat piece of symbolism, the SLD had recently helped the retailer Debenham's to restore the Gladstone Library in what had once been the Scottish Liberal Club on Edinburgh's Princes Street, a reminder of the party's Gladstonian heyday.[83] Wallace was doubtless conscious he could become the first Liberal to serve in government since Sir Archibald Sinclair was Secretary of State for Air from 1940 to 1945.[84]

NOTES

1. The SLP had backed the 'Scottish Liberal Democrats' nomenclature at a special council meeting in Edinburgh in January 1988. 'To call the new party the Alliance', quipped one delegate, 'is like calling a new ship the Titanic' (*Guardian*, 11 January 1988).
2. Charles Kennedy and Jim Wallace had once envisaged a situation in which both would vie for leadership of a merged party. They agreed, recalled Wallace, that 'whichever of us was better placed, the other would back him' (G. Hurst, 2006, *Charles Kennedy: A Tragic Flaw*, London: Politico's, 63).
3. See P. Lynch (1998), 'Third Party Politics in a Four Party System: The Liberal Democrats in Scotland', *Scottish Affairs* 22:1, 16–32.
4. Ibid. Perhaps apocryphally, this 'looser' membership included those who had contributed produce to annual SLD fundraising sales. Bernard Ponsonby, who worked at Clifton Terrace for more than a year, recalled 'various worthies from the Borders . . . brandishing lists containing the names of people who had once bought a raffle ticket but had never really parted with hard cash to join the party' (Bernard Ponsonby to the author, 20 February 2021).
5. See *Glasgow Herald*, 25 January 1990.
6. S. Hames (2020), *The Literary Politics of Scottish Devolution:*

Voice, Class, Nation, Edinburgh: Edinburgh University Press, 182.

7. The implication of 'non-unionist' would shift over time, but in the late 1980s it generally referred to parties – the Liberal Democrats, Labour and the SNP – which favoured some sort of constitutional reform.

8. See P. Lynch (1996), 'The Scottish Constitutional Convention 1992–5', *Scottish Affairs* 15:1, 1–16.

9. See B. Crick & D. Millar (1991), *Making Scotland's Parliament Work: Standing Orders for the Parliament of Scotland*, Edinburgh: Centre for Scottish Public Policy.

10. O. Dudley Edwards (ed.) (1989), *A Claim of Right for Scotland*, Edinburgh: Polygon, 87.

11. Sandra Grieve to the author, 28 February 2021.

12. *Glasgow Herald*, 12 March 1992.

13. *Guardian*, 7 February 1992. Robertson Sullivan later said he would vote 'yes' in an independence referendum (*Scotsman*, 19 May 1998).

14. SLD (1992), *Sovereignty & Integration: The Case for a Scottish Parliament*, Edinburgh: Scottish Liberal Democrats, 1–2.

15. Nicol Stephen had also been at one point Scotland's youngest councillor aged 22.

16. P. Lynch (1999), 'In From The Fringes? The Scottish Liberal Democrats', *Journal of Liberal Democrat History* 22.

17. See C. Rennard (2018), *Winning Here – My Campaigning Life: Memoirs Volume 1*, London: Biteback, 149–53, for a full account of the Kincardine & Deeside by-election. Writing in February 1992, Malcolm Bruce maintained that the by-election result was 'in large measure an expression of the resurgence, both political and cultural, of Scotland's national identity, of the Scottish people's impatience with a remote London government's ignorance of Scottish feelings and values' (SLD, *Sovereignty & Integration*, preface).

18. *Herald*, 2 January 1992.

19. See Scottish Liberal Democrats (1992). *Changing Scotland and Britain for Good: The Scottish Liberal Democrat Manifesto for 1992*. Dorset: Liberal Democrat Publications.

20. *Herald*, 7 April 1992.

21. See G. Hurst, 84.

22. *Glasgow Herald*, 26 March 1992.

23. M. Dyer (1992), 'The 1992 General Election in Grampian', *Scottish Affairs* 1:1, 27–35.

24. L. Bennie, J. Brand & J. Mitchell (1997), *How Scotland Votes: Scottish Parties and Elections*, Manchester: Manchester University Press, 149.

25. P. Lynch (1998), 29.
26. Lord Grimond died aged 80 in October 1993.
27. *Sunday Times*, 27 April 1997.
28. *Independent*, 22 September 1995.
29. *Herald*, 6 May 1992.
30. *Scotsman*, 19 March 1993.
31. *Herald*, 15 March 1993.
32. See R. Waddell & D. Gorrie (1991), *The P.R. Debate and the Constitutional Convention*, Edinburgh: Scottish Liberal Democrats.
33. An internal consultation had overwhelmingly rejected a 50:50 gender split.
34. See A. Brown (1996), 'Women's Political Representation in Scotland: Progress Since 1992', *Scottish Affairs* 14:1, 73–89.
35. Sandra Grieve to the author, 28 February 2021.
36. E. Breitenbach & F. Mackay (2001), *Women and Contemporary Scottish Politics: An Anthology*, Edinburgh: Polygon, 242–3. Attempts to exempt party political candidate selections from this legislation by including a clause in what became the *Scotland Act 1998* were unsuccessful.
37. See P. Jones (1997), 'Labour's Referendum Plan: Sell-out of Act of Faith', *Scottish Affairs* 18:1, 1–17. The 1991 SLD conference had adopted an electoral system it called 'STV Plus'.
38. See Scottish Liberal Democrats (1995). *The Final Steps: Towards the Completion of the Scottish Constitutional Convention's Scheme for a Scottish Parliament*. Edinburgh: Scottish Liberal Democrats.
39. *Herald*, 18 January 1995.
40. *Herald*, 21 August 1995.
41. *Herald*, 21 August 1995.
42. *Independent*, 20 January 1992.
43. SLD (1994). *Unlocking Scotland's Potential: The Scottish Liberal Democrat Vision for Europe*. Edinburgh: Scottish Liberal Democrats.
44. See P. Lynch (1994), 'The 1994 European Elections in Scotland: Campaigns and Strategies', *Scottish Affairs* 9:1, 45–58.
45. SLD (1992), *Democracy and Accountability: A new local government structure for Scotland*, Edinburgh: Scottish Liberal Democrats.
46. M. McVicar, G. Jordan & G. Boyne (1994), 'Ships in the Night: Scottish Political Parties and Local Government Reform', *Scottish Affairs* 9:1, 80–96.
47. In 1992, five Liberal Democrat councillors on Borders Regional Council demanded the resignation of Sir David Steel's constitu-

ency agent, Riddle Dumble, who sat as an Independent member of the council and was not even a member of the party. Andy Myles, the Scottish Liberal Democrat chief executive, admitted that it was a 'mildly anomalous' situation (*Herald*, 25 November 1992).
48. Bernard Ponsonby to the author, 21 February 2021.
49. Bruce had studied at St Andrews and Strathclyde before working for the North East of Scotland Development Agency.
50. P. Lynch (1998), 27.
51. P. Ashdown (2000), *The Ashdown Diaries: Volume One 1988–1997*, London: Allen Lane, 442.
52. *Glasgow Herald*, 2 November 1996.
53. *Herald*, 27 April 1994. George Robertson, Labour's Shadow Scottish Secretary, attempted to pressure Jim Wallace into getting Christopher Mason to drop the referendum plan. Wallace refused (Lord Wallace to the author, 13 February 2021).
54. SLD (1996), *Alex in Wonderland: The True Cost to Scotland of the SNP's Economic Policy*, Edinburgh: Scottish Liberal Democrats, 1.
55. Including Peter Lynch, who later committed a mea culpa to print.
56. *Daily Mail*, 3 May 1997.
57. Paddy Ashdown wanted Scottish Liberal Democrat MPs to abstain on the Referendums (Scotland & Wales) Bill, but at the Committee Stage they voted against Clause 1 and forced a division to remove one of the questions. None of this had an effect but nevertheless demonstrated the party's lingering unhappiness at Labour's 1996 U-turn.
58. *Herald*, 6 August 1997.
59. D. Denver, J. Mitchell, C. Pattie & H. Bochel (2000), *Scotland Decides: The Devolution Issue and the Scottish Referendum*, London: Routledge, 158.
60. *Independent*, 22 September 1998.
61. *Herald*, 23 September 1997.
62. This included Lord Jenkins of Hillhead reviewing the House of Commons' electoral system. He recommended moving to an Additional Member System (similar to that planned for Scotland, Wales and London) in 1998, but his proposals gathered dust, as did a proposed referendum.
63. P. Ashdown (2001), *The Ashdown Diaries: Volume Two 1997–1999*, London: Allen Lane, 64–5.
64. M. Campbell (2008), *Menzies Campbell: My Autobiography*, London: Hodder and Stoughton, 144.
65. Lord Wallace to the author, 15 February 2021.
66. *Sunday Times*, 5 April 1998.
67. *Herald*, 24 September 1998.

68. *Herald*, 7 December 1998.
69. *Daily Mail*, 8 December 1998.
70. *Herald*, 13 March 1998.
71. *Financial Times*, 16 March 1998.
72. *Herald*, 31 December 1998.
73. Lyon won a seat, Ascherson did not. Ascherson later became a confirmed supporter of independence if not the SNP.
74. This, as it happened, did not take place, even when Scotland's 72 MPs were reduced to 59 at the 2005 general election. As part of the Scottish Executive after 1999, the SLD argued against a reduction in MSPs.
75. *Herald*, 25 November 1998.
76. P. Lynch (1998), 32.
77. See SLD (1999), *Raising the Standard: Scottish Parliament Manifesto 1999*, Edinburgh: Scottish Liberal Democrats.
78. H. Macdonell (2009), *Uncharted Territory: The story of Scottish devolution 1999–2009*, London: Politico's, 9.
79. M. Ritchie (2000), *Scotland Reclaimed: The inside story of Scotland's first democratic parliamentary election*, Edinburgh: Saltire Society, 61.
80. N. McEwen (2002), 'The Scottish National Party after devolution: progress and prospects', in G. Hassan & C. Warhurst (eds), *Tomorrow's Scotland*, London: Lawrence & Wishart, 61.
81. M. Ritchie, 62.
82. *Scotsman*, 15 April 1999.
83. Gina Davidson (1998) 'We're glad to have you back again', *Edinburgh Evening News*, 31 August 1998.
84. Sir Archibald's grand-daughter, Veronica Linklater, had taken her seat as a Liberal Democrat member of the House of Lords a few months after the 1997 general election.

9

In and Out of Government: 1999–2021

The Scottish Liberal Democrats joined the new Scottish Parliament in May 1999 as a minor party which had become used to punching above its weight. It remained Scotland's fourth party, gaining fewer votes and MSPs than the apparently 'toxic' Scottish Conservatives, but entered devolved government via a coalition, as widely anticipated, with the Scottish Labour Party. This could be seen as the natural culmination of a less formal partnership between the two parties that had lasted for more than two decades. It won 17 seats, a figure at the top end of the party's expectations, and the largest number of Scottish Liberal parliamentarians since the 1920s.

Scottish Liberal Democrat leader Jim Wallace approached coalition negotiations better prepared than his Labour counterpart, the Secretary of State for Scotland, Donald Dewar. Wallace consulted his party and elected colleagues throughout, while preparation was key. David Laws, a future Cabinet minister but at that point a Westminster researcher for Malcolm Bruce MP, had outlined a possible partnership agreement in a paper commissioned by the Scottish party.[1]

The SLD negotiating team comprised Wallace, Ross Finnie, Nicol Stephen (who had gained the constituency seat of Aberdeen South), Iain Smith, Laws, Denis Robertson Sullivan and Andy Myles. To assist the overall process, two party groups had arranged to go through each other's manifestos subject by subject in order to identify areas of agreement. Some Labour figures had qualms. Henry McLeish, for example, considered Scottish Liberal Democrats to be 'a diverse and sometimes eccentric lot who had subjected us [Labour politicians] to virulent attacks at local level'.[2] On one occasion during the talks, Dewar made deprecatory remarks about one policy idea he considered 'Liberal nonsense'. On being told that it had actually appeared in Labour's manifesto, the Secretary of State for Scotland 'laughed wholeheartedly'.[3]

An impasse over tuition fees was harder to laugh off, not least because Prime Minister Tony Blair tried several times to have the abolition commitment dropped via Paddy Ashdown, who was also nervous lest the failure of coalition talks in Scotland undermine his UK realignment 'project'. Blair, who seemed unaware that devolution might involve policy divergence, eventually agreed to an independent review of fees to break the logjam.[4] 'This has been a triumph for Jim,' noted Ashdown in his diary. 'He has shown great courage and succeeded in negotiating a superb deal for Scotland and the Party. He will get hell from the Party for a bit, but he will get through it. Scotland will benefit, and so will he.'[5]

The party's reward was four ministers including two in the Cabinet, one of whom was Jim Wallace as Deputy First Minister and Justice Minister. Numerically, the SLD could have argued for a fifth but this would have forfeited its entitlement to 'Short' money,[6] an important consideration given its financial position. The partnership agreement was signed on 14 May 1999 amid the modernist curves of the new Museum of Scotland in Edinburgh. Wallace got on well with the cerebral Dewar, and the agreement meant each was kept in the loop via access to each other's ministerial papers. At European Parliament elections in June, meanwhile, the SLD gained an MEP for the first time, the legal academic Elspeth Attwooll.[7] Sir David Steel also relinquished his party membership to become the new parliament's first Presiding Officer.

The challenges faced by junior parties in coalitions were well known, so Wallace's challenge was to maintain a distinct party identity while fending off accusations that he was little more than a Scottish Labour poodle. This he managed well, though Wallace recalled getting the feeling that 'Donald thought we should suspend the natural right and instinct of an opposition party to oppose. He certainly could be tetchy if attacked too much.'[8] The SLD, after all, remained in opposition at Westminster, and it was on reserved matters that the party sometimes found itself at odds with its coalition partners. Initially, the SNP tried to drive wedges between the Scottish Executive parties by sponsoring opposition day debates on reserved issues. The coalition responded by agreeing to disagree in any division, or by tabling a joint amendment which acknowledged both parties' position.[9]

The Scottish Executive's decision to repeal Thatcher-era legislation prohibiting the 'promotion' of homosexuality in schools provided an early coalition test, and on an issue which was clearly devolved. Wallace was diplomatic, but the 2000 SLD spring conference railed against businessman Brian Souter and Cardinal Winning for, in the words of former party chief executive Andy Myles, 'importing the worst excesses of American politics' into its 'Keep the Clause' billboard campaign.[10] Scottish Liberals also played a prominent role in delivering land reform – a longstanding Liberal issue – as well as freedom of information legislation.

Other matters tended to come to a head shortly before elections. In January 2001, for example, Scottish Liberal Democrat MSPs threatened to rebel over proposals concerning free personal care for the elderly, which forced the new First Minister Henry McLeish to commit. Although this placed a huge spending burden on local authorities, it came to be considered a core achievement and was heavily trumpeted in future elections by the SLD. A tie-up scheme for fishing vessels, on the other hand, caused difficulties. Despite committing a significant sum to decommissioning, the Executive lost an important vote when some SLD MSPs failed to vote in favour. Tavish Scott, a junior minister and the MSP for Shetland, resigned. The vote was reversed the following week.

Wallace performed solidly as Deputy First Minister, as well as Acting First Minster following Donald Dewar's premature death in October 2000. Indeed, opposition leaders – including Alex Salmond – were surprised to find themselves put in their place at First Minister's Questions by someone they had expected to be a walkover. As Minister for Agriculture, Ross Finnie was also widely judged to have deftly handled an outbreak of foot-and-mouth disease. Henry McLeish, Dewar's successor, rated both, recalling 'a degree of trust and honour in Jim that I did not experience from some in my own party'.[11]

The BBC journalist Brian Taylor viewed Finnie and Wallace as 'like family GPs, always there, always reliable'. The party, he noted, was careful to publish frequent updates detailing their coalition triumphs, though continuing to come up with policies

which were 'populist, distinctly liberal but capable of implementation by a coalition' proved difficult.[12] There were no immediate dividends judging by opinion polls, with the party struggling
to reach double figures. Scottish Liberal Democrat candidates
also came behind the Scottish Socialist Party at by-elections in
Ayr (for the Scottish Parliament) and Hamilton (for the House
of Commons).

At the 2001 UK general election, the SLD talked up their
impact in devolved government, while the party benefitted more
generally from the popular (and thoroughly Scottish) Charles
Kennedy, who had led the federal party since August 1999.[13]
The party's successes in 1997 meant it had more seats to defend
than ever before. On polling day, the SLD gained 16.4 per cent
of the vote (an increase of 3.4 per cent) and, more to the point,
overtook the Conservatives to become Scotland's third party
in terms of seats *and* votes, for the first time since before the
Second World War.[14] Jim Wallace appeared to have convinced
voters that he and his party were still worth voting for, even
now that devolution had been delivered.

Measured against pre-election polling of less than 10 per cent,
it was an even better result. Thereafter, pressure from Liberal
Democrat activists to introduce proportional representation
(PR) for local government elections increased. The messy resignation of Henry McLeish as First Minister in November 2001
provided Wallace with another stint as Acting First Minister
as well as an opportunity to push for the single transferable
vote. Jack McConnell, the new Labour First Minister, appeared
amenable, promising 'greater urgency' and privately pledging
to deliver by 2007. Wallace found McConnell 'pragmatic' and
easy to deal with. 'I knew that Jack was on our side on PR,' he
recalled, 'but we realised he had some sensitive handling issues
in his own party.'[15]

Wallace clearly envisaged the coalition lasting for some time.
In an interview in November 2001, he said he could not see the
SNP being strong enough to lead a coalition in 2003. The academic Peter Lynch predicted that the party would be 'central to
coalition formation for years to come' and depicted the SLD as
the 'great winners of devolution':

> Somewhere along the line, the party changed from being a radical,
> oppositionalist, agenda-setting pressure party – seeking to promote

issues and ideas – to one which could anticipate its policies actually being implemented by its own Ministers rather than derided by its opponents.[16]

Wallace turned out to be more correct than Lynch, although Scottish Labour were no pushovers. Opponents of PR pointed out that the 1999 partnership agreement referred only to 'progress towards electoral reform' rather than any specific scheme. The Scottish Liberal Democrat conference in April 2002, however, demanded a Bill by the next Scottish Parliament elections.

Polling suggested the party would pick up a few seats in 2003, but in the event it held steady.[17] Wallace had campaigned on 'a social democratic manifesto with liberal trimmings', proposing a review of the devolution settlement in 2009, a needs-based replacement for the Barnett formula and possible use of the Scottish Variable Rate to finance increased spending. A backdrop to the campaign had been the Iraq conflict, which provided a useful point of differentiation between the anti-war Liberal Democrats and generally supportive Scottish Labour Party.

But electoral success (or, more accurately, consistency) hid weaknesses, organisationally, geographical and political. Even in 2003, the SLD had declining membership, a plethora of 'paper' branches and little presence in Glasgow or the West of Scotland, where most voters were located.[18] This, noted Peter Lynch, prevented 'the Lib Dems from being a national party ... Instead, a provincial politics of patchwork priorities dominates'.[19] Finances were, as ever, a problem. Although the Scottish party was in better shape than it had been in the 1970s, it had still relied on 'federal' funding to fight devolved elections in 1999 and 2003, as well as assistance with policy development and even general administration north of the border.[20]

PEAK SCOTTISH LIBERAL DEMOCRAT

Given the 'rainbow' nature of the 2003 Holyrood elections, at which the Greens and Scottish Socialists gained 6 and 7 MSPs respectively, the Scottish Liberal Democrats did well to retain 17 seats; it also gained the Edinburgh South constituency seat from its senior coalition partner. Scottish Labour's loss of six seats also gave the Scottish Liberal Democrats an additional Cabinet minister in future leader Nicol Stephen.[21] It helped that the two coalition parties did not really threaten each other electorally so, unlike in the 2010 UK coalition, there was no need to undermine each other electorally.

In the negotiations that followed the 2003 election, the junior coalition partner secured agreement on free eye and dental checks, while a Bill proposing STV for three- and four-member local council wards appeared later that year, further evidence of SLD influence. Not everyone in the senior coalition party was happy. The outspoken Labour minister Sam Galbraith, for example, attacked electoral reform as a 'right-wing' Liberal policy which was being forced upon him and his Labour colleagues.

Another Labour minister, Jackie Baillie, thought SLD ministers 'really decent people' but found the party's backbenchers 'hugely difficult to work with' and 'just off the wall'.[22] Her Liberal Democrat ministerial colleagues would probably have agreed. Tension often manifested itself at MSP group meetings, where 'ministers would report on what was happening and then the purists and the awkward squad would wade in'. Mike Rumbles, one of several perennial rebels, was later made chief whip 'so he would behave',[23] a containment strategy that turned out to be successful.

There were other tensions. Labour's determination to crack down on youth crime unnerved the Liberals. Labour regarded its coalition partners as soft on such matters and took back the justice portfolio after the 2003 election, during which Jack McConnell and Jim Wallace clashed over plans to jail the parents of delinquents (a policy later diluted to point of irrelevance). One aide spoke highly of Wallace in such situations: 'If we ever got confused about the angle, Jim would always bring it back to core liberal principles, then work from there to find a pragmatic way forward'.[24]

It was perhaps significant that the 2004 Liberal Democrat publication, *The Orange Book: Reclaiming Liberalism*, included no Scottish contributor and little on constitutional reform,[25] a curious omission given SLD involvement in the Scottish Executive. The 2003–7 Scottish Parliamentary term also witnessed some pork-barrel politics, with the SLD getting Skye Bridge tolls abolished and restoration of the Waverley railway line, both of huge benefit in Liberal Democrat-held constituencies.[26] In an interview, Jim Wallace even claimed his party was responsible for most of the coalition's successful policies.

Many voters appeared to agree. At the 2005 UK general election, the Scottish Liberal Democrats peaked, gaining a further two MPs (despite Scotland's constituencies being cut from 72 to 59) and 22.6 per cent of the vote, well ahead of the SNP (led once again by Alex Salmond following a comeback in 2004) and the Conservatives. It also proved to be the high watermark for Liberal Democrats across Great Britain. The federal party ran an almost presidential campaign based upon the popularity of its leader, the Ross, Skye and Lochaber MP Charles Kennedy. This included huge posters emblazoned with Kennedy's face, many of which ended up in Scotland's largest city. The SLD was perhaps surprised to come within 2,000 votes of winning Glasgow North at that election, the seat closest to that captured by Roy Jenkins back in 1982.

Jim Wallace chose to go out on a high, ending his political career 'midstream at a happy juncture'.[27] He was succeeded by Nicol Stephen, who became Minister for Enterprise and Lifelong Learning as well as Deputy First Minister. 'Stephen was solid, if uncharismatic,' was one typical judgement from a journalist. 'He was not a terribly good platform speaker but he had served the party for a long time, in both Westminster and Holyrood, and was respected.'[28]

This electoral buoyancy continued in February 2006 when Willie Rennie (a former SLD chief executive) fought the Westminster constituency of Dunfermline and West Fife at a by-election. Chris Rennard, the federal party's campaign supremo, persuaded the party to spend the maximum permitted sum of £100,000 on the campaign, which few expected the SLD to capture (although it had come second in the 2005 general election). A meeting of SLD MPs at Westminster even leaked, including the conclusion that the party had no prospect of success,[29] a not unreasonable prediction given the resignation of Charles Kennedy as federal Liberal Democrat leader following weeks of turmoil within the party. Further media headlines involved often lurid tales concerning those jostling to succeed him.[30] Another Scottish MP, Sir Menzies Campbell, became acting leader. The backdrop to the by-election could hardly have been less precipitous for the party.

In Rennie, however, the party had found an energetic candidate with strong Fife roots. The party even portrayed him as the Liberal Democrat version of 'Oor Willie', with a specially produced cartoon featuring him sitting on a bucket.[31] Local foot-soldiers were thin on the ground during a freezing January, but the party brought in many of its best campaigners from across Scotland and the rest of Great Britain. Rennie recalled leading:

> Afternoon and evening canvassing sessions seven days a week for the bulk of the campaign and when not doing interviews or debates visited almost every shop and business in the constituency. The micro campaigning focussed on personal and local issues seeking to resolve problems with issues as diverse as parks to personal finance. The team of four caseworkers were fed with my daily returns scribbled on scraps of paper often soaking wet from the winter rain.[32]

Rennie's campaign also exploited Scottish Executive in-fighting over tolls on the Forth Road Bridge, while Rennard hit upon the idea of inviting Charles Kennedy (who remained popular in Scotland) to make his first post-resignation appearance in the constituency. Despite some opposition, Kennedy agreed to visit Dunfermline on the final Thursday before polling day. Rennard's gamble paid off. In what he described as one of the 'most politically effective and personally emotional scenes' he had ever witnessed at an election played out on Dunfermline's High Street. Liberal Democrat MPs descended on the seat, while every SLD member was invited too. Sensing the ground shift, federal party leadership candidates – which included neighbouring MP, Sir Menzies Campbell – rearranged their diaries for the Friday after polling day.

Willie Rennie won the seat by 1,800 votes, the first ever Liberal/Liberal Democrat gain from Labour at a Scottish by-election, and the first Labour had lost in Scotland since Govan in 1988. He became the UK party's 63rd MP at Westminster, while Sir Menzies was prominent in the extensive coverage that followed, something Chris Rennard believed was 'a significant factor' in Campbell becoming yet another Scottish leader of the federal party a few weeks later.[33] Dunfermline and West Fife, meanwhile, joined the ranks of great Liberal by-election upsets. 'For five weeks the party had been treated as a joke as it endured regicide, alcoholism, sex scandals, infighting and public scorn,' wrote the journalist Greg Hurst. 'Victory in Dunfermline & West Fife confounded the Lib Dems' critics.'[34]

The following month, David Steel (another former UK party leader) published *Moving to Federalism – A New Settlement for Scotland*, an indication the party was thinking ahead to the next Holyrood election, when it anticipated the need to provide a constitutional 'offer' for voters. In his 2003 Donald Dewar Memorial Lecture, Steel had made his position clear:

> No self-respecting Parliament should expect to exist permanently on 100% handouts determined by another Parliament, nor should it be responsible for massive public expenditure without any responsibility for raising revenue in a manner accountable to its electorate.

So in his 2006 report,[35] Lord Steel argued for a 'broadly federal solution', although he acknowledged it was unlikely the UK could become 'truly federal' in the absence of English support. He also preached 'fiscal federalism',[36] with Holyrood becoming more responsible for raising the cash it spent, gaining borrowing powers and a 'needs-based equalisation formula' to replace Barnett.[37] This was far-sighted thinking which anticipated the future contours of Scottish political discourse. Two of these proposals (greater fiscal autonomy and borrowing powers) later became legislative reality.

During the summer of 2006 there were a couple of opinion polls which suggested a three-way split between Labour, the Liberal Democrats and SNP, with the academic Bill Miller even suggesting that the SLD might even emerge as the largest party at the 2007 election. Nicol Stephen entered that Holyrood campaign with his party having delivered on PR for local government but with little new to say: the headline commitment of his manifesto (written in the first person) were more hours of physical education in schools. As the historian Catriona M. M. Macdonald has observed, with:

> . . . home rule won, early land reform anticipated and proportional representation the voting mechanism that had elevated them into a position of power, there was little left in the traditional Liberal arsenal that the Lib Dems could offer the Scottish public that was now uniquely their own.[38]

They were, in other words, victims of their own success. Election broadcasts did their best to build up Stephen as a dynamic electoral contender, as well as a forceful, vigorous personality, when in fact he was rather shy and diffident ('I need', he admitted himself, 'to build my profile'). Media coverage was dominated by coalition speculation should the SNP emerge, as some polls suggested, the largest single party. While Liberal Democrat voters generally wanted their party to renew its vows with Labour, the electorate more generally liked the idea of a new relationship between the SLD and the SNP. As Martin Laffin observed, 'their participation as junior partners in a coalition government . . . enhanced rather than damaged their electoral prospects'.[39]

There was, on paper, a degree of policy overlap: both the SNP and SLD emphasised environmental issues, both were committed to replacing the council tax with a local income tax while, perhaps most importantly, both favoured some sort of constitutional change. In a pre-election conference speech, Nicol Stephen had sounded an ecumenical note, although one of his MSPs, Jamie Stone, undermined this by attacking the Nationalists as 'xenophobic'. The party was, as it had been since the 1960s, split on how to handle its rival third party.

A major sticking point was the Liberal Democrats' refusal to countenance an independence referendum. The retiring MSP Donald Gorrie unhelpfully stirred the pot, saying his party should 'never say never' to a plebiscite, thus the issue ended up obscuring 'the rest of the Lib Dem agenda, and the party's campaign never really got past the first hurdle'.[40] Spooked by the prospect of an SNP victory, Gordon Brown – who was about to succeed Tony Blair as Prime Minister – met with UK Liberal Democrat leader Sir Menzies Campbell. Brown wondered if there was 'common ground' on which their two parties might 'tackle the SNP together', and the possibility that a third coalition agreement could be reached, assuming they won enough seats.

As in 1999, when Paddy Ashdown and Tony Blair had discussed the first Scottish coalition, this put the federal party leader in a difficult position. 'We practise institutional and constitutional devolution in our party,' Campbell told Brown; he promised to speak to Nicol Stephen, but was aware of 'a mood among some Lib Dems against going into a new coalition with Labour'.[41] The pair met again on election day. Campbell not only shared Brown's concern at the prospect of an SNP government, but a subsequent campaign for independence.

On election day the SLDs held steady, its constituency vote slightly up and its regional list showing slightly down. The party lost three constituency seats (including Nora Radcliffe, who was defeated by Salmond in Gordon) and gained Dunfermline (building on its Westminster by-election success). Overall, the party was down just one seat on 2003, although it had expected to make gains. The loss of Euan Robson in Roxburgh & Berwickshire and a near miss with Jeremy Purvis in Tweeddale, Ettrick and Lauderdale gave the party a 'sense of mortality'. 'The halcyon days were gone,' recalled Michael Moore, 'and after that point worries about an existential threat to the party were never far away.'[42]

Concurrent council elections were also fought for the first time under STV, a direct result of the first Labour-Liberal Democrat partnership agreement. But while it had been argued that this would allow the SLD to gain councillors in previously 'Liberal Democrat-free areas', its tally of councillors actually fell from 175 to 166, leaving the Scottish Liberal Democrats further bruised and disappointed.

On the Friday following the election, Nicol Stephen and Tavish Scott joined Sir Archy Kirkwood and others at Menzies Campbell's Edinburgh home for a pizza-fuelled 'summit' on what to do next. None could see a Lib Dem/SNP coalition 'working in practice', while Scott and Campbell were clear there should be 'no deal with the SNP'. Brown called Campbell the following morning, leading Sir Menzies to fear being 'portrayed as the heavy hand of Westminster telling the Scottish parliamentarians what to do'.[43]

It was Alex Salmond's working assumption that the SLD would form part of an SNP-led coalition, together with 2 Scottish Greens (down from 7 in 2003). The 16 Scottish Liberal Democrat MSPs gathered at an Edinburgh hotel the same day Brown spoke to Campbell for the last time. They agreed to stand by the party's campaign position that there could be no talks unless the SNP dropped its demand for an independence referendum. Salmond reacted badly to what he considered an 'ultimatum' when he and Nicol Stephen finally spoke by telephone, and the SNP leader suggested a 'creative' compromise whereby a referendum could proceed (its legality appears not to have been discussed), but with each coalition party campaigning for a different outcome.[44]

But as Menzies Campbell put it, the 'feeling in the party was strongly against a coalition with the SNP and the mood in the country was against a deal to keep Labour in power when it had lost the election'.[45] Several further phone calls failed to resolve the impasse and both sides accepted that this meant the formation of a 'minority' SNP Scottish Executive. In any case, the numbers were not there – even a Lib Dem-SNP deal would still have lacked an overall majority. An agreement could even have split the party, not least because many SLD MSPs simply did not trust Alex Salmond.

Lindsay Paterson has argued that the Scottish Liberal Democrats should have entered a new coalition on the basis of a multi-option referendum: 'A clear rejection of independence, and a clear way ahead, may well then by now have been the outcome.'[46] Indeed, one of those close to these events said 'we should have been open to working with the SNP. We didn't exist in Scottish politics to be a caravan in Labour's back yard.'[47] But this was conjecture. Looking back, Jim Wallace reckoned the 1999–2007 coalitions had ensured Holyrood was 'established on a firm foundation. If anything, the criticism by 2007 was that it had become predictable and boring.'[48]

CLINGING ON TO POLITICAL RELEVANCE

Out of office, the Scottish Liberal Democrats lost their main selling point since the late 1980s, and particularly since entering government in 1999: political relevance. The 'hung' Scottish Parliament, however, still presented theoretical opportunities. In June 2007, the Liberal Democrats joined forces with other unionist parties to force the Scottish Executive (soon to be renamed the Scottish Government) to see through the Edinburgh trams project, although in other policy areas the SLD chose to support the SNP, including a Bill to abolish the compromise graduate endowment scheme it had helped introduce in 2000. As a sort of quid pro quo, the Scottish Government planned to promote the Liberal Democrats' policy of two hours' extra PE in schools. Ultimately, however, they could not agree on a local income tax: the SNP wanted, paradoxically, a national rate, the SLD local flexibility.

Complacently, there was a widespread belief at Holyrood that the SNP would not last until Christmas. The Scottish Liberal Democrats also joined Labour and the Conservatives to form the cross-party Calman Commission to consider further powers for the Scottish Parliament, as suggested by the Steel Commission in 2006. Of all the parties, the SLD had the most to contribute, although this was far removed from the sort of pressure its MSPs and ministers had once been able to exert on Labour while in office. Jim Wallace, now Lord Wallace, joined the Calman Commission as one of two Liberal Democrat representatives. As one Scottish party staffer recalled:

> We thought the SNP would soon fall apart. After six months things became really tough. What was the point of the Lib Dems? We were almost going through a grieving process. We'd lost MSPs, we lost staff, lost money and of course we lost morale. And it turned out that our view of how long voters would give/tolerate the SNP was massively out of kilter with reality. What if we had reached a deal? We'd have ended up facilitating a policy we didn't agree with, and it would have blocked out the sun: for the next four years that's all we would've talked about.[49]

Robert Brown, who was for a short time SLD business manager at Holyrood, recalled staging a 'sit in' on the front bench to ensure his party's MSPs retained two places there rather than surrender them to the SNP and be 'shoved over into an uncomfortable position in the Tory section'.[50]

There were some modest achievements. Nicol Stephen garnered headlines when he said the Scottish Government's unprecedented decision to 'call in' a planning application from Donald Trump for a £1 billion golf resort plan in the north-east of Scotland had the 'smell of sleaze'. First Minister Alex Salmond hit back that the SLD leader was 'unelectable'. Some said the same of Scottish MP Sir Menzies Campbell, who resigned as UK Liberal Democrat leader in October 2007 following relentless media and internal party criticism.

Less than a year later, in July 2008, Nicol Stephen also resigned to spend more time with his wife and four young children. Tavish Scott, the former Cabinet minister Ross Finnie and perennial rebel Mike Rumbles all vied for the Scottish Liberal Democrat crown. Finnie argued that the party's message had 'become blurred and lacking a distinctive Liberal Democrat edge', squeezed between the SNP-Labour duopoly and merely responding to a debate, 'the terms of which have been set by another party'.[51]

This was a shrewd diagnosis of where the party found itself a year after leaving office, but not enough to win a leadership election. Tavish Scott decisively beat Finnie and Rumbles but found it difficult to establish his authority for precisely the reasons articulated by one of his defeated rivals. In a radio interview Scott suggested, not incorrectly, that politicians and the media were 'too obsessed by endless talk about referendums and the constitution', but it was a curious observation ahead of the Calman Commission's final report, in which the Liberal Democrats had been so heavily involved.

By 2010, by which point Scott had been leader for two years, it was difficult to associate any memorable speech, policy or campaign with his stewardship, his call for a 2p tax cut having made little impact, not least because it coincided with the Great Financial Crash of 2007–8. 'Tavish loved politics,' recalled an aide, 'but once he became leader, he found it much harder to cut through beyond the Holyrood bubble.'[52] Events at Westminster, meanwhile, were about to make his job even harder.

COALITION REDUX

The 2010 UK general election appeared to offer the Scottish Liberal Democrats another shot at political relevancy. Not only did the party retain its 11 Scottish MPs (a tally roughly in proportion to its 18.9 per cent of the vote),[53] but a 'balanced' parliament propelled the UK party into government for the first time since 1945. Many in the SLD were not exactly enthusiastic at the prospect of a Con-Dem coalition, an unnatural fit in a Scottish context. Only Charles Kennedy, however, abstained at a crunch party meeting, an indication of his concern as to the likely impact on Welsh and Scottish elections due in May 2011.[54]

The party, in Scotland as well as federally, was between a rock and a hard place: if it remained aloof, then another election threatened Liberal Democrat gains, and if it did coalesce with the Conservatives, they would struggle to gain credit for any policy concessions. 'We knew the risks,' reflected Michael Moore, one of several SLD MPs who gained ministerial office as a result of the pact, 'no one was particularly comfortable about what the next few years might look like.'[55]

The Conservatives' relative weakness in Scotland, meanwhile, meant the Cabinet post of Secretary of State for Scotland went to a Scottish Liberal Democrat MP, Danny Alexander, who was succeeded a few weeks later by Michael Moore following the resignation of David Laws.[56] Although Nick Clegg's U-turn on raising university tuition fees did not apply in Scotland, it still proved damaging given that the Scottish Liberal Democrats were associated with reform in 1999–2000 (the graduate endowment scheme) and complete abolition in 2007–8.

Alex Salmond predicted that the coalition would spell disaster for the Liberal Democrats at the next Scottish Parliament election. It proved a brutally accurate prediction: the party lost all its mainland constituencies amid an SNP tsunami, retaining only Orkney, Shetland and three list MSPs. Its vote share sank to just 7.9 per cent in constituency seats and 5.3 per cent on the regional list, a mere third of its 2007 support. Scotland, like the rest of the UK, also rejected the Alternative Vote in a nation-wide referendum held the same day. At a Westminster by-election in Inverclyde a week later, the SLD attracted just over 2 per cent of the vote.

The 2012 local government elections saw the party further humbled. Around 16 incumbent Liberal Democrat councillors sought re-election under a different banner (several for the SNP) and the party's vote share was halved to 6.6 per cent, its poorest showing since the 1970s. It was left without a single councillor on half of Scotland's 32 unitary councils. Tavish Scott resigned shortly after as leader. 'We were just defeated,' recalled one former Westminster staffer. 'We'd run out of ideas, and Lib Dems were expected to have policies.'[57]

As the academic Malcolm Harvey summarised, in just five years 'the collective representation of the party in Scotland had dropped from 193 MPs, MSPs and councillors in 2007 to 87 in 2012.' This, he added,

> ... had a direct impact on the ability of the party to campaign: fewer representatives means fewer seats to defend, fewer seats to defend means less motivation for activists to knock on doors, less motivation means a less active membership, and a less active membership means an inability to seriously challenge incumbents, meaning fewer opportunities to return representatives.

Only 3,000 Scottish members remained.[58]

In a speech two months after the 2011 Holyrood election, Alex Salmond issued a 'come and join us' call to Scottish Liberal Democrats, arguing that their 'honourable tradition' of 'Home

Rule' for Scotland (within the UK) was under threat from the present Liberal Democrat leadership, which had 'become Conservative with a capital C – exactly the wrong approach for Scotland'.[59] Salmond had spotted a political opportunity to further grow SNP support, but in reality his own party's 'catch all' ideology had relentlessly squeezed the socially liberal territory in Scotland once occupied by the SLD. 'People used to accuse the Liberal Democrats of being all things to all people,' quipped the Scottish Green Party co-leader Patrick Harvie, 'but they were never as good at it as the SNP.'[60]

A *Little Yellow Book* published in 2012 demonstrated, according to the new party leader Willie Rennie, 'that Scottish Liberal Democrats are an intellectual force in the land'.[61] One of its editors later considered it part of the post-2011 'grieving process'.[62] Also part of the grieving process was the 'Devo Plus' campaign chaired by former MSP Jeremy Purvis, which attempted to progress 'fiscal federalism'. Rennie, a former SLD chief executive, brought a degree of stability to the party; comfortable with campaigning and articulate in the Holyrood chamber, he also ensured it remained visible. But, in essence, it was difficult for the SLD to preach social liberalism while federal Liberal Democrats were in a coalition with a party it had gained electoral strength by advocating *against*. This fact, as the academic Adam Evans has pointed out, not only contradicted 'the traditional positioning of the Scottish Liberal Democrats, but also key narratives in Scottish political culture'.

Indeed, Evans has argued that the coalition served to exacerbate and expose weaknesses which had long afflicted Liberal Democrats in Scotland and Wales. While Scottish Liberal Democrat MPs and ministers were kept in the loop, MSPs and senior figures in Edinburgh were not. One Scottish staffer had the sense that Nick Clegg and UK Liberal Democrats 'looked down on the Scottish party', with even Scottish UK leaders announcing policies which took no account of devolution, 'despite us being a federal party advocating a federal UK'.[63] Meetings of the federal executive committee would often see Scottish and Welsh members 'jumping up and down together saying that it isn't just about England'.[64] Elsewhere, Evans doubted the UK Liberal Democrats' federalist credentials, both in terms of party structures and given 'the absence of clear thinking within the party on what a federal Britain would look like'.[65]

The 2011–16 Scottish Parliamentary term, meanwhile, was dominated by the build-up to an independence referendum. In Scotland, Willie Rennie did his best to push the party's vision of a 'strong Scotland' within a 'federal UK', while at Westminster, coalition Liberal Democrats tempered Conservative instincts to force a quick referendum on the SNP, so that Westminster rather than Holyrood called the shots. Scottish Liberal Democrats in particular feared this would play into the SNP's hands. A key player in this respect was the Secretary of State for Scotland. In David Laws' account:

> Mike Moore . . . was low-key, unflashy and mild-mannered. These might have seemed like weaknesses in a politician. But Mike also proved to be a patient, strategic, respected and sure-footed. Inch by inch, he secured all of the objectives that the coalition government set itself for the referendum question and timing. And in the slippery world of Scottish politics, he had steadily built up a reputation for himself as trustworthy and reasonable.[66]

It was Lord Wallace, now Advocate General for Scotland, who first suggested using a Section 30 Order (under the *Scotland Act 1998*) to facilitate a referendum on an unambiguous statutory basis. Indeed, Moore and Wallace did more than most to ensure that a fair and legal independence referendum took place, which was ironic given the party's opposition to such a move since 1999. The SLD certainly influenced the resulting 'Edinburgh Agreement' but ended up falling between two camps. As Rennie put it at the federal party's 2012 conference: 'We don't want Scotland to break from the rest of the UK but we do want to change it.'[67]

To that end, Rennie asked Sir Menzies Campbell to lead another commission ahead of the referendum, something that was criticised on the basis that the Calman reforms had not yet reached fruition. The (first) Campbell Commission reported in 2012 and argued for a 'radical' allocation of tax and borrowing powers to Holyrood, which would allow the Scottish Parliament to raise around two thirds of its own revenue. 'A rejection of independence', added Sir Menzies, 'will enable Scotland to continue down the track towards a modern, pluralist and federal relationship with the other parts of the United Kingdom'.[68]

Otherwise, the party's strategy was to campaign for a 'no' vote alongside Labour and the Conservatives under the

'Better Together' banner. Each SLD MP embarked on a 'Road to Referendum' tour, with some visiting up to 30 town and village halls during the summer of 2014. Rennie said the party would act as 'the guarantors of change', a similar argument to that used before the 1997 devolution referendum. 'Liberal Democrats have wanted home rule for a hundred years,' he said at the 2012 Scottish conference. 'A Scotland with the powers to run our home affairs but proud to share the wins and share the risks with the United Kingdom family of nations'.[69] That the federal party's annual conference took place in Glasgow in September 2013 was an attempt to underline this point.

A few weeks later there occurred a sudden change of personnel. Although Michael Moore could not claim to be a household name (*The Times* even used a photograph of the Scottish Secretary to illustrate a story about civil servants), his stock had risen as a result of his tactful role in negotiating the Edinburgh Agreement. He might, as the journalist John Rentoul wrote, 'be counted the most successful Liberal Democrat in the Cabinet, and, even, the man who saved the United Kingdom'.[70] Moore's political style was the antithesis of Alex Salmond's, and many within the Scottish party had come to believe that Moore lacked the aggressive edge to tackle the referendum campaign itself.

Taking this advice at face value, Nick Clegg (who had little feel for Scottish politics) dismissed Moore in October 2013 and replaced him with Alistair Carmichael, something which came as 'a complete surprise to Mike, and a massive blow to him'. It also came as a shock to many SLD MSPs. Journalists were briefed that the Orkney & Shetland MP was more of a 'street fighter', but within weeks of his appointment he was soundly beaten by Nicola Sturgeon (with whom Moore had a good relationship) in a televised debate for which he seemed ill prepared. Carmichael 'never entirely regained his confidence'[71] and there were soon suggestions he would himself be replaced by Scottish Liberal Democrat MP Jo Swinson.[72]

Danny Alexander, the Chief Secretary to the Treasury and another Scottish MP, remained influential, particularly after March 2014 when, according to David Laws, he 'became the new but unofficial head of the No campaign in London'. Everything UK ministers did or said regarding the referendum as well as contingency planning for the last few weeks of the campaign were directed by Alexander with the 'full backing' of the Prime

Minister, Chancellor and Nick Clegg. He also spent much of the summer in Scotland supporting the 'Better Together' campaign. The Deputy Prime Minister believed Alexander 'played an absolute blinder' in the final weeks of the campaign, co-ordinating Better Together's final big push in the face of narrowing polls and mobilising business voices to speak out against independence.[73]

Nick Clegg was concerned about Labour haemorrhaging votes to the SNP, although the Scottish Liberal Democrats had to contend with a nationalist (or 'Home Rule') wing of their own, most prominently represented by Judy Steel. They were wooed by SNP leader Alex Salmond, who in one referendum campaign speech made a direct pitch to Liberal 'Home Rulers', casting independence as a completion of that party's century-long Home Rule 'journey'. He knew what he was doing. On 18 September 2014, 43 per cent of Liberal Democrats voted 'yes', higher than the 31 per cent of Labour supporters and the Scottish Conservatives' 2 per cent.[74] As Tony Blair had observed in his memoirs, you could 'never be sure where nationalist sentiment ends and separatist sentiment begins'.[75]

A PYRRHIC VICTORY

The majority 'no' vote on 18 September 2014 proved to be a Pyrrhic victory for all the Unionist parties. Adding to Liberal Democrat woes was its inability to take any credit for policy wins within the UK Government coalition (increasing, for example, the personal taxation allowance). Worse, Liberal Democrat ministers actually became scapegoats for some of the coalition's more unpopular policies, such as tripling tuition fees in England, having 'pledged' that there would be no increase.

There was, at least, a continuing influence in the constitutional domain. The second report of the (Sir Menzies) Campbell Commission had been published in spring 2014. This recommended an extension of the Scottish Parliament's fiscal powers as well as its constitutional 'entrenchment'.[76] 'Campbell II' also proposed that the Secretary of State for Scotland convene a meeting 30 days after the referendum to 'secure a consensus for further extension of powers to the Scottish Parliament consistent with continued membership of the United Kingdom and to be included in party manifestos for the 2015 general election'.[77]

This and, more to the point, narrowing opinion polls, compelled the Scottish Conservatives and Scottish Labour to work
up their own proposals for further powers (Ruth Davidson had
previously spoken of Calman as a 'line in the sand'). A YouGov
poll giving 'Yes' a lead also created a sense of panic which led
to former premier Gordon Brown setting out a post-referendum
timescale (with David Cameron's agreement) for what became
the Smith Commission, as announced on 19 September 2014.[78]
Its SLD representatives were Michael Moore and Tavish Scott,
who fought Conservative resistance to the partial devolution of
welfare they and others supported.

Smith published its recommendations just over two months
later, which included several ideas first outlined in the 2006
Steel Commission report and in Campbell II, though neither
Steel nor the SLD got much credit. Presenting Smith to the
House of Lords, Lord Wallace ended with a rhetorical flourish:

> The cause of Home Rule has been at the heart of Scottish politics
> since the days of Gladstone. This agreement provides a modern
> blueprint for Scottish Home Rule within our strong United
> Kingdom. Home Rule for Scotland can open the door to constitu-
> tional reform for the whole of the UK. We can deliver Home Rule
> all around.[79]

As the 2015 general election approached, the federal Liberal
Democrats 'had originally ruled out Scotland', believing the
prospect of holding on to seats there would be too difficult. But
in December 2014 Ryan Coetzee, Nick Clegg's South African-
born election supremo, headed north to meet the Scottish campaign team as internal polling showed that 10 out of 11 seats
were now SNP-facing. Victoria Marson, the federal party's head
of strategic seat operations, said the only way to win was for the
SLD to present 'themselves as the only viable pro-UK party that
could beat the SNP'.[80]

The Liberal Democrats also dominated the 2015 campaign
in an unhelpful way. Just after Nicola Sturgeon's triumph in
the first televised leaders' debate, a Liberal Democrat special
adviser at the Scotland Office leaked a memo based on a con-
versation between the French consul general in Edinburgh and
the First Minister, who had apparently indicated that her pre-
ferred election outcome was another Conservative government.
'Nikileaks', as it was dubbed on Twitter, rumbled on for around

a year, reflecting badly on a party that had once punched above its weight in Scottish politics.

The 2015 SLD manifesto, meanwhile, was launched at a café in South Queensferry, which again spoke to the party's diminished status. Willie Rennie warned of another independence referendum and urged Scots to 'vote intelligently' in order to keep out the SNP, a plea for tactical voting echoed by Nick Clegg on a campaign visit to Scotland. Clegg also 'totally' ruled out any arrangement with the SNP, saying his party could never 'help establish a government which is basically on a life support system, where Alex Salmond could pull the plug any time he wants'.[81] As the campaign drew to a close, Liberal Democrat HQ in London sent a last-minute 'urgent communication' which panicked the Scottish party. 'They're coming to shut us down,' Rennie reportedly told aides, with internal polling now suggesting a complete wipe out.[82]

On polling day, it was the Liberal Democrats – in Scotland and across the UK – who were left on life support, losing 10 of their 11 Scottish MPs,[83] with only former Scottish Secretary Alistair Carmichael (the focus of the Nikileaks row) narrowly retaining Orkney & Shetland. A few weeks later, Charles Kennedy – who had led the UK party to its 2005 triumph – died aged only 55, not long after losing his seat. At Holyrood elections a year later, the party won North East Fife and Edinburgh Western constituencies from the SNP with healthy swings, but lost two list seats and was pushed into fifth place by the Scottish Greens. The result was spun as a success because of the two constituency gains, but the number of SLD MSPs remained at a modest five. But then commentators had predicted that the party would be left, as at Westminster, with only Orkney and Shetland.

The party, as in the 1920s and '30s, had retreated to the Scottish periphery. Mike Rumbles later observed that the SLDs 'did rather better in the 2003 elections and even the 2007 election than our colleagues in Westminster did after being in coalition government'.[84] This, however, was to compare apples with pears. Not only had the Labour-Liberal Democrat coalitions of 1999–2007 involved two parties with a similar ideological outlook, but the economic climate was such that money was easily found for SLD commitments. Importantly, neither had been true of the 2010–15 UK Conservative-Liberal Democrat coalition.

At the 2017 UK general election, all the party could do was revive its tried-and-tested strategy of targeting a small number of constituencies, the priority being Orkney & Shetland, where Carmichael had survived a legal attempt to unseat him in the wake of the Nikileaks incident. During the 'snap' election campaign, the party appeared spirited yet irrelevant, although it managed to gain three additional seats despite its vote share dropping to just 6.8 per cent. It had benefitted from a degree of anti-SNP tactical voting, but with four MPs and five MSPs the party was at least back in the game, if still a shadow of its former self. Scottish party leader Willie Rennie focused on two policy issues – early years education and mental health – winning some policy concessions from the Scottish Government and a degree of 'cut through' with voters.

At another UK general election in December 2019, the Scottish Liberal Democrats retained four MPs, though not the same ones (it gained North East Fife from the SNP). Neither the self-promotion by UK party leader Jo Swinson as a potential Prime Minister nor the Liberal Democrats' attempt to increase support as the 'party of Remain' proved credible.[85] Swinson even lost her East Dunbartonshire seat to the SNP. A subsequent 'Election Review' was reported as describing Swinson's national campaign as a 'car crash' with 'unclear' 'Local-Regional-National connections', together with a lack of 'collaboration and communication' between London and the Scottish and Welsh parties.[86]

The loss of Swinson's seat avoided, however, what might have been a contentious debate had she wished to continue as leader. Alex Salmond's former spin doctor, Kevin Pringle, took to suggesting that the Liberal Democrats 'junk' their 'damaged' brand north of the border and 'revive the old Scottish Liberal Party as an autonomous force of the radical centre'. 'Scottish Liberalism was an honourable part of our politics,' added Pringle, 'it would be good to see it back.'[87]

In December 2020, Lord Steel, a long serving Scottish Liberal official, MP, peer and former UK party leader, made what he assumed to be his last political speech at the Scottish Liberal Club, proposing an 'elected senate' as the 'keystone to federalism'.[88] Steel had recently retired from the House of Lords he now sought to abolish.[89] In February 2021, Willie Rennie once again charged former federal leader Lord Campbell of Pittenweem with refreshing the SLD case for a federal UK. 'The status quo has fractured,' said Rennie, 'and the failures of the United Kingdom must be addressed if we want our future to flourish.'[90]

This, *Bring Our Country Together*, was published in April 2021 and drew together familiar pledges intended as an alternative to independence or the status quo.[91] 'Scottish Liberal Democrats were central to the foundation of the Scottish Parliament, fair votes in council elections and more powers for Holyrood,' said Willie Rennie at the launch. 'Now we want to go further with federal UK, fair votes for the whole UK, a reformed House of Lords, a written constitution and power devolved across the nations and regions of the UK.'[92]

This fed into the party's manifesto for elections to the Scottish Parliament the following month, which turned out to be what Rob Johns called an 'as you were' election; few seats changed hands in a contest which remained largely an expression of support for or opposition to independence.[93] The Scottish Liberal Democrats went from five seats to four, and although Willie Rennie doubled his majority in North East Fife, he soon announced his resignation as leader after a decade at the helm.

Alex Cole-Hamilton, the MSP for Edinburgh Western, won the leadership election unopposed in August 2021. From a younger generation than his predecessor, it fell to him to position the party within an increasingly polarised Scottish and UK political environment. Committed to re-joining one union (the European Union) and reforming another (the UK), it remained to be seen how the federalist Scottish Liberal Democrats would emerge from a second independence referendum – long promised by the SNP – which many believed would take place before (or perhaps as a consequence of) the next Westminster election due by early 2025.

NOTES

1. R. Finnie (1999), 'Diary of Scottish Liberal Democrat Negotiator: Ross Finnie MSP', *Scottish Affairs* 28:1, 51–6. The SLD's executive had, in anticipation of a possible coalition with Labour, published a 'coalition framework' earlier that year. This made clear that any coalition agreement had to be approved by a two-thirds majority of both the executive and the parliamentary party.

2. H. McLeish (2004), *Scotland First: Truth and Consequences*, Edinburgh: Mainstream, 89.
3. W. Alexander (ed.) (2005), *Donald Dewar: Scotland's first First Minister*, Edinburgh: Mainstream, 156.
4. Corporate lawyer Andrew Cubie was later asked to chair the inquiry, while academic Richard Kerley was also asked to look at PR for local government, another sticking point between Labour and the Liberal Democrats.
5. P. Ashdown (2001), *The Ashdown Diaries: Volume Two 1997–1999*, London: Allen Lane, 458.
6. Named after Labour MP and minister Ted Short, this funding to support opposition parties was introduced in 1975.
7. Attwooll served until 2009, when she was succeeded by former MSP and minister George Lyon. He lost his seat at the 2014 European Parliament election.
8. W. Alexander (ed.), 155.
9. Lord Wallace to the author, 13 February 2021.
10. BBC News online, 'Section 28 debate gets personal', 26 March 2000.
11. H. McLeish, 169.
12. B. Taylor (2002), *Scotland's Parliament: Triumph and Disaster*, Edinburgh: Edinburgh University Press, 203 & 216.
13. Many Liberal Democrats believed there was an understanding between Charles Kennedy and Menzies Campbell that an early resignation by Paddy Ashdown in the 1997 Parliament would see Campbell seek the leadership with the other's support and vice versa if Ashdown stood down late in that Parliament. The fact that Ashdown stood down in the middle of the Parliament made this apparent Kennedy/Campbell understanding difficult (private information).
14. The SLD had come second in terms of seats at the 1997 and 2001 general elections.
15. L. Davidson (2005), *Lucky Jack: Scotland's First Minister*, Edinburgh: Black & White, 182.
16. P. Lynch (2002), 'Partnership, plurality and party identity: the Liberal Democrats after devolution', in G. Hassan & C. Warhurst (eds), *Tomorrow's Scotland*, London: Lawrence & Wishart, 83; 87–8 & 96.
17. SLD MSP Robert Brown even believed there was 'potential to overtake the SNP if all went well. Hubris on my part as it turned out!' (Robert Brown to the author, 18 February 2021).
18. See M. Keating (ed.) (2020), *The Oxford Handbook of Scottish Politics*, Oxford: Oxford University Press, 301–19.
19. P. Lynch (2002), 86.

20. A. Evans (2015), 'The Squeezed Middle? The Liberal Democrats in Wales and Scotland: A Post-Coalition Reassessment', *Scottish Affairs* 24:2, 163–86.
21. Taking a fifth minister meant the SLD lost its entitlement to Short money.
22. T. A. W. Stewart (ed.) (2019), *The Scottish Parliament in its own words: an oral history*, Edinburgh: Luath, 62.
23. Anonymous interview, 20 August 2018.
24. Anonymous interview.
25. That said, Charles Kennedy did provide an introduction.
26. See M. Keating (2010), *The Government of Scotland: Public Policy Making after Devolution* (second edition), Edinburgh: Edinburgh University Press.
27. Enoch Powell's much-quoted maxim in a study of Joseph Chamberlain was that: 'All political lives, unless they are cut off in midstream at a happy juncture, end in failure, because that is the nature of politics and of human affairs' (E. Powell, 1977, *Joseph Chamberlain*, London: Thames and Hudson, 151).
28. H. Macdonell (2009), *Uncharted Territory: The story of Scottish devolution*, London: Politico's, 187.
29. C. Rennard (2018), *Winning Here – My Campaigning Life: Memoirs Volume 1*, London: Biteback, 411–12.
30. See G. Hurst (2006), *Charles Kennedy: A Tragic Flaw*, London: Politico's, 1–23, for a full account of Kennedy's resignation.
31. J. Ault (ed.) (2015), *By-Elections: Essays of the Nations*, Penryn: Institute of Cornish Studies, 152. The editor of the *Sunday Post*, home to the real 'Oor Willie' cartoon, was unhappy at the allusion.
32. J. Ault, 155.
33. C. Rennard, 413–16.
34. G. Hurst, 242.
35. This was largely drafted by David Paterson, the party's head of communications and policy between 2004 and 2008.
36. This term derived from a 2004 pamphlet of the same title written by the SLD's then finance spokesman Jeremy Purvis.
37. D. Steel (2006), *The Steel Commission: Moving to Federalism – A New Settlement for Scotland*, Edinburgh: Scottish Liberal Democrats, 54; 113; 117–19.
38. C. M. M. Macdonald (2009), *Whaur Extremes Meet: Scotland's Twentieth Century*, Edinburgh: John Donald, 221.
39. M. Laffin (2007), 'The Scottish Liberal Democrats', *Political Quarterly* 78:1, 147–55.
40. P. Jones (2007), 'The SNP's Victory in the 2007 Scottish Parliament Elections', *Scottish Affairs* 60:1, 6–23.

41. M. Campbell (2008), *Menzies Campbell: My Autobiography*, London: Hodder and Stoughton, 277–8.
42. Interview with Michael Moore, 7 March 2021.
43. M. Campbell, 280–1.
44. See D. Torrance (2010), *Salmond: Against the Odds*, Edinburgh: Birlinn, 243–45 for a full account of the aborted negotiations.
45. M. Campbell, 280–81.
46. L. Paterson (2015), 'Utopian Pragmatism: Scotland's Choice', *Scottish Affairs* 24:1, 22–46.
47. Private information.
48. J. Wallace (2019), 'A New Voice in the Land' in J. Johnston & J. Mitchell (eds), *The Scottish Parliament at twenty*, Edinburgh: Luath Press, 152.
49. Anonymous interview.
50. Cllr Robert Brown to the author, 18 February 2021.
51. *Herald*, 26 July 2008.
52. Anonymous interview.
53. Willie Rennie failed to hold his by-election gain in Dunfermline and West Fife but was elected to the Scottish Parliament a year later.
54. Sir Menzies Campbell also expressed reservations but voted for the deal on the basis that as the party's immediate past leader he could not be disloyal to Nick Clegg.
55. Interview with Michael Moore, 7 March 2021.
56. Alexander became Chief Secretary to the Treasury. Later, the SLD MP Mike Crockart resigned as Michael Moore's PPS in December 2010 over the UK Government's proposed rise in tuition fees.
57. Private information.
58. M. Harvey (2014), 'The Scottish Liberal Democrats and the 2014 Independence Referendum' in K. Adamson & P. Lynch (eds), *Scottish Political Parties and the 2014 Independence Referendum*, Cardiff: Welsh Academic Press, 68.
59. Angus Macleod (2011), 'Salmond reaches out to disappointed Lib Dems', *The Times*, 9 July 2011.
60. *Holyrood*, 27 February 2012.
61. R. Brown & N. Lindsay (eds) (2012), *The Little Yellow Book: Reclaiming the Liberal Democrats for the People*, Peterborough: Liberal Futures, 9.
62. Cllr Robert Brown to the author, 18 February 2021.
63. Anonymous interview. Cable, recalled one aide, 'thought he understood Scotland because he'd been a Glasgow councillor in the 1970s'. A lecturer at Glasgow University, Cable contested Glasgow Hillhead for Labour in 1970 and served as a Glasgow

Corporation councillor for the Maryhill ward between 1971 and 1974. Another former adviser believes Cable 'did actually understand Scotland. He saw the bigger picture' (anonymous interviews).

64. A. B. Evans (2015).
65. A. B. Evans (2014), 'Federalists in name only? Reassessing the federal credentials of the Liberal Democrats: An English case study', *British Politics* 9:3, 355–6.
66. D. Laws (2016), *Coalition: The Inside Story of the Conservative-Liberal Democrat Coalition Government*, London: Biteback, 438–39.
67. W. Rennie (2012), Speech to Liberal Democrat conference, 25 September 2012.
68. Sir M. Campbell (2012), *Federalism: the best future for Scotland: The report of the Home Rule and Community Rule Commission of the Scottish Liberal Democrats*, Edinburgh: Scottish Liberal Democrats, 19.
69. W. Rennie (2012), Speech to Scottish Liberal Democrat conference, 4 March 2012.
70. J. Rentoul (2012), 'The man who saved the Union: Lib Dem Michael Moore is Westminster's answer to James Bond', *Independent on Sunday*, 4 November 2012.
71. D. Laws, 439.
72. Private information.
73. D. Laws, 440–43.
74. See A. McHarg et al. (2016), *The Scottish Independence Referendum: Constitutional and Political Implications*, Oxford: Oxford University Press.
75. T. Blair (2010), *A Journey*, London: Hutchinson, 251.
76. Legally, entrenchment was not possible in the absence of a codified or written constitution.
77. M. Campbell (2014), *Campbell II: The second report of the Home Rule and Community Rule Commission*, Edinburgh: Scottish Liberal Democrats, 5.
78. Liberal Democrats, both Scottish and English, were furious at the Prime Minister's decision to announce plans for 'English Votes for English Laws' at the same time (see D. Laws, 448–9).
79. HL Debs 27 November 2014 Vol 757 c1045.
80. J. Pike (2015), *Project Fear*, London: Biteback, 206.
81. *The Times*, 25 April 2015.
82. J. Pike, 210.
83. Sir Malcolm Bruce in Gordon and Sir Menzies Campbell in North-East Fife had decided not to stand.
84. T. A. W. Stewart, 64.

85. P. Sloman (2020), 'Squeezed Out? The Liberal Democrats and the 2019 General Election', *Political Quarterly* 91:1.
86. M. Pack (2020), *2019 Election Review: Report*, London: Liberal Democrats.
87. Kevin Pringle (2019), 'Bring back the Scottish Liberals for a real centrist renaissance', *Sunday Times Scotland*, 3 March 2019.
88. *The Times*, 3 December 2020.
89. Steel had recently quit the party following a report from the Independent Inquiry into Child Sexual Abuse, which had looked at allegations regarding his late colleague Cyril Smith. Although a Scottish Liberal Democrat inquiry cleared Steel (it was alleged he had failed adequately to tackle Smith regarding his actions), Steel proved unable adequately to defend himself during the Independent Inquiry and resigned lest a further party investigation trigger wider resignations from the party.
90. W. Rennie (2021), 'Federalism', Scottish Liberal Democrats website.
91. Scottish Liberal Democrats (2021), *Bring Our Country Together*, Edinburgh: Scottish Liberal Democrats.
92. *Scotsman*, 9 April 2021.
93. Rob Johns (2021), 'As You Were: The Scottish Parliament Election of 2021', *Political Quarterly* 92:3.

Conclusion:
Whither Scottish Liberalism?

In the run up to the 2021 Scottish Parliament elections – held as the UK emerged from a long, gruelling lockdown – Willie Rennie, leader of the Scottish Liberal Democrats (SLD) since 2011, repackaged an old rallying cry. 'As we recover from the pandemic,' he argued, 'a federal UK would allow us to chart a course together that allows us to reflect our common interests and our more local needs.'

Rennie also alluded to strained inter-governmental relations and rising support for Scottish and Welsh independence:

> I believe that the United Kingdom will only be secure when its constitution clearly recognises the shared sovereignty of all four constituent parts of the Union and finds a way to ensure that the UK Government, the governments of Scotland, Wales, Northern Ireland and the various parts of England can work together with rather than grandstanding for political advantage.

Lord Campbell of Pittenweem, a former UK Liberal Democrat leader and chairman of the old Scottish Liberal Party, added that:

> In the 1980s and '90s, Scottish Liberal Democrats worked across party lines to build the case for a powerful Scottish Parliament and succeeded ... Despite this ... the SNP seek to offer the people of Scotland a binary choice – the status quo or independence. As Scottish Liberal Democrats we reject that.[1]

The lofty rhetoric from Rennie and Campbell disguised the reality that the Scottish Liberal Democrats were no longer in a position to deliver either a federal UK or indeed fend off the SNP. With just five Members of the Scottish Parliament and four

Members of the UK House of Commons, the party had been reduced to a minor political player. It had been in such a situation before, but it was no less painful for that historical reality.

All political parties like to tell stories about themselves, and these usually leave out inconvenient details. As Eugenio F. Biaghini has observed, under leaders from Gladstone to Asquith, the Liberal Party proved itself 'good at managing and absorbing Celtic separatism, turning a potentially destructive force into an important asset for both the stability of the United Kingdom and the electoral success of their own party'.[2] In the late 19th century, therefore, a hegemonic – and therefore morally superior – Liberal Party functioned 'as the party of Scottish aspirations'. This gave rise to claims of a consistent and unbroken commitment both to Home Rule for Scotland and federalism, but neither was entirely true.

Gladstone had spoken of 'Home Rule all round' rather than true federalism, while Ireland was always his main focus and priority. Such rhetoric certainly helped win votes, and indeed Scottish Liberal success during the 19th century (much like the SNP's in the early 21st) can be measured primarily in electoral terms. Having helped deliver the Great Reform Act of 1832, Whigs and Liberals were rewarded with majority after majority in Scotland. By the 1880s, the consolidated Scottish Liberal Party had benefitted hugely from two further extensions of the franchise. It failed, however, to capitalise on another in 1918; indeed votes for women and the working classes ultimately robbed Liberals in Scotland (and indeed in the rest of the UK) of its status as a natural party of government.

In the interim, Scottish Liberals had worked hard to address unfinished business from the 19th century while updating their platform in an attempt to see off the threat posed by Labour. Anti-landlordism ran deep in the party – resentment at their opposition to the 1832 Act lingered for decades – which meant the party responded nimbly to an electoral challenge from crofting candidates in the 1880s and 1890s. Time was made for land reform legislation in the famously 'congested' Imperial Parliament and that challenge dissipated. In the 1910s, Lord Pentland tried to promote smallholdings, and while his Act proved a damp squib, the sentiment acted as a bridge between the old and new liberalism, keeping the party electable in the process.

Disestablishment, however, was a notable failure, regularly preached by the Scottish party but never delivered (unlike in Ireland and Wales). Despite a myriad of resolutions and even a government-backed Bill in 1894, the Liberal leadership in London generally ignored the Scottish party on this issue (but not the Welsh party, which played a cannier game). By the early 20th century, disestablishing and disendowing the 'national' Church of Scotland lacked the salience it once had, especially as the wounds of the 1843 Disruption healed. Nevertheless, Scottish Liberals tended to be more secular in their views, less hidebound by clerical orthodoxy.

This was given its fullest expression by the Education Act 1918, which brought generally poorer Catholic schools into the Kirk-dominated state sector and guaranteed their religious independence. Having devolved a degree of legislative power to the Church of England Assembly in 1919, a Liberal Secretary for Scotland also followed suit by recognising the spiritual autonomy of the Church of Scotland with another Act in 1921. Although far from disestablishment, it nevertheless separated church(es) and state a little more, reducing the size and scope of government – a key liberal aim – in the process. Robert Munro, sponsor of both Acts, emerges as a great reforming Liberal Scottish Secretary.

In other respects, the size of the state was expanding in the inter-war period, and here the Scottish Liberals were less nimble. Although the Liberal governments of 1906–18 made great strides when it came to social reform, Scottish Liberals viewed policies such as National Insurance, old-age pensions and a minimum wage as a bit too radical, fearful they would scare off its middle-class supporters. While Lloyd George and Asquith laid the foundations of the UK's welfare state, their Scottish colleagues were caught between their opposition to socialism and the obvious demand for progressive social policies from an expanding electorate.

A failure in this respect was that of personnel. In 1888 Keir Hardie had offered himself as a Scottish Liberal candidate but was rebuffed in snobbish terms. Although the party's overly aristocratic leadership had been balanced with radical middle-class MPs and activists by the early 20th century, by the 1920s this was a drawback given the further extension of the franchise to the industrial working classes. Their representatives were nowhere to be seen on the Scottish Liberal benches and the Duke of Montrose no longer looked like the face of contemporary Scotland. The pre-occupations of middle-class Liberals – temperance, disestablishment, etc. – proved of little interest to factory workers.

The Scottish Liberal party also suffered from hubris. As John Buchan perceptively observed in 1911, 'its members seemed to assume that their opponents must be lacking either in morals or mind'. Such a mindset rarely sustains a party indefinitely, however invincible it might look. Sure enough, just a decade later Liberals appeared to many voters in Scotland to be reactionary defenders of established interests. By the time Asquith redefined Liberalism during the Paisley campaign of 1920, it was too little too late.

Ironically, the apparent settlement of the Irish Question in 1921 – devolution for Northern Ireland, Dominion status for the Irish Free State – robbed the Liberals of a rallying cry and contributed to their decline. Home Rule for Scotland was, like disestablishment, another undelivered pledge from the late 19th century. Gladstone and Asquith kicked it into the long grass, even as it became linked to Ireland in an ambitiously holistic attempt to reform the United Kingdom of Great Britain and Ireland. As with disestablishment, the Scottish tail failed to wag the English dog.

'Scotch home rule must wait', remarked Sir Henry Campbell-Bannerman, 'until the sluggish mind of John Bull is educated up to that point.' But the mind of John Bull viewed Home Rule and disestablishment as peculiarly Scottish issues which could be fudged and delayed. There were, as a consequence, a myriad of false dawns. In 1913 a Liberal Scottish Secretary, Thomas McKinnon Wood, declared Home Rule to be close, but this too was kicked into the long grass. While Scottish Liberal publications continued to quote that pledge well into the 1940s, other parties – initially Labour but most successfully the Scottish Unionists – harnessed Scottish nationalist sentiment to their own ends.

That the policy of Irish Home Rule had split the Scottish Liberals hardly helped. Opposition to that goal was particularly marked in Scotland, which had religious, industrial and familial links to the Protestants of Ulster. Co-operation between Liberal Unionists and Scottish Conservatives recalibrated Scottish party politics, with Liberal Unionism – strong in many parts of Scotland – acting as a gateway drug for many hitherto hostile Scots to vote Tory for the first time. In 1912 the two parties merged, which allowed the resulting Scottish Unionist Party to become the sort of well-organised broad church the Scottish Liberals had once been. Within a decade, Unionism had eclipsed Liberalism as Scotland's party of choice.

All parties like to claim synchronicity with nation, and in doing so the Scottish Liberals helped forge the nationalist-unionist mythology of Scotland as a radical, egalitarian nation held back by an English conservative majority. But if Liberals were truly the party of Scottish national interests, then their failure to make good on the logic and rhetoric of Home Rule alienated another section of its once considerable support. Frustrated by this Liberal failure, dedicated Home Rulers started to defect to Labour in the 1890s, further weakening its nationalist credentials and therefore its electoral dominance.

Scottish Liberals only shifted unequivocally in favour of Home Rule for Scotland (and Wales) at the very moment its power to deliver both waned. The party had dominated for so long precisely because it was such a broad church – Imperialist *and* anti-Imperialist, Radical *and* Whig – but from 1922 onwards large portions of its congregation looked elsewhere for salvation: right-leaning Liberals defected to the Unionists and left-leaning to Labour. Failure begat failure. Despite a modest revival in 1923, by the mid-1920s Scottish Liberals had been reduced to a bunch of squabbling factions united only by a name and the electoral glories of the previous century. Minutes of executive meetings from the inter-war years do not make edifying reading.

The Scottish Liberal Party (as it formally became after the Second World War) became intellectually moribund, apparently unsure of what it stood for. After all, what could Scottish Liberals hope to deliver that Tories could not economically or Labour socially? Although the party was sustained for a while by various coalitions and 'national' governments, they all tended to smother what distinctive Scottish Liberal ethos still existed. A proposed merger with the Liberal-Nationals in the late 1940s failed, and the party nearly disappeared. Grand squabbles between the Scottish Liberal Association executive and party grassroots in the late 19th century had by the 1950s become puerile spats between a dwindling number of part-time office holders.

Following Jo Grimond's election in 1950, however, the party sensed an opportunity to rebuild. Grimond – married to one of the Asquith clan – demonstrated that the Scottish Liberal caste system of the late 19th century was alive and well. But the party learned not to spread itself too thinly, instead targeting particular seats, usually those with pockets of historic Liberal support in the rural Highlands and Islands and Borders. A recognisably Scottish leadership also began to emerge for the first time since the 1920s. The hitherto overlooked Lady Glen-Coats almost single-handedly held the party together as chair, while Grimond's 'New Liberalism' reminded voters that individualism was central to Scottish Liberalism. John Bannerman, a dedicated Home Ruler, helped mould the party in its contemporary form.

Only in the late 1960s, when Scottish party politics became more competitive on the basis of the constitutional question, did the Scottish Liberal Party's goal evolve from 'Home Rule all round' to 'federalism', the key figure in this respect being Jeremy Thorpe. But even then the 'f' word was not fleshed out in any meaningful sense. Scottish Liberals spoke of 'phased' federalism, an elegant way of acknowledging that their English (if not Welsh) colleagues were divided as to how England might be governed within a British federation.

Nevertheless, the Scottish Liberal Party of the 1960s was impressive, particularly given its recent existential fragility. It adopted a far-sighted 'regional' strategy, evidence it was beginning to think strategically as well as tactically. Its candidates reflected this new-found vitality, although until 1964 there were a lot of brilliant second places in by-elections and not enough mediocre firsts. The party's campaigning also became more vigorous as well as focused. It was a pioneer in the realm of what became known as 'community politics', not least in local government, which Scottish Liberals began to take seriously in the 1960s and '70s, rightly viewing it as a basis upon which parliamentary gains could be made.

Momentum, properly harnessed, is a third party's friend, and the Scottish Liberals took full advantage. They earned the right to be taken seriously at the 1964 general election, and built on that success with David Steel's by-election win in the Borders and further gains in 1966. It helped that the Overton

Window had shifted in the Liberals' favour, with Scottish voters attracted by a party advocating individualism and Home Rule. Once the party realised that a (majority) Liberal dawn was not imminent and instead embraced its third-party status, it began to see results. Both Grimond and Steel spoke of 'realignment', which at a UK level meant Labour-Liberal co-operation and in Scotland also encompassed the Scottish National Party.

Nationalist realignment proved difficult given that by the late 1960s it was clear that Scottish Liberals and the SNP were competing for the same voters. Russell Johnston attempted to draw a philosophical line between the two during his conference speeches, but the SNP were populist and the Liberals (still) a middle-class debating society. Johnston's belief that upon gaining devolution Scotland would 'shed outright nationalism' and revert back to traditional debates between left, right and centre proved naïve. The 1970s saw lots of previously Scottish Liberals switch to the SNP, increasing third-party competition at Liberal expense.

A remaining point of differentiation between the two parties was Europe. In 1973 the Scottish Liberal Party advocated a referendum on the UK's accession to the then European Economic Community (the English party did not). But even this was removed when the SNP pivoted towards Europe in 1988. There also emerged a curious separation between the Scottish party leadership and voters, at first on Europe (when there was a referendum in 1975) and later on support for a Scottish Assembly (1979) and Parliament (1997). It seemed that Scottish Liberals were not as constitutionally progressive as the party believed them to be, something that perhaps reflected its status as a repository for refugees from the two main parties. At one Scottish by-election in 1991 Scottish Liberal support for devolution was even seen as having soured its victory and dampening support at the 1992 general election.

By this point, realignment of a sort had been realised: the SDP-SLP 'Alliance' – something that allowed the two parties to mount a major third-party challenge across Scotland – led to a formal merger in 1988 and subsequent co-operation between the new Scottish Liberal Democrat party and Scottish Labour. This proved fruitful, extending into devolved government (1999–2007) and beyond to the Scottish independence referendum campaign (2011–14). The most significant legacy of Scottish

Liberal Democracy, therefore, lies in the field of constitutional reform, over which it paradoxically exercised more influence as a third rather than as a main party.

The Scottish Constitutional Convention presented a major opportunity for the SLD, particularly after the SNP withdrew. Jim Wallace in particular played a strong hand when it came to shaping the future devolution settlement's use of proportional representation. At the same time this legacy was incomplete and lopsided. Lord Rosebery had despaired of Gladstone's failure to take Scotland seriously in the 1880s and there remained something of that tension even when Scots acted as federal party leader (Charles Kennedy, for example, and Sir Menzies Campbell) and a fifth of the party's MPs came from Scotland. A belief in organisational and constitutional federalism masked the fact that the Edinburgh and London leadership were often at loggerheads, even when HQ in London helped professionalise the Scottish party.

The failure remained that of a century earlier, a vagueness when it came to adequately spelling out what a federal United Kingdom would actually look like, how to get there and, crucially, how to persuade the English party to take such an holistic goal seriously. But in a purely Scottish context the party had obvious appeal, especially as support for devolution became an unequivocal vote winner. Thereafter, the Scottish Liberal Democrats presented themselves as the 'guarantors of home rule', while Wallace did his best to prevent the party falling into what he called the 'trap' of 'seeing home rule as an end in itself'.

In this he was not entirely successful, although that does not detract from the very real achievements of Scottish Liberal Democrats between 1999 and 2007, when the party pursued a productively pragmatic path rather than the dogma of undiluted federalism. At points, that coalition Scottish Executive was rocky but, looking back, what is striking was its stability, especially when contrasted with the UK Conservative-Liberal Democrat coalition that followed in 2010. Euan Roddin has suggested that two-thirds of Scottish Executive policies delivered by 2003 began life as Liberal Democrat initiatives, while by 2007 it was possible to add PR for local government to that record.

It is difficult not to conclude, therefore, that the Scottish party was rather better at deriving policy and electoral benefits from coalition politics than Nick Clegg et al. between 2010 and 2015. It even revisited Liberal policies associated with the 19th-century party, such as land reform. The Scottish Liberal Democrats moved from protest to power seamlessly, although they remained organisationally weak and geographically concentrated. Despite further advances, most notably at the 2005 UK general election, the party did not manage to break out of its middle-class, rural and historic strongholds.

To its credit, the party attempted to keep ahead of the constitutional curve with the 2006 Steel Commission, and although its focus on greater fiscal autonomy later came to pass, the SLD got little credit. By 2007 Scottish Liberal Democrats were victims of their own success. The party manifesto of that year was not exactly fizzing with intellectual energy, while its leader, Nicol Stephen, lacked the heft of his predecessors. Stephen's failure to reach a deal with the SNP over a referendum also robbed the party of influence it had enjoyed in some form since the late 1980s. After only eight years it once again ceased to be a party of government.

The 2010 UK Conservative-Liberal Democrat coalition further distanced the Scottish Liberal Democrats from the electoral mainstream in Scotland, which remained hostile to the Conservatives. This decimated the Scottish party at the 2011 Holyrood election, while further co-operation during the independence referendum proved to be another nail in the electoral coffin, robbing it of all but a single Scottish seat at the 2015 UK general election. Indeed, victory in that referendum proved Pyrrhic for all three parties now simplistically classed as 'unionist'.

The trouble was that the 2010–15 coalition – even though it boasted the first Liberal Scottish Secretaries since the Second World War – flew in the face of the traditional positioning of the SLD, as well as key narratives in Scottish political culture. These were often more rhetorical than real – Scotland, like the rest of the UK, had rejected the Alternative Vote in a 2011 referendum – but this nationalistic frame inevitably aided the SNP, with whom Scottish Liberals had long competed electorally.

Figures like Russell Johnston and David Steel had worked hard to differentiate their nationalism ('Home Rule') from their opponents' (independence), but they tread such a fine line that by 2007–15 many Scots (and a large chunk of their own supporters) failed to discern the boundary. As Tony Blair observed in his memoirs, you could 'never be sure where nationalist sentiment ends and separatist sentiment begins'. Federalism might have been tidier, but it appeared undeliverable; independence, with all its complexities, was just a referendum vote away.

At the same time, it would be churlish to hold the Scottish Liberals responsible for not having delivered a federal UK, something that would have required a majority, or at least a Liberal-led government. Jim (now Lord) Wallace continued to speak of delivering 'Home Rule all round' after 2017, but there was a definite sense that the constitutional ship had sailed. The debate in Scotland after 2014 became polarised between 'independence' and (unreformed) 'Union', which left little room for a Liberal middle way. By 2021 the Scottish Liberal Democrats were what their Scottish Liberal predecessors had been a century before, a minor party of the Scottish middle class increasingly squeezed between political rivals. The disproportionate number of Scottish Liberal Democrat peers in the House of Lords merely underlined its reduced status.

Still, political success is not measured by elections alone. The Scotland of 2021 is transformed – and indeed liberalised – from that of 1921. Home Rule of some form is its natural form of government, its councils and parliament are elected by proportional representation, but most striking is the nation's liberal frame of mind, socially, politically, constitutionally. By the early 21st century liberal ideas and reforms were championed by parties across the political spectrum – even the Scottish Conservatives. This had not always been the case, for despite widespread narratives to the contrary (many perpetrated by Liberals), Scotland was not particularly liberal in its attitudes until the early 21st century. When polled throughout the second half of the 20th century on three standard issues – abortion, homosexuality and divorce – Scots were often more conservative than the English.

By the time Liberal Democrats entered devolved government in 1999 Scottish attitudes were beginning to converge with those in England. A row over the 'promotion' of homosexuality in schools (via section 2A of the Local Government Act 1986) was unpleasant but represented the last gasp of the old, illiberal Scotland. By 2021 liberal individualism had triumphed, economically and culturally, but small efficient government – another key Liberal aim – had not. Events such as the Great

Financial Crash, Brexit and the Cronavirus pandemic had made sure of that. So, the fact that most Scots were reluctant to vote Liberal Democrat in the 2020s did not mean they were not liberal by temperament and belief, far from it. And that this was true owed something to the influence of Scottish Liberalism in all its manifestations between 1832 and 2021.

NOTES

1. David Bol, 'Scottish Lib Dems draw up five-point blueprint for federal UK', *Herald*, 1 March 2021.
2. E. F. Biagini (ed.) (1996), *Citizenship and Community: Liberals, Radicals and Collective Identities in the British Isles, 1865–1931*, Cambridge: Cambridge University Press, 14.

Appendix 1 – Party Leaders

PRESIDENTS

Scottish Liberal Association

Lord Rosebery (1881)
Earl of Stair (1881–4)
Earl of Fife (1884–6)
Lord Rosebery (1886–1900)[1]
Sir Henry Campbell-Bannerman (1900–8)
H. H. Asquith (1909–18)[2]

Scottish Liberal Party

Sir Archibald Sinclair, 1st Viscount Thurso (1946–65)
Andrew Murray (1960–1)
John (later Lord) Bannerman (1963–9)
Ray (Lady) Bannerman (1969–76)
Robert L. Smith (1976–82)
Fred McDermid (1982–3)
George Mackie (1983–8)

---

[1] When the SLA amalgamated with the National Liberal Federation of Scotland in December 1886, Lord Rosebery remained president.

[2] Asquith was only elected to succeed CB as president of the SLA on 9 February 1909.

CHAIRS

Scottish Liberal Federation

Sir William Robertson (1918–21)
Sir Donald Maclean (1921–5)
Sir John Anthony (1925–33)
Sir William M. Baird (1933–5)
Philip Kerr, 11th Marquess of Lothian (1935–46)

Scottish Liberal Party

Lady Glen-Coats (1946–8)
Dr L. T. Gray (1948–52)
John G. Wilson (1952–4)
Charles H. Johnston (1954–6)
John Bannerman (1956–65)
George Mackie (1965–70)
Russell Johnston (1970–3)
Robert L. Smith (1973–5)
Menzies Campbell (1975–7)
Terry Grieve (1977–80)
Fred McDermid (1980–2)
Ross Finnie (1982–6)
John Lawrie (1986–7)
Christopher Mason (1987–8)

Scottish Liberal Democrats

Sandra Grieve (1993)

LEADERS

Scottish Liberal Party

Russell Johnston (1973–88)

Scottish Liberal Democrats

Malcolm Bruce (1988–92)
Jim Wallace (1992–2005)
Nicol Stephen (2005–8)

Tavish Scott (2008–11)
Willie Rennie (2011–21)
Alex Cole-Hamilton (2021–)

DEPUTY LEADERS

Scottish Liberal Democrats

Michael Moore (2002–10)
Jo Swinson (2010–12)
Alistair Carmichael (2012–)

Appendix 2 – Election Results

WESTMINSTER ELECTION RESULTS, 1832–2019

Election year	Vote share %	Number of MPs	Seats uncontested	Total no. of seats
1832	79	43	15	53
1835	62.8	38	23	53
1837	54	33	22	53
1841	60.8	31	29	53
1847	81.7	33	37	53
1852	72.6	33	33	53
1857	84.7	39	38	53
1859	66.4	40	45	53
1865	85.4	42	37	53
1868	82.5	51	26	58
1874	68.4	40	22	58
1880	70.1	52	12	58
1885	53.3	51	5	70
1886	53.6	43	9	70
1892	53.9	51	0	70
1895	51.7	39	5	70
1900	50.2	34	3	70
1906	56.4	58	1	70
1910 (Jan.)	54.2	58	0	70
1910 (Dec.)	53.6	58	12	70
1918	19.1	25 (coalition)	8	71
	15	8 (independent)		
1922	17.7	12 (National Lib)	3	71
	21.5	15 (Liberal)		
1923	28.4	22	4	71
1924	16.6	8	3	71

Election year	Vote share %	Number of MPs	Seats uncontested	Total no. of seats
1929	18.1	13	0	71
1931	13.5	15	8	71
1935	6.7	7 (National Lib)	1	71
	6.7	3 (Liberal)		
1945	5	0	0	71
1950	6.6	2	0	71
1951	2.7	1	0	71
1955	1.9	1	0	71
1959	4.1	1	0	71
1964	7.6	4	0	71
1966	6.8	5	0	71
1970	5.5	3	0	71
1974 (Feb.)	8	3	0	71
1974 (Oct.)	8.3	3	0	71
1979	9	3	0	71
1983	24.5*	8 (5 Liberals)	0	72
1987	19.2*	9 (7 Liberals)	0	72
1992	13.1	9	0	72
1997	13	10	0	72
2001	16.4	10	0	72
2005	22.6	11	0	59
2010	18.9	11	0	59
2015	7.5	1	0	59
2017	6.8	4	0	59
2019	9.5	4	0	59

Sources: F. W. S Craig (1981), *British Political Facts 1832–1980*, Chichester: Parliamentary Research. Services; R. Parry (1988), *Scottish Political Facts*, Edinburgh: T. & T. Clark; House of Commons Library.

SCOTTISH PARLIAMENT ELECTION RESULTS, 1999–2021

Election year	Constituency vote	Regional vote	Number of MSPs	Total no. of seats
1999	14.2	12.4	17	129
2003	15.4	11.8	17	129
2007	16.2	11.3	16	129
2011	7.9	5.2	5	129
2016	7.8	5.2	5	129
2021	6.9	5.1	4	129

Sources: House of Commons Library.
* Fought as the Liberal/SDP Alliance.

Bibliography

PRIMARY SOURCES

Clement Davies Papers, National Library of Wales
Gladstone Papers, British Library
J. J. Reid Papers, National Library of Scotland
Scottish Liberal Party Papers, National Library of Scotland
SDP Scotland Papers, Glasgow Caledonian University
1st Viscount Thurso Papers, Churchill Archives Centre, University of
    Cambridge
Gordon Wilson Papers, National Library of Scotland

SECONDARY SOURCES

Alexander, W. (ed.) (2005), *Donald Dewar: Scotland's first First Minister*, Edinburgh: Mainstream.

Ashdown, P. (2000), *The Ashdown Diaries: Volume One 1988–1997*, London: Allen Lane.

—— (2001), *The Ashdown Diaries: Volume Two 1997–1999*, London: Allen Lane.

Asquith, H. H. (1920), *The Paisley Policy*, London: Cassell.

Ault, J. (ed.) (2015), *By-Elections: Essays of the Nations*, Penryn: Institute of Cornish Studies.

Ball, S., A. Thorpe and M. Worley (2005), 'Elections, Leaflets and Whist Drives: Constituency Party Members in Britain between the Wars' in M. Worley (ed.), *Labour's Grass Roots: Essays on the Activities of Local Labour Parties and Members, 1918–45*, London: Routledge.

Bennie, L., J. Brand & J. Mitchell (1997), *How Scotland Votes:*

Scottish Parties and Elections, Manchester: Manchester University Press.

Biagini, E. F. (ed.) (1996), *Citizenship and Community: Liberals, Radicals and Collective Identities in the British Isles, 1865–1931*, Cambridge: Cambridge University Press.

Blair, T. (2010), *A Journey*, London: Hutchinson.

Bochel, J., D. Denver & A. Macartney (eds) (1981), *The Referendum Experience: Scotland 1979*, Aberdeen: Aberdeen University Press.

Breitenbach, E. & F. Mackay (2001), *Women and Contemporary Scottish Politics: An Anthology*, Edinburgh: Polygon.

Brown, R. & N. Lindsay (eds) (2012), *The Little Yellow Book: Reclaiming the Liberal Democrats for the People*, Peterborough: Liberal Futures.

Buchan, J. (1940), *Memory Hold-the-Door: The Autobiography of John Buchan*, London: Hodder and Stoughton.

Bulpitt, J. (1983), *Territory and Power in the United Kingdom: An Interpretation*, Manchester: Manchester University Press.

Burness, C. (2003), *Strange Associations: The Irish Question and the Making of Scottish Unionism, 1886–1918*, East Linton: Tuckwell Press.

Butler, D. E. & A. King (1965), *The British General Election of 1964*, London: St Martin's Press.

Butler, D. E. & R. Rose (1966), *The British General Election of 1966*, London: Macmillan.

Cameron, E. A. (2010), *Impaled Upon a Thistle: Scotland Since 1880*, Edinburgh: Edinburgh University Press.

Campbell, J. (2014), *Roy Jenkins: A Well-Rounded Life*, London: Jonathan Cape

Campbell, Sir M. (2008), *Menzies Campbell: My Autobiography*, London: Hodder and Stoughton.

—— (2012), *Federalism: the best future for Scotland: The report of the Home Rule and Community Rule Commission of the Scottish Liberal Democrats*, Edinburgh: Scottish Liberal Democrats.

—— (2014), *Campbell II: The second report of the Home Rule and Community Rule Commission*, Edinburgh: Scottish Liberal Democrats

Checkland, S. (1988), *The Elgins 1766–1917: A tale of aristocrats, proconsuls and their wives*, Aberdeen: Aberdeen University Press.

Checkland, S. & O. Checkland (1989), *Industry and Ethos: Scotland 1832–1914*, Edinburgh: Edinburgh University Press.

Chrimes, S. B. (ed.) (1950), *The General Election in Glasgow: February, 1950*, Glasgow: Jackson.

Coupland, Sir R. (1954), *Scottish & Welsh Nationalism: A Study*, Glasgow: Collins.

Coutts, B. (1988), *Bothy to Big Ben: an autobiography*, Aberdeen: Aberdeen University Press.

Crewe, I. & A. King (1995), *SDP: The Birth, Life and Death of the Social Democratic Party*, Oxford: Oxford University Press.

Crick, B. & D. Millar (1991), *Making Scotland's Parliament Work: Standing Orders for the Parliament of Scotland*, Edinburgh: Centre for Scottish Public Policy.

Davidson, L. (2004), *Lucky Jack: Scotland's First Minister*, Edinburgh: Black & White.

Davidson, R. & G. Davis (2012), *The Sexual State: Sexuality and Scottish Governance, 1950–80*, Edinburgh: Edinburgh University Press.

De Groot, G. J. (1993), *Liberal Crusader: The Life of Sir Archibald Sinclair*, London: C. Hurst & Co.

Denver, D., J. Mitchell, C. Pattie & H. Bochel (2000), *Scotland Decides: The Devolution Issue and the Scottish Referendum*, London: Routledge.

Dickson, A. & J. H. Treble (eds) (1992), *People and Society in Scotland Volume III, 1914–1990*, Edinburgh: John Donald.

Dudley Edwards, O. (ed.) (1989), *A Claim of Right for Scotland*, Edinburgh: Polygon.

Dutton, D. (2004), *A History of the Liberal Party*, Basingstoke: Palgrave Macmillan.

Dyer, M. (1996), *Men of Property and Intelligence: The Scottish Electoral System prior to 1884*, Aberdeen: Scottish Cultural Press.

—— (1996), *Capable Citizens and Improvident Democrats: The Scottish Electoral System 1884–1929*, Aberdeen: Scottish Cultural Press.

Egan, M. (2009), *Coming into Focus: The Transformation of the Liberal Party 1945–64*, Riga: VDM Verlag Dr Müller.

Finlay, R. J. (1994), *Independent and Free: Scottish Politics and the Origins of the Scottish National Party 1918–1945*, Edinburgh: John Donald.

—— (2004), *Scotland 1914–2000*, London: Profile.

Fraser, W. H. (2000), *Scottish Popular Politics: From Radicalism to Labour*, Edinburgh: Polygon.

Fry, M. (1987), *Patronage and Principle: A Political History of Modern Scotland*, Aberdeen: Aberdeen University Press.

Grieve, S. (1991), 'Women in the Scottish Liberal Democrats', in *A Woman's Claim of Right in Scotland: Women, Representation and Politics*, Edinburgh: Polygon.

Grimond, J. (1979), *Memoirs*, London: Heinemann.

—— (1983), *A Personal Manifesto*, Oxford: Martin Robertson.

Hames, S. (2020), *The Literary Politics of Scottish Devolution: Voice, Class, Nation*, Edinburgh: Edinburgh University Press.

Hanham, H. J. (1959), *Elections and Party Management: Politics in the time of Disraeli and Gladstone*, London: Longmans.

—— (1969), *Scottish Nationalism*, Cambridge, MA: Harvard University Press.

Harvey, M. (2014), 'The Scottish Liberal Democrats and the 2014 Independence Referendum' in K. Adamson & P. Lynch (eds), *Scottish Political Parties and the 2014 Independence Referendum*, Cardiff: Welsh Academic Press.

Hill, C. W. (1976), *Edwardian Scotland*, Edinburgh & London: Scottish Academic Press.

Hurst, G. (2006), *Charles Kennedy: A Tragic Flaw*, London: Politico's.

Hutchison, I. G. C. (1986), *A Political History of Scotland 1832–1924: Parties, Elections and Issues*, Edinburgh: John Donald.

—— (2001), *Scottish Politics in the Twentieth Century*, Basingstoke: Palgrave.

—— (2020), *Industry, Reform and Empire: Scotland, 1790–1880*, Edinburgh: Edinburgh University Press.

Jenkins, R. (1991), *A Life at the Centre*, London: Macmillan.

—— (1994), *Asquith*, London: Papermac.

Johnston, R. (1979), *Scottish Liberal Party Conference Speeches 1971–1978*, Edinburgh: Bookmag.

Keating, M. (2010), *The Government of Scotland: Public Policy Making after Devolution* (second edition), Edinburgh: Edinburgh University Press.

—— (ed.) (2020), *The Oxford Handbook of Scottish Politics*, Oxford: Oxford University Press.

Kellas, J. G. (1968), *Modern Scotland: The Nation since 1780*, London: Pall Mall Press.

Kennedy, J. (2015), *Liberal Nationalisms: Empire, State, and Civil Society in Scotland and Quebec*, Montreal: McGill-Queen's University Press.

Kennedy, L. (1995), *In Bed with an Elephant: A Journey through Scotland's Past and Present*, London: Bantam Press.

Koss, S. (1976), *Asquith*, London: Allen Lane.

Laws, D. (2016), *Coalition: The Inside Story of the Conservative-Liberal Democrat Coalition Government*, London: Biteback.

Lynch, P. (2002), 'Partnership, plurality and party identity: the Liberal Democrats after devolution', in G. Hassan & C. Warhurst (eds), *Tomorrow's Scotland*, London: Lawrence & Wishart.

MacCormick, J. (1955), *The Flag in the Wind: The Story of the National Movement in Scotland*, London: Victor Gollancz.

Macdonald, C. M. M. (2009), *Whaur Extremes Meet: Scotland's Twentieth Century*, Edinburgh: John Donald.

Macdonell, H. (2009), *Uncharted Territory: The story of Scottish devolution 1999–2009*, London: Politico's.

McEwen, N. (2002), 'The Scottish National Party after devolution: progress and prospects', in G. Hassan & C. Warhurst (eds), *Tomorrow's Scotland*, London: Lawrence & Wishart.

McHarg, A. et al. (2016), *The Scottish Independence Referendum: Constitutional and Political Implications*, Oxford: Oxford University Press.

Mackie, G. (1963), *Policy for Scottish Farming*, Edinburgh: Scottish Liberal Party.

—— (2004), *Flying, Farming and Politics: a liberal life*, Stanhope: Memoir Club.

Maclay, J. (1950), *Liberalism and the Present Situation*.

McLeish, H. (2004), *Scotland First: Truth and Consequences*, Edinburgh: Mainstream.

McManus, M. (2001), *Jo Grimond: Towards the Sound of Gunfire*, Edinburgh: Birlinn.

McMillan, J. (1969), *Anatomy of Scotland*, London: Leslie Frewin.

Mercer, J. (1978), *Scotland: The Devolution of Power*, London: John Calder.

Miller, W. L. (1981), *The End of British Politics? Scots and English Political Behaviour in the Seventies*, Oxford: Clarendon.

Munro, R. (1930), *Looking Back: Fugitive Writings and Sayings*, London: Thomas Nelson.

Murray, A. C. (1945), *Master and Brother: Murrays of Elibank*, London: John Murray, 1945.

Murray, C. de B. (1938), *How Scotland is Governed*, Edinburgh & London: The Moray Press.

Oxford & Asquith, Earl of (1920), *Memories and Reflections I*, London: Cassell.

Pack, M. (2020), *2019 Election Review: Report*, London: Liberal Democrats.

Paterson, L. (1994), *The Autonomy of Modern Scotland*, Edinburgh: Edinburgh University Press.

—— (ed.) (1998), *A Diverse Assembly: The Debate on a Scottish Parliament*, Edinburgh: Edinburgh University Press.

Pentland, Lady (1928), *Memoir of Lord Pentland*, London: Methuen.

Pickard, W. (2011), *The Member for Scotland: A Life of Duncan McLaren*, Edinburgh: John Donald.

Pike, J. (2015), *Project Fear*, London: Biteback.

Powell, E. (1977), *Joseph Chamberlain*, London: Thames and Hudson.

Purvis, J. (2004), *Fiscal federalism: A new model for financing the Scottish Parliament within the UK*, Edinburgh: Scottish Liberal Democrats.

Purvis, J., J. Steel & D. Torrance (eds) (2015), *Militant for the Reasonable Man: Celebrating David Steel's Fifty Years as a Parliamentarian*, Edinburgh: Birlinn (privately distributed).

Reid, A. (ed.) (1885), *Why I Am a Liberal: Being Definitions and Personal Confessions of Faith by the Best Minds of the Liberal Party*, London: Cassell.

Rennard, C. (2018), *Winning Here – My Campaigning Life: Memoirs Volume 1*, London: Biteback.

Rhodes, R. James, *Rosebery*, London: Orion.

Ritchie, M. (2000), *Scotland Reclaimed: The inside story of Scotland's first democratic parliamentary election*, Edinburgh: Saltire Society.

Scottish Land Enquiry Committee (1914), *Scottish Land: Rural and Urban*, London

SDP/Liberal Alliance (1987), *The Alliance programme for Government: The Time Has Come For Scotland*, Edinburgh/Glasgow: Scottish Liberal Party/SDP.

SLA (1884), *Third Midlothian Campaign: Political Speeches Delivered in August and September 1884 by the Right Hon. W. E. Gladstone, M.P.*, Edinburgh: Scottish Liberal Association.

—— (1900), *Current Politics From a Liberal Standpoint: A Handbook for the Use of Liberals*, Edinburgh & Glasgow: Scottish Liberal Association.

——(1905), *Current Politics From a Liberal Standpoint: A Handbook for the General Election*, Edinburgh & Glasgow: Scottish Liberal Association.

Scottish Liberal Club (1885), *The Rosebery Banquet: Edinburgh, 13th November 1885*, Edinburgh: Edinburgh University Press (privately printed).

SLD (1989), *Sovereignty & Integration: The Case for a Scottish Parliament*, Edinburgh: Scottish Liberal Democrats.

—— (1992), *Changing Scotland and Britain for Good: The Scottish Liberal Democrat Manifesto for 1992*, Dorset: Liberal Democrat Publications.

—— (1992), *Democracy and Accountability: A new local government structure for Scotland*, Edinburgh: Scottish Liberal Democrats.

—— (1994), *Unlocking Scotland's Potential: The Scottish Liberal Democrat Vision for Europe*, Edinburgh: Scottish Liberal Democrats.

—— (1995), *The Final Steps: Towards the Completion of the Scottish Constitutional Convention's Scheme for a Scottish Parliament*, Edinburgh: Scottish Liberal Democrats.

—— (1996), *Alex in Wonderland: The True Cost to Scotland of the SNP's Economic Policy*, Edinburgh: Scottish Liberal Democrats.

—— (1999), *Raising the Standard: Scottish Parliament Manifesto 1999*, Edinburgh: Scottish Liberal Democrats.

—— (2021), *Bring Our Country Together*, Edinburgh: Scottish Liberal Democrats.

SLF (1925), *Liberal Principles and Aims adopted by the Scottish Convention of Liberals*, Edinburgh & Glasgow: Scottish Liberal Federation.

—— (1928), *The Scottish Countryside*, Glasgow: Scottish Liberal Federation.

—— (1929), *Our Scottish Sea Fisheries: Their Present Plight, and the Liberal Remedy*, Edinburgh & Glasgow: Scottish Liberal Federation.

—— (1937), *A Policy for Scotland: Interim Report of the Industrial Policy Committee*, Edinburgh & Glasgow: Scottish Liberal Federation.

SLP (1949), *Scottish Self Government*, Edinburgh: Scottish Liberal Party.

—— (1950), *Manifesto of the Scottish Liberal Party: The Scottish Party of Progress*.

—— (1962), *Scottish Self Government*, Edinburgh: Scottish Liberal Party.

—— (1970), *Scottish Self Government: The Views of the Scottish Liberal Party*, Edinburgh: Scottish Liberal Party.

—— (1972), *Oil: the key to Scotland's future*, Edinburgh: Scottish Liberal Party.

Smout, T. C. (1986), *A Century of the Scottish People 1830–1950*, London: Collins

Steel, D. (1968), *Out of Control: A Critical Examination of the Government of Scotland*, Edinburgh: Scottish Liberal Party.

—— (1970), 'Federalism' in N. MacCormick (ed.), *The Scottish Debate: Essays on Scottish Nationalism*, London: Oxford University Press.

—— (1989), *Against Goliath: David Steel's Story*, London: Weidenfeld & Nicolson.

—— (2006), *The Steel Commission: Moving to Federalism – A New Settlement for Scotland*, Edinburgh: Scottish Liberal Democrats.

Stewart, T. A. W. (ed.) (2019), *The Scottish Parliament in its own words: an oral history*, Edinburgh: Luath.

Taylor, B. (2002), *Scotland's Parliament: Triumph and Disaster*, Edinburgh: Edinburgh University Press.

Thorpe, J. & G. Mackie (1967), *The Liberal Crusade – People Count: The Liberal Plan for Power*, Edinburgh: Scottish Liberal Party.

Torrance, D. (2006), *The Scottish Secretaries*, Edinburgh: Birlinn.

—— (2010), *Salmond: Against the Odds*, Edinburgh: Birlinn.

—— (2012), *David Steel: Rising Hope to Elder Statesman*, London: Biteback

Unknown (1882), *The Scottish Liberal Members and their Pledges on the Church Question in 1880*, Edinburgh.

Urwin, D. W. (1965), 'The Development of the Conservative Party Organisation in Scotland until 1912', *Scottish Historical Review*.

Vincent, J. (1972), *The Formation of the British Liberal Party 1857–68*, Harmondsworth: Pelican.

Waddell, R. & D. Gorrie (1991), *The P. R. Debate and the Constitutional Convention*, Edinburgh: Scottish Liberal Democrats.

Wallace, J. (2019), 'A New Voice in the Land' in J. Johnston & J. Mitchell (eds), *The Scottish Parliament at twenty*, Edinburgh: Luath Press.

Waugh, A. S. (2019), *Sir Henry Campbell-Bannerman: A Scottish Life and UK Politics 1836–1908*, London: Austin Macauley.

Young, D. (1971), *Scotland*, London: Cassell.

YSS (1911), *Manifesto and Appeal to the Scottish People on Scottish Home Rule*, Glasgow: Young Scots Society.

JOURNAL ARTICLES

Ball, S. R. (1982), 'Asquith's Decline and the General Election of 1918', *Scottish Historical Review* 61:171, 44–61.

Baxter, K. (2013), '"The advent of a woman candidate was seen . . . as outrageous": Women, party politics and elections in interwar Scotland and England', *Journal of Scottish Historical Studies* 33:2, 260–83.

Brooks, D. (1985), 'Gladstone and Midlothian: The Background to the First Campaign', *Scottish Historical Review* lxiv.

Brown, A. (1996), 'Women's Political Representation in Scotland: Progress Since 1992', *Scottish Affairs* 14:1, 73–89.

Brown, J. (1968), 'Scottish and English Land Legislation 1905–11', *Scottish Historical Review* 47:143, 72–85.

Brown, S. J. (1992), '"Echoes of Midlothian": Scottish Liberalism and the South African War, 1899–1902', *Scottish Historical Review* 71:191/192, 156–83.

Cameron, E. A. (1993), 'Politics, Ideology and the Highland Land Issue, 1886 to the 1920s', *Scottish Historical Review* 72:193, 60–79.

—— (2006), '"A far cry to London": Joseph Chamberlain in Inverness, September 1885', *The Innes Review* 57, 36–53.

—— (2008), '"Rival foundlings": the Ross and Cromarty by-election, 10 February 1936', *Historical Research* 81:213, 507–30.

—— (2018), 'The 1918 Reform Act, Redistribution and Scottish Politics', *Parliamentary History* 37:1, 101–15.

Dyer, M. (1992), 'The 1992 General Election in Grampian', *Scottish Affairs* 1:1, 27–35.

—— (2003), '"A Nationalist in the Churchillian Sense": John MacCormick, the Paisley by-election of 18 February 1948, Home Rule and the Crisis in Scottish Liberalism', *Parliamentary History* 22:3, 285–307.

Evans, A. B. (2014), 'Federalists in name only? Reassessing the federal credentials of the Liberal Democrats: An English case study', *British Politics* 9:3, 346–58.

—— (2015), 'The Squeezed Middle? The Liberal Democrats in Wales and Scotland: A Post-Coalition Reassessment', *Scottish Affairs* 24:2, 163–86.

Finnie, R. (1999), 'Diary of Scottish Liberal Democrat Negotiator: Ross Finnie MSP', *Scottish Affairs* 28:1, 51–56.

Johns, R. (2021), 'As You Were: The Scottish Parliament Election of 2021', *Political Quarterly* 92:3, 493–99.

Jones, P. (1997), 'Labour's Referendum Plan: Sell-out of Act of Faith', *Scottish Affairs* 18:1, 1–17.
—— (2007), 'The SNP's Victory in the 2007 Scottish Parliament Elections', *Scottish Affairs* 60:1, 6–23.
Kellas, J. G. (1964), 'The Liberal Party and the Scottish Church Disestablishment Crisis', *English Historical Review* lxxix, 31–46.
—— (1965), 'The Liberal Party in Scotland 1876–1895', *Scottish Historical Review* 44:137, 1–16.
Kelley, R. (1964), 'Asquith at Paisley: the Content of British Liberalism at the End of Its Era', *Journal of British Studies* 4:1, 133–59.
Laffin, M. (2007), 'The Scottish Liberal Democrats', *Political Quarterly* 78:1, 147–55.
Lloyd-Jones, N. (2014), 'Liberalism, Scottish Nationalism and the Home Rule Crisis, c.1886–93', *English Historical Review* 129:539, 862–87.
Lynch, P. (1994), 'The 1994 European Elections in Scotland: Campaigns and Strategies', *Scottish Affairs* 9:1, 45–58.
—— (1996), 'The Scottish Constitutional Convention 1992–5', *Scottish Affairs* 15:1, 1–16.
—— (1998), 'Third Party Politics in a Four Party System: The Liberal Democrats in Scotland', *Scottish Affairs* 22:1, 16–32.
McVicar, M., G. Jordan & G. Boyne (1994), 'Ships in the Night: Scottish Political Parties and Local Government Reform', *Scottish Affairs* 9:1, 80–96.
Packer, I. (1996), 'The Land Issue and the Future of Scottish Liberalism in 1914', *Scottish Historical Review* 75:199, 52–71.
Paterson, L. (2015), 'Utopian Pragmatism: Scotland's Choice', *Scottish Affairs* 24:1, 22–46.
Petrie, M. (2018), 'Anti-Socialism, Liberalism and Individualism: Rethinking the Realignment of Scottish Politics, 1945–1970', *Transactions of the Royal Historical Society* 28, 197–217.
Savage, D. C. (1961), 'Scottish Politics, 1885–6', *Scottish Historical Review* 40:130, 118–35.
Simon, A. (1975), 'Church Disestablishment as a Factor in the General Election of 1885', *The Historical Journal* 18:4, 791–820.
Sloman, P. (2020), 'Squeezed Out? The Liberal Democrats and the 2019 General Election', *Political Quarterly* 91:1.
Smyth, J. J. (2003), 'Resisting Labour: Unionists, Liberals, and Moderates in Glasgow between the wars', *Historical Journal* 46:2, 375–401.
Stewart, J. (1999), '"This Injurious Measure": Scotland and the 1906

Education (Provision of Meals) Act', *Scottish Historical Review* 78:205, 76–94.

Stewart, T. A. W. (2019), '"A disguised Liberal vote" – third-party voting and the SNP under Gordon Wilson in Dundee during the 1970s and 1980s', *Contemporary British History* 33:3, 357–82.

Thompson, M. K. (2016), 'Defining Liberalism', *The Innes Review* 67:1, 6–30.

Walker, W. M. (1970), 'Dundee's Disenchantment with Churchill: A Comment upon the Downfall of the Liberal Party', *Scottish Historical Review* 49:147, 85–108.

UNPUBLISHED THESES

Akroyd, R. J. (1996), *Lord Rosebery and Scottish Nationalism 1868–1896*, PhD thesis: University of Edinburgh.

McLeod, I. (1978), 'Scotland and the Liberal Party, 1880–1900: Church, Ireland and Empire – A Family Affair', M. Litt. thesis: University of Glasgow.

Millar, G. F. (1994), *The Liberal party in Scotland, 1843–1868: electoral politics and party development*, PhD thesis: University of Glasgow.

Torn, N. (2012), *From the birth of 'The Gladstone' to the death of W. E. Gladstone: The Scottish Liberal Club, 1879–1898*, Dissertation: University of Edinburgh.

NEWSPAPERS AND PERIODICALS

Aberdeen Weekly Journal
Daily Mail
Financial Times
Glasgow Herald/Herald
Guardian
Holyrood
Independent
Journal of Liberal History
National Review
People's Journal
Scottish Liberal Bulletin
Scottish Review
Spectator
Sunday Mail

Sunday Times
The Times

INTERVIEWS

Alan Blair
Cllr Robert Brown
Lord Campbell of Pittenweem
Matthew Clark
Sandra Grieve
Michael Moore
David Paterson
Bernard Ponsonby
Lord Rennard
Euan Roddin
Lord Steel of Aikwood
Lord Wallace of Tankerness
Sir Graham Watson

Index